JUSTICE AND THE AMERICAN METROPOLIS

GLOBALIZATION AND COMMUNITY

Susan E. Clarke, Series Editor
Dennis R. Judd, Founding Editor

(continued on page 269)

JUSTICE AND THE
AMERICAN METROPOLIS

**CLARISSA RILE HAYWARD AND
TODD SWANSTROM, EDITORS**

Globalization and Community 18

University of Minnesota Press
Minneapolis
London

Published by the University of Minnesota Press
111 Third Avenue South, Suite 290
Minneapolis, MN 55401-2520
http://www.upress.umn.edu

Library of Congress Cataloging-in-Publication Data

Justice and the American metropolis / Clarissa Rile Hayward and Todd Swanstrom, editors.

    p. cm. — (Globalization and community ; v. 18)

    Includes bibliographical references and index.

    ISBN 978-0-8166-7612-5 (hc : alk. paper) — ISBN 978-0-8166-7613-2 (pb : alk. paper)

    1. Urban policy—United States.   2. Urbanization—United States.
3. Sociology, Urban—United States.   4. Equality—United States.
5. Justice.   I. Hayward, Clarissa Rile.   II. Swanstrom, Todd.

    HT123.J87 2011

    303.3'720917320973—dc23   2011017083

CONTENTS

IV. JUSTICE AND INSTITUTIONS

ACKNOWLEDGMENTS

This book was born over lunch at Miss Saigon, a Vietnamese restaurant in "The Loop," a cultural district in a streetcar suburb of St. Louis, Missouri. Even though we taught at different institutions (Clarissa at Washington University and Todd at the University of Missouri–St. Louis) and were trained in different specialties (normative political theory and empirical urban politics), we found that we shared many interests and points of view. Over the course of lunch, we began to zero in on what struck us as a glaring anomaly. Metropolitan injustices were as acute as ever. Indeed, a few blocks north of Miss Saigon were neighborhoods and schools that imposed enormous burdens on children who were trying to succeed in life. At the same time, it struck us that very few observers, whether in academia or in the popular press, expressed moral outrage at these metropolitan injustices.

Something had changed. In the 1960s, social justice issues were at the forefront of debates about American cities and their suburbs. But starting in the late 1970s and 1980s, discourse shifted markedly, to the point where it became dominated by economic considerations—by concerns about efficient production and service provision, for example, and competitiveness in the globalized economy. Granted, these are important topics. But addressing them should not foreclose addressing questions of justice.

At that lunch we decided to hold a conference on justice and the American metropolis, one that would bring political theorists concerned with justice to the table with empirical scholars of urban politics, urban history, and urban political economy. The result is the present volume, which aims to put justice back in the forefront of debates about American urban policy.

Justice and the American Metropolis would not have been possible without the generous financial assistance of four programs at Washington University in St. Louis: the Political Theory Research Group, the American Culture Studies Program, the Center for New Institutional Social Sciences, and the Center for the Study of Ethics and Human Values. The Des Lee Collaborative Vision at the University of Missouri–St. Louis also contributed to the conference's success.

Our debts to individuals are no less great than our debts to institutions. Alana Bame put her tremendous energy and organizational skills to work planning the conference. Heather Sloan-Randick kept track of the money. Colin Gordon, chair of the history department at the University of Iowa, not only shared his deep knowledge of St. Louis history with conference participants but also guided us on an eye-opening tour of the city. Brandon Nelson helped us draft responses to the first versions of the authors' chapters, and Jennifer Edwards helped with manuscript preparation.

We are grateful, as well, to those conference participants who served as chairs or discussants or presented research that does not appear in the present volume. These include Susan Clarke, Adrienne Davis, Peter Dreier, Gerald Early, Wayne Fields, Maggie Garb, Marilyn Friedman, Terry Jones, Ian MacMullen, Larry May, Linda Nicholson, Andrew Rehfeld, David Robertson, Tommie Shelby, Lauren Silver, and Kit Wellman.

Thanks also to those who have responded to the arguments presented in this volume, including audience members at the 2009 Justice and the American Metropolis Conference at Washington University and participants in panel discussions at the 2009 and 2010 meetings of the American Political Science Association. Pieter Martin, editor at the University of Minnesota Press, and Susan Clarke, editor of the Globalization and Community Series, understood immediately what kind of a book we wanted to publish and why it was important. We thank them for their support. Finally, we want to thank the anonymous reviewers who pressed us, and all the contributors, to clarify and sharpen our arguments.

Last, but not least, we want to thank the staff at Kaldi's coffeehouse, where we met regularly to discuss the book, for never kicking us out, no matter how long we stayed.

INTRODUCTION

Thick Injustice

CLARISSA RILE HAYWARD AND TODD SWANSTROM

A MODEST TWO-STORY BRICK HOME sits at 4600 Labadie Avenue in the heart of St. Louis's North Side. Nothing sets this house apart from its neighbors but a small metal plaque, which commemorates its role in the landmark Supreme Court decision *Shelley v. Kraemer* (334 U.S. 1 [1948]). In October 1945, J. D. and Ethel Shelley, an African-American couple, purchased 4600 Labadie. At that time, the house was covered by a deed restriction that prohibited occupancy by "any person not of the Caucasian race" and specifically by "people of the Negro or Mongolian Race" (quoted in *Shelley v. Kraemer* 334 U.S. 1 [1948]). A white couple, Fern and Louis Kraemer, were the plaintiffs, chosen to represent the Marcus Avenue Improvement Association (whose covenants covered a total of fifty-seven parcels in the vicinity of 4600 Labadie) because Fern's mother had been a party to the 1911 agreement that originated the covenant. In its *Shelley v. Kraemer* decision, the U.S. Supreme Court ruled that, although as private contracts racial deed restrictions were legal, state enforcement of such contracts violated the equal protection clause of the Fourteenth Amendment.

Following *Shelley v. Kraemer*, major civil rights triumphs in the second half of the twentieth century opened up important new opportunities for African-Americans, especially for middle-class blacks. But segregation persisted. Although after 1950 the black population expanded into the previously all-white neighborhood around 4600 Labadie, for most African-Americans in North St. Louis this change represented not the achievement of equality or equal opportunity so much as a move from the compacted Jim Crow ghetto to the lower-density ghetto of the post–civil rights movement years.

In the second half of the last century, the neighborhood in which the house at 4600 Labadie sits experienced significant population loss. By the year 2000, the census tract in which the house is sited was 98.6 percent black (U.S. Census Bureau 2003). At that time, a full 21.3 percent of the neighborhood's residents lived below the poverty level, and the median value of single-family homes in the area was less than half that for the St. Louis metropolitan area as a whole (U.S. Census Bureau 2003). In North St. Louis as in similar neighborhoods throughout the United States, African-Americans had gained access to places from which they had previously been excluded. But that gain proved a weak foundation for equalizing resources and opportunities.

We begin this volume with the tale of 4600 Labadie because its fate mirrors—"in stark and dramatic form"—that of so many ghettoized places in older American cities.[1] In the second half of the twentieth century, the city of St. Louis lost over half a million people, its population dropping from almost 860,000 in 1959 to below 350,000 in 2000, a decline of nearly 60 percent (U.S. Census Bureau 1980; U.S. Census Bureau 2003). By 1990, St. Louis was among America's "hypersegregated" metropolitan areas (Massey and Denton 1993, 76).[2] White, middle-class residents had moved en masse to the new suburbs in west St. Louis County, leaving behind weak housing markets and hollowed-out institutions. Not only people but also capital had fled the city, and with capital went jobs. Between 1977 and 2002, the city lost a full two-thirds of its manufacturing jobs, falling from 92,600 to just 25,500 (Testa 2006). With joblessness came poverty. By the turn of the twenty-first century, the city's poverty rate had reached a staggering 22.4 percent, double that of the St. Louis metropolitan area as a whole (U.S. Census Bureau 2003).

In short, racial segregation and concentrated social and economic deprivation failed to change significantly following *Shelley v. Kraemer*. In his penetrating history of the racial patterns of development in St. Louis, the historian Colin Gordon argues the principal reason is that "a tangle of private practices and public policies . . . overlapped and outlasted the legal life of the restrictive deed covenant," while producing the very effects deed restrictions were designed to produce (Gordon 2008, 83). Among the relevant practices and policies are the Federal Housing Administration (FHA) and Veteran's Administration (VA) mortgage programs, which notoriously excluded American blacks through the 1960s; the exclusionary zoning laws prevalent even today in affluent, majority-white suburbs—laws that, although not explicitly racially targeted, have predictable racially segregating effects; and local government laws, which grant municipalities the powers to regulate land use and to raise and spend taxes on public schooling and other services that they make available to residents only (Hayward 2003).

At the start of the twenty-first century, these practices and policies ensure that, in places like the neighborhood surrounding 4600 Labadie, gross inequalities of resources, opportunities, and powers endure. However, political debate about American cities and suburbs today typically fails to acknowledge and address these inequalities. In the 1960s and early 1970s, social justice concerns were central to debates about urban policy in this country, but in the decades since political discourse about cities has focused predominantly on economic considerations.[3]

In the 1960s, public discourse about urban problems was permeated by a sense of moral indignation—even shame. In the nation's capitol, in the press, and in city halls and civic associations throughout the United States, a wide-ranging debate about inequality and racial hierarchy— a debate about *justice*—took the American metropolis as its subject.[4] A case in point is the report of the so-called Kerner Commission, which famously proclaimed that "our nation is moving toward two societies, one black, one white—separate and unequal" (Kerner Commission 1968, 1). The Kerner Commission report expressed a clear sense of moral outrage at the living conditions of urban blacks. It even assigned moral responsibility for those conditions: "What white Americans have never fully understood, but what the Negro can never forget, is that white society is deeply implicated in the ghetto. White institutions created it, white institutions maintain it, and white society condones it" (2). The authors of the report argued unambiguously that the appropriate agency for addressing ghetto poverty was the federal government: "Only a commitment to national action on an unprecedented scale can shape a future compatible with the historic ideals of American society" (23). They continued: "The major need is to generate new will—the will to tax ourselves to the extent necessary to meet the vital needs of the nation" (23).

Conditions in urban neighborhoods like the North St. Louis neighborhood that surrounds 4600 Labadie Avenue are no less inequitable today than they were fifty years ago. Yet, today, it is almost impossible to imagine a presidential commission calling for massive federal intervention to rectify those conditions, let alone assigning blame for them to white Americans. Why the shift? One possible explanation is simply that dominant beliefs about justice have shifted: the socialist and communalist normative frameworks of the 1960s have given way to more individualistic and market-oriented beliefs. In the first section of this chapter, we make the case that ideological shifts alone cannot account for the decline of discourse about metropolitan justice. The inequalities and hierarchies that characterize North St. Louis and countless urban and inner-ring suburban communities are unjust according to a very wide range of competing normative theories. These include Marxist and post-Marxist accounts of justice, Rawlsian liberalism, communitarianism, and even philosophical libertarianism.

Political discourse about justice in the metropolis has declined, not only and not principally because of changing beliefs, but also crucially because of changes in the structure of unjust power relations. At the start of the twenty-first century, American cities and their suburbs are sites of what we call *thick injustice*: unjust power relations that are deep and densely concentrated, as well as opaque and relatively intractable. We argue that the historical roots of metropolitan injustice, its relation to the structure of local governance in the United States, and its imbrication with physical place render it difficult to see and difficult to assign responsibility for it—and hence difficult to change.

Our focus, in other words, is one particular form of what Edward Soja calls "spatial (in)justice" (Soja 2010), namely, injustice generated over time by institutional structures, including structures that segregate metropolitan space by race and class. To be sure, not all injustice takes this form. Injustice plays out at multiple scales and in the context of a broad array of power relations, including global hierarchies and inequalities, U.S. federal institutions and practices (e.g., federal deregulation of subprime mortgage lending), and relations among workers and capitalists. Still, thick injustice in the metropolis is a major source of enduring inequality and hierarchy and one that is particularly difficult to comprehend and challenge.

The principal aim of this volume is to help render thick injustice more legible, and hence more tractable, in order to put questions of justice back at the forefront of deliberations about urban politics and policy.[5] The product of a conference held on the campus of Washington University in St. Louis—just a few miles from the house at 4600 Labadie—*Justice and the American Metropolis* brings normative political theorists concerned with questions of justice to the table with scholars of urban politics, urban history, and urban political economy. Its impetus is our shared sense that recent political shifts in the United States, including the election of the first former community organizer and African-American to the office of president, open up possibilities for promoting justice in policy domains where questions of justice have, for decades, been marginalized.[6]

Theories of Justice and the American Metropolis

Although political discourse about American cities and suburbs tends to neglect questions of justice, social and political theory provides a wide array of conceptual and analytic resources with which to criticize, on principled grounds, the metropolitan status quo. People with a very wide range of beliefs about justice, we argue in this section, should repudiate the inequalities of resources, opportunities, and powers that characterize the contemporary metropolis.

Let us begin with Marx. As is well known, Marx's critique of capitalism centers on its organization of the process of production (1978a, 1978b). It is not principally inequality of *resources* that renders the status quo in the American metropolis illegitimate by this view. Instead, it is the fact that those who own the means of production—not only the means to produce consumer goods but also the means to produce urban and suburban places—disproportionately control, and benefit from, metropolitan growth. Indeed, private, profit-driven development drove the segregation of the neighborhood near 4600 Labadie over the course of the last century, both the socioeconomic and the racial segregation that grew so pronounced in St. Louis and its suburbs. Those who built new houses and new communities and then sold them at a profit *benefited* when they marketed exclusivity to the wealthy and racially privileged. They benefited when they extracted high rents from the poor and racially marginalized. Profit-oriented developers benefited (a Marxian would underscore) at the expense of those who did not own, and who could not control, urban and suburban space. Thus for the geographer David Harvey, the root of injustice in the contemporary metropolis is the capitalist market economy, which works to the advantage of the property-owning class and the disadvantage of those who do not own the means of production (see, e.g., Harvey 1973, 1989, 1996, 2000). Justice, by his view, requires social control of urban and suburban space: the elimination of "rent, interest, and profit [so that] . . . socially necessary labour . . . produc[es] . . . socially beneficial use values" (Harvey 1973, 235).[7]

Post-Marxian scholars draw attention to not only the uneven distribution of the means of production but also, more generally, the metropolitan relations of social, political, and economic privilege and disadvantage. The contemporary metropolis, they argue, is a site of *structural inequality*—that is, of asymmetries in access to resources, opportunities, and the capacity to participate in collective decision making, which are built into laws, institutions, and other structural forms (Hayward 2009, 112–13). Think of the FHA and the VA mortgage programs cited in the introduction to this chapter or the jurisdictional boundaries that separate affluent St. Louis County municipalities and school districts from poor suburban jurisdictions and from St. Louis city. To be sure, urban spaces can be important sites of resistance and transformative change (Foucault 1986; Kohn 2003; Massey 1994; Soja 1996, 2010). But as scholars like the political theorist Iris Marion Young emphasize, spatial segmentation and racial and class-based segregation can also render injustice invisible and hence depoliticize it. "Making privilege invisible to the privileged," Young writes, "has the effect of inoculating against what sense of injustice they might have . . . The everyday separation of the lives of the more and less privileged that is part of the process of residential racial segregation makes it unnecessary for the privileged to think about social injustice except in the most abstract terms" (Young 2000, 208).

It is not only social and political theory on the philosophical Left, however, that gives us grounds to be strongly critical of the status quo in the American metropolis. John Rawls, in what is arguably the most influential contemporary liberal theory of justice, argues that the circumstances of people's birth—their luck in such contingent matters as whether they happen to be born poor or wealthy, black or white, residents of a ghettoized neighborhood in North St. Louis or an exclusive suburb in St. Louis County—are "morally arbitrary" (Rawls 1971). Material resources, such as income and wealth, Rawls suggests, should be distributed equally unless an unequal distribution benefits the least well-off.[8] Hence in the case of metropolitan St. Louis, a Rawlsian would ask whether segregation, along with the unequal distribution of collective goods, motivates people to work hard, save, and invest, and thus increases aggregate well-being. If so (she would ask), does growth "trickle down," benefiting even the most disadvantaged residents of North St. Louis and similar neighborhoods?

The available evidence suggests the answer to both questions is a resounding no. Comparative analyses of spatial inequality show segregation does *not* promote productivity and growth.[9] What is more, studies of the contextual effects of concentrated poverty show that any benefit the least well-off might derive if segregation *did* increase productivity would be overwhelmed by the enormous costs and burdens that they bear.[10] The normative implications are clear. By the Rawlsian view, justice demands revising the status quo in order to improve the condition of the urban poor and those who are disadvantaged by racial inequalities and hierarchies.

Not only Rawlsian liberals but also their communitarian critics would find the state of the contemporary metropolis unjust.[11] Consider Michael Walzer's argument in *Spheres of Justice* that different goods should be distributed according to different principles in different "spheres" (e.g., the sphere of education or of work) and that justice requires the relative autonomy of spheres vis-à-vis one another (Walzer 1983). According to Walzer, although it may be legitimate to distribute income and wealth according to market principles, it is illegitimate to allow that distribution to affect people's educational opportunities, their civil liberties, or political powers. Justice does not require the *equal* distribution of all goods, but it imposes limits on the *significance* of any form of inequality. In Walzer's words, when justice obtains, "there may be many small inequalities, [but] inequality will not be . . . summed up across different goods, because the autonomy of distributions will tend to produce a variety of local monopolies held by different groups of men and women" (Walzer 1983, 17).

For a communitarian such as Walzer, the principal problem in the St. Louis case is that the unequal distribution of income and wealth infects so many spheres. For example, it grants the advantaged disproportionate access to basic public goods, including police protection and education.[12] It produces inequalities in access to important opportunities as well, such as the opportunity to access labor markets and compete for jobs and to access consumer goods.[13] It produces inequalities in important political powers, such as the power to participate effectively in making those collective decisions (e.g., land use decisions) that profoundly shape life chances. Although justice in the metropolis does not necessarily require the large-scale redistribution of income and wealth, it does require defanging inequalities of income and wealth, ensuring that the affluent cannot use their money to purchase goods that ought to remain outside money's sphere.

"Very well," we imagine a skeptic objecting at this point in our argument. "Multiple left and liberal philosophical schools condemn as unjust the status quo in the American metropolis. But that hardly means it is unjust according to the normative beliefs of *most people*. What about more conservative thinkers? After all, in the contemporary United States—and surely in the St. Louis suburbs of your example—liberals and leftists are not the majority. To persuade me that power relations in America's cities and suburbs are unjust according to a 'very wide range of competing normative theories,' you would need to persuade me they are unjust even to thinkers on the Right."

To address this challenge, we now consider our case from the perspective of what is arguably the most sophisticated account of philosophical libertarianism to date: Robert Nozick's classic *Anarchy, State, and Utopia* (1974). Justice, Nozick argues, requires a "night watchman" state, which provides basic security for all but, beyond that, refrains from intervening in people's choices. Just distributions, in his analysis, are whichever distributions are arrived at when people acquire things in a fair way and then engage in free market exchanges with one another. *Contra* Marx, Rawls, and Walzer, Nozick underscores that just distributions can be extremely inegalitarian. In the St. Louis case, the status quo distribution would be fair, then, so long as income, wealth, and other resources had been acquired in a way that was fair (in the sense of free from coercion) and then transferred from individual to individual in a fair way(through free exchanges, gifts, or inheritance).

One need only state this claim to see that our case fails even the libertarian test. Think back to what is often (still) called "the discovery of America." Original acquisition took the form of outright expropriation. At the start of black–white relations in the United States, first distributions were rooted in enslavement, coerced labor, and exploitation. Even if we confine our historical analysis to black–white relations in the twentieth-century metropolis, we cannot help but conclude that contemporary distributive patterns are *not* the product of free and fair exchange. Instead they are the product of (among other forms of coercion) a dual-housing market created and maintained by institutions such as the racially restrictive covenants that were the subject of *Shelley v. Kraemer*. To be sure, libertarians will not agree with Marxians or post-Marxist theorists, or with Rawlsian liberals or communitarians, when it comes to articulating a *positive* vision of justice in the metropolis. Still, even Robert Nozick acknowledges that justice requires what he calls "the rectification of injustice in holdings" (Nozick 1974, 152). In cases, such as the case of metropolitan St. Louis, in which income, wealth, and other resources were not acquired fairly, and in which market exchanges were not free and fair, justice, by his view, cannot be attained.[14]

Metropolitan inequalities and hierarchies are unjust, then, even for libertarians and others on the political Right who conceive justice as a matter of market freedom. Hence the rightward shift in U.S. politics in the last decades of the twentieth century is insufficient to account for the decline of political discourse about metropolitan injustice. In the remainder of this chapter, we make the case for an alternative explanation. An important cause of the shift in political discourse over the past fifty years, we suggest, is the rise of what we call *thick injustice*. Injustice in the American metropolis is "thick" in more than one sense of that word. It is thick in the very basic sense of "deep," "dense," and "extending far down from the surface." It is thick, in addition, in the sense of "obscure" and "difficult to penetrate" (*OED* 1989). Our principal claim is that three characteristics of contemporary metropolitan injustice render it thick: the deep historical roots of unjust power relations in America's cities and suburbs, their interaction with the institutional structure of local governance in the United States, and their embeddedness in physical places. These traits obscure metropolitan injustice, we argue, making it "difficult to penetrate." They thereby make it difficult to assign moral responsibility for injustice and to motivate collective action to change it.

Thick Injustice and History

William Faulkner famously wrote, "The past is never dead. It's not even past" (Faulkner 1994, 535). In the American metropolis today, the past lives on in the historical roots of contemporary injustice . Deep historical roots are, by definition, hard to perceive. The historical roots of contemporary injustices are obscure to members of the post-civil-rights-movement generations and especially to current beneficiaries of those injustices, who very often do not see them, let alone see themselves as implicated in them.

Because legal barriers to equal opportunity in housing, lending, education, and employment were largely eliminated in the wake of the civil rights movement, Americans below the age of fifty have no direct memory of the Jim Crow era, when laws explicitly discriminated against blacks. Nor do many Americans "remember" historical injustices indirectly by attending to the ways they shape present relations of power. This historical amnesia is, in a sense, understandable. Much has changed since the 1960s. Racial attitudes, to cite one important factor, have changed dramatically. In the words of the social theorists Michael Omi and Howard

Winant, today it is "impossible to argue *for* segregation or *against* racial equality" (Omi and Winant 1994, 140). By the view of many American whites, the only inequalities that remain are the product of personal preferences and freedom of association (see, e.g., Hochschild 1995). Although one may lament that people prefer to live with others whom they perceive to be racially "like" themselves (this view suggests), it is not reasonable to express moral indignation at that preference, let alone to assign moral responsibility for racial injustice to those who hold it. Nor does government have a legitimate role to play in changing segregated living patterns.

We take issue with this position. Metropolitan injustices are like the layers of the earth. To examine only the topsoil is to miss the sediment below, which provides some with solid ground for upward mobility and political empowerment while miring others in the sociopolitical equivalent of quicksand. If we are to understand contemporary injustice, then we must dig down to the layers that mark its historic origins. To that end, let us consider once more the private and public acts of discrimination in housing that were cited at the start of this chapter: the racial zoning laws, the racially restrictive covenants, the New Deal housing policies, and the other collective decisions that set in motion processes whose momentum is still felt in the metropolis today. These historic acts of discrimination—along with discriminatory practices in lending, employment, and education—helped shape contemporary conditions whereby ostensibly race-neutral policies have predictably racially biased effects.

In St. Louis, as in so many older metropolitan areas, the historic exclusion of blacks from much of the city and its suburbs, along with their exclusion from federal mortgage programs like the FHA and VA programs, meant their exclusion from rising property values in precisely those places that benefited most from collective investment through the second half of the twentieth century (Lipsitz 2006). As is well known, home equity represents the majority of wealth for most American households. The historic bias against black home ownership contributed hugely to what is now a tenfold gap in median wealth between blacks and whites (Mishel, Bernstein, and Allegretto 2007, 278). Historic discrimination in housing contributed not only to contemporary inequalities of wealth but also to contemporary inequalities of access to public education (Rusk 2008) and other locally controlled public services. It contributed to inequalities in access to higher education (which covaries with wealth) and to the capital that entrepreneurs need for business investments (Shapiro 2004).

Decisions made and actions taken in the American metropolis today can be formally unbiased and wholly race neutral, but due to our long history of racist practices and institutions, they can produce racially discriminatory effects. Consider the practice of highway and redevelopment planning. Planners are trained and incentivized to site interstates and other major public projects efficiently, which of course means to site them on relatively inexpensive land. Due to past discrimination, inexpensive land is disproportionately owned and occupied by black residents and black business owners. As is well known, during the Urban Renewal years, intentional discrimination fueled what critics called "Negro removal."[15] But *even absent intentional discrimination*—even in the context of contemporary civil rights laws, which dramatically curtail it—planning for economically efficient development places disproportionate social, economic, and psychological burdens on poor and black Americans.[16]

Similarly, mortgage interest tax deductions—again, formally race-neutral—disproportionately benefit whites, due to our history of racial discrimination in housing and lending. Even programs aimed at historic preservation are, in effect, biased against African-American architectural heritage, since blacks historically had fewer resources with which to hire elite architects (Saito 2009).

Many readers of this volume will be familiar with the U.S. Supreme Court's controversial 2005 *Kelo* decision, which ruled that the use of eminent domain to transfer land from one private owner to another for the purposes of economic development was a permissible "public use" under the "Takings Clause" of the Fifth Amendment (*Kelo v. City of New London et al.* 545 U.S. 469 [2005]). The majority ruled in *Kelo* that state actors can seize land from private owners, not only for highways and other public projects, but also for redevelopment by private actors if redevelopment is judged likely to promote "economic rejuvenation" (*Kelo v. City of New London et al.* 545 U.S. 469 [2005]). Critics of the decision emphasize the Court's exceedingly broad interpretation of "public purpose."[17] More pertinent for our purposes, however, is the fact that the majority ignored the systematic biases its decision produced. Justice O'Connor, in her dissent, wrote that "the fallout from this decision will not be random." She explained, "The beneficiaries are likely to be those citizens with disproportionate influence and power in the political process, including large corporations and development firms. As for the victims, the government now has license to transfer property from those with fewer resources to those with more" (*Kelo v. City of New London et al.* 545 U.S. 469 [2005], O'Connor, dissenting). In a separate dissent, Justice Thomas emphasized the burden borne by African-Americans, whom he noted are disproportionately displaced by urban redevelopment (*Kelo v. City of New London et al.* 545 U.S. 469 [2005], Thomas, dissenting). But notwithstanding claims to the contrary made in *amicus* briefs filed on behalf of the plaintiff by the National Association for the Advancement of Colored People (NAACP), the American Association of Retired Persons (AARP), the Southern Christian Leadership Conference (SCLC), and others, the majority asserted that New London's proposed development plan was neutral in its effects because it was "not adopted 'to benefit a particular class of identifiable individuals'" (*Kelo v. City of New London et al.* 545 U.S. 469 [2005]).

This claim illustrates well our larger point about the relation between historical amnesia and thick injustice, which, it is worth emphasizing, is not limited to specifically racial forms of inequality. Susette Kelo, whose $56,000 house was seized to make room for a proposed redevelopment project by the multibillion-dollar drug conglomerate Pfizer, was poor, female, and white. Not only racial discrimination but also *any* past injustice that shapes current relations of power—gender discrimination, for example, or exploitative or otherwise unjust labor practices—can produce contemporary injustices that are "thick" in the sense of "difficult to penetrate." They can contribute to the creation and the maintenance of stark inequalities and profound social hierarchies: injustices that, when viewed ahistorically, may seem neither to harm nor to advantage any "particular class of identifiable individuals."

Thick Injustice and Institutions

Almost a quarter century before *Kelo*, in its 1974 decision, *Milliken v. Bradley*, the Supreme Court ruled that remedies for racial segregation in America's schools cannot be metropolitan-wide in scope—in other words, they cannot cross the jurisdictional lines that define urban and suburban school districts—unless it is proven that "a constitutional violation within one district" produced "a significant segregative effect in another" (*Milliken v. Bradley* 418 U.S. 717 [1974]). "Specifically," the majority wrote, "it must be shown that racially discriminatory acts of the state or local school districts, or of a single school district, have been a substantial cause of interdistrict segregation. Thus an interdistrict remedy might be in order where the racially discriminatory acts of one or more school districts caused racial segregation in an adjacent district, or where district lines have been deliberately drawn on the basis of race" (*Milliken v. Bradley* 418 U.S. 717 [1974]). Absent proof that intentional acts taken across district lines caused interdistrict segregation, however, metropolitan-wide remedies were unconstitutional, the Court declared. In such cases, court-mandated desegregation efforts must stop at school district boundaries.

We recall this oft-cited Supreme Court ruling to illustrate the second cause of thick injustice in the contemporary American metropolis. Injustice is "thick" due not only to its deep historical roots but also to the structure of the legal and political institutions of American local governance. This legal–political structure has changed dramatically since the early years of the last century. Consider the St. Louis case once more: through much of the twentieth century, the poor and the affluent alike, blacks and whites, and longtime residents and new urban immigrants, lived side by side, and they lived *within the city's jurisdictional boundaries.* City government was, at least in principle, capable of addressing problems of segregation, inequality, and other forms of urban injustice. In early twentieth-century St. Louis, as throughout the United States, city government, for all its flaws, provided poor and minority communities with a solid institutional base from which to press their demands and make their voices heard. Big-city machines provided patronage jobs, which served as a first rung up the ladder of mobility for immigrants (Erie 1988). Even as recently as the 1960s, the war on poverty provided federal grants to large cities. Hence, at the time when big cities began electing African-Americans to the mayor's office (starting with the election of Carl Stokes in Cleveland in 1967), city government was a prize worth capturing.

But in the American metropolis today, the suburbanization of the urban population, along with the dramatic decentralization and privatization of governance, has created a complex and fragmented institutional structure. In 2007, there were 89,476 local governments in the United States, including 39,044 general-purpose governments (U.S. Bureau of the Census 2007). The St. Louis metropolitan area alone has over three hundred general-purpose governments, which, as Gerald Frug emphasizes in his chapter for this volume, are authorized to engage in a wide range of political decision making. For example, suburban municipalities can make land-use decisions without consulting neighboring governments. They can pass ordinances that literally "zone out" those with few resources (e.g., by prohibiting multifamily dwellings or by requiring large lot sizes or large setbacks from the road). Municipalities can tax their residents, and they can use the revenue generated to provide public services—including, crucially, public education—that they can make available only to residents within their borders. Thus affluent, predominantly white suburbs, like the St. Louis suburbs of Clayton and Ladue, can make decisions that foster inequality and exclusion—decisions that profoundly affect those St. Louisans who cannot afford the high cost of living in these suburbs—and they can do so without appearing to act in a way that is discriminatory or otherwise unjust.

Frug's claim is that just as power relations cross municipal boundaries, so should the franchise in local elections. People who work in Ladue, for instance, but cannot afford to live there should be politically enabled to help influence the local laws and policies that affect them (e.g., the zoning policies that currently prohibit the type of housing that would enable them to live there). A change like this, which would help reduce intermunicipal inequalities of political power, would benefit not only residents of older cities like St. Louis but also residents of older, inner-ring suburbs like the St. Louis suburb of Wellston.[18] As Margaret Weir emphasizes in her chapter, such suburbs place low-income and disadvantaged people in a kind of "double jeopardy": not only are they resource poor but they also lack access to the public, private, and nonprofit institutions that empower similar residents of central cities.[19]

Fragmentation, then, is a significant institutional trend that contributes to the "thickening" of metropolitan injustice. As Susan Fainstein shows in her chapter, privatization is another such trend. Between what Fainstein calls the "concessionary period" (1965–74) and the period of "privatized redevelopment" (1982–present), the pronounced shift from public- to private-sector-led redevelopment has obscured metropolitan injustices. At midcentury, urban redevelopment and renewal was administered by powerful state bureaucracies, which used eminent domain to displace poor and working people, especially African-Americans and members of other disadvantaged groups. Although the distribution of redevelopment's benefits and burdens was deeply unjust, at least the agents of that injustice were easy to identify.

Today, by contrast, large urban redevelopment projects are very often led by private sector actors, with government serving only as a junior partner. *Kelo* notwithstanding, the displacement that results is typically the product of gentrification and rising property values rather than the direct force of "the federal bulldozer" (Anderson 1964). People do not necessarily see the inegalitarian distribution of redevelopment's benefits and burdens as a matter of injustice. They do not necessarily experience moral outrage, assign moral responsibility, and act politically to challenge redevelopment's outcomes. After all, when you are forced out of your home not by your government but by anonymous market forces, to whom do you protest?

The institutional context of metropolitan injustice has shifted, in short, from powerful state institutions with clear centers of decision making to diffuse decision points comprising multiple public and private actors. It has changed from a top-down, government-centered structure, with bright lines of authority and responsibility, to a more decentralized, society-centered system. One might imagine that smaller, autonomous governments, working together with nongovernment actors, would ensure citizens better access to the political decision-making process. The new institutional environment is relatively open and accessible (one might think) and hence relatively democratic. Our claim, to the contrary, is that the new institutional context is less democratic than the system it replaced: less responsive, that is, to the needs and the claims of the governed. The new institutional environment helps render metropolitan injustice thick because when no one is in charge, no one seems responsible. No city mayor or city council—indeed, no identifiable political agent—seems responsible for, and at the same time capable of addressing, deep and enduring metropolitan injustices.

Thick Injustice and Place

In the contemporary American metropolis, place powerfully shapes what people can do and what they can be. Poor African-Americans are more than three times as likely as poor whites to live in areas of concentrated poverty, like the area surrounding 4600 Labadie (Jargowsky 2003, 10). Living in high-poverty neighborhoods has significant negative effects, even controlling for relevant individual-level characteristics, including poverty itself (see Dreier, Mollenkopf, and Swanstrom 2004, ch. 3). Poor people who live in high-poverty neighborhoods suffer higher rates of disease, for instance, than poor people who live in mixed-income neighborhoods. They are more likely to be victims of crime; they pay more for groceries and for other retail items; and they receive inferior public services.

Place differentially distributes life chances, what is more, through the so-called spatial mismatch of jobs and housing (Ellen and Turner 2003). Privileged places, where housing costs are high, also tend to be job-rich, while disadvantaged places tend to be job-poor. Although markets, in theory, tend toward equilibrium (a shortage of affordable housing in one part of a metropolitan region should be corrected, as increased demand motivates entrepreneurs to build), exclusionary zoning and similar land-use practices prevent markets from responding to demand. And there is a distinct racial component to the job–housing mismatch: more minorities, especially African-Americans, live in places that are more distant from jobs than otherwise similar whites do (Raphael and Stoll 2002).

Before the civil rights movement, the spatial dimension of injustice was easy to see. American blacks were compelled to live in overcrowded ghettos, characterized by physically deteriorated infrastructure and inferior public services, including separate and unequal schools. They were compelled to live in such places by agents of the state and by racially privileged private actors (e.g., white realtors). Starting in the 1960s, however, civil rights activists, motivated by an acute sense of injustice, forced the dismantling of state-sponsored segregation. Today, the American state does not dictate where members of different racial groups can and cannot live, and private discrimination in housing is forbidden by the 1968 Fair Housing Act. Still, place-based inequality, including racial inequality, persists. As john powell notes, "Space and land use policies remain an important way—perhaps the *most* important way—that we racially distribute opportunities and burdens in the United States" (powell 2009, 23).

Some political theorists have emphasized that the spatial concentration of the oppressed can promote resistance to unjust institutions and practices. Concentrating the disadvantaged, their claim is, enables them to interact and communicate with one another and then to mobilize and act collectively to challenge injustice (see, e.g., Kohn 2003; Imbroscio 2010). What is more, the concentration of unjust power relations in particular places can help highlight them even for the privileged and hence attract critical attention. Consider St. Louis, which went from having no black ghettos at the end of the nineteenth century to being "hypersegregated" by the 1970s.[20] Clearly, the concentration of racial injustice in the so-called black ghetto helped midcentury progressive reformers see it.

In the wake of the civil rights movement, however, when the segregated metropolis is produced and reproduced not by the positive actions of the state so much as by the weight of history and the structure of local governance, the fact that injustice is rooted in place makes it *thick injustice*.[21] The places where poverty is concentrated (inner cities and inner-ring suburbs) are places that most privileged Americans rarely see. If poverty were spread throughout the St. Louis metropolitan area, then the average St. Louisan would be much more likely to encounter it as part of her everyday life. She would not only see poverty and its effects in her neighborhood, in her local schools, and in other public places she would also encounter, in her *political* life, significant collective problems associated with poverty, such as high crime rates, public health problems, and low levels of academic achievement and attainment.

Place makes injustice thick, then, when it hides it away. Place also makes injustice thick by imbuing it with the innocence of personal preference, market competition, and choice. As Edward Soja puts it, "Rather than being seen as modifiable injustices or violations of civil rights, distributional inequalities [across space] have most often been buried under claims that they are the normal, expected, and unavoidable consequences of urban living. For some observers, they may even be viewed as ultimately contributing to the greater public good as products of individualized freedoms of choice, as noted for the multiplication of gated communities" (Soja 2010, 48).

Consider the intuitively appealing approach to thinking about place that has been elaborated by public choice theorists and popularized in everyday political discourse.[22] A multiplicity of local governments, this view suggests, each offering a distinct package of public services and tax expenditure levels, enables people to select that combination of services and taxes that best meets their needs. I might chose to live in an affluent suburb, paying high taxes for good schools, because I have children and highly value their education. You might choose a downtown loft because you have no children and prefer lower taxes. By this view, any municipality that offers a package that no one wants will be forced to change, or it will risk "going out of business"—losing residents, that is, and tax dollars—as people express their dissatisfaction by "voting with their feet."

One need not delve far into the public choice literature, however, to see the problems with this approach. It defines the differential ability to pay for public services (or for any of the other collective goods that are, in the contemporary metropolis, attached to place of residence) as a difference in people's *preferences* alone. It thus implies, implausibly, that those who lack resources prefer not to live in safe neighborhoods, have access to good jobs, or send their children to good schools. The public choice approach relies, what is more, on the baldly counterfactual assumption that people are free to move wherever they choose, and it assumes that household income is independent of residential location.[23] In short, although the "marketplace of governments" may respond to (some of) the preferences and desires of the racially privileged and the resource rich, it largely fails to serve the needs of the poor, working class, and those who encounter racial discrimination in their search for housing.

Let us return to our counterfactual argument and imagine again that the risk of suffering ill health, joining the ranks of the unemployed, or becoming a victim of violent crime was distributed *equally* across the physical space of metropolitan St. Louis. Imagine that place made *no difference whatsoever* in people's access to public services and private goods. This time, however, imagine that pronounced inequalities among racial and other groups obtain. Whites are significantly safer and healthier than blacks. Whites have access to the best public schools in the metropolitan area, while blacks attend clearly inferior schools. Absent attachment to place, the injustice of such racial inequality would be readily apparent. Stripped of place effects, the injustice of white, middle-class privilege and poor, black disadvantage would be easy to see.

Place makes injustice thick when it hides it away from the privileged. Place makes injustice even thicker when it hides *the relationship between the power and the privilege of some and the disadvantage of others.* "I live in Clayton," I might think, "because I work hard and use my earnings to buy the education I want for my children. My fellow citizen cross town lives in St. Louis City and sends his children to failing schools. His situation is unfortunate, but it has nothing to do with my choice and my preference." Although at midcentury the concentration of poverty and powerlessness in the Jim Crow ghetto drew attention to racial and other forms of injustice, in the post–civil rights movement years, place helps naturalize and obscure unjust power relations.

Conclusion and Overview

In 1945, when J. D. and Ethel Shelley purchased their two-story brick house at 4600 Labadie, the injustice they confronted was easy to see. State-enforced deed restrictions prohibited the couple from purchasing or occupying this house for the simple reason that they were "not of the Caucasian . . . [but] of the Negro . . . Race" (*Shelley v. Kraemer* 334 U.S. 1 [1948]). Clearly identifiable individual and collective actors—Fern and Louis Kraemer, for example, the Marcus Avenue Improvement Association, and the State Supreme Court Justices in Missouri—took clearly identifiable actions, which directly and predictably affected the Shelleys.

Today, more than a half-century later, the North St. Louis neighborhood in which 4600 Labadie sits remains racially segregated. It is now overwhelmingly African-American rather than white. It is a high-poverty neighborhood in which residents are significantly more likely than the average St. Louisan to be unemployed or underemployed, to be victims of crime, and to drop out of high school. But the injustice 4600 Labadie's current residents face is (as the *OED* puts it) "difficult to penetrate." It is thick injustice, we have argued, because of its deep historical roots, its relation to America's fragmented and privatized system of local governance, and its embeddedness in the physical space of North St. Louis.

Who is responsible for metropolitan injustice today? As we have emphasized throughout this chapter, it is difficult to point a finger at the agent or the agents who are *morally responsible*. When the Kerner Commission report was published in 1968, it was a relatively straightforward matter to identify those agents who had made concrete decisions, the foreseeable effects of which were to produce and reproduce injustice. At the start of the twenty-first century, by contrast, unjust power relations are reproduced through the uncoordinated actions of multiple actors, the effects of which are often unintended. They are produced by the choices and the actions of agents (e.g., home buyers and sellers, developers and planners, urban and suburban elected officials) pursuing reasonable ends (such as personal satisfaction, professional success, or reelection) within a metropolitan context that renders the combined effects of their choices unjust.

Injustice that is thick in this sense must be analyzed through not only the lens of moral responsibilitybut also the lens of *political responsibility* (Hayward and Lukes 2008). As Iris Young (among others) has argued, political responsibility is a matter less of blameworthiness than of the shared obligation to work to understand, criticize, and change those unjust outcomes to which multiple agents contribute, even if unconsciously (Young 2004). In this volume, political theorists and empirical scholars of urban politics grapple with the complex problem of metropolitan injustice. If it is successful, then unjust relations that are the product of uncoordinated, sometimes historically remote decisions can be moved into the realm of conscious political action. Understanding, criticizing, and informing efforts to change metropolitan injustice is our aim.

The remainder of the volume is divided into four parts. In Part I, "The Roots of Injustice in the American Metropolis," three political theorists ask foundational questions about what justice requires in cities and suburbs today. We open with Stephen Macedo's "Property-Owning Plutocracy: Inequality and American Localism" in which the author makes the case that local institutions in the American metropolis shape citizens' identities, motivations, and interests in ways that make them "stakeholders in inequality." Justice, in Macedo's view, requires changing institutions, including local political jurisdictions and the institution of home ownership. Next, Loren King's "Public Reason and the Just City" draws on John Rawls's work on "public reason" to make the case that we should evaluate proposed laws, policies, and institutions with a view to discerning whether the reasons used to justify them respect the equal political standing and basic interests of all affected. In King's view, metropolitan justice is less substantive than procedural; it requires political processes that encourage respectful engagement across lines of difference and spaces in which those with unpopular values might pursue their (reasonable) ends. Margaret Kohn's "Public Space in the Progressive Era" closes the first part. Drawing on work by Progressive thinkers who understood the education of democratic citizens to be closely linked to the creation of public space, Kohn makes the case that authentically public space is a necessary, if not sufficient, condition for prompting the privileged to question their unexamined beliefs and perceptions and for augmenting the power of the oppressed. Public space, properly designed, her claim is, can enable the difficult work of democratic political engagement across difference.

Part II, "Rethinking Metropolitan Inequality," begins with Douglas Rae's "Two Cheers for Very Unequal Incomes: Toward Social Justice in Central Cities," in which the author shows that most metropolitan inequality is *among*, rather than *within*, municipalities. Rae argues, counterintuitively, that justice may require *increasing* inequality within disadvantaged municipalities (such as St. Louis City) by attracting and working to retain high-income residents. In "Beyond the Equality–Efficiency Tradeoff," Clarence Stone argues that urban policy is often framed as an either–or choice between equality and efficiency. The alleged dichotomy between growth and redistribution is rooted in the assumption that policies should be evaluated with reference to their immediate effects on the interests of isolated individuals. Stone proposes, instead, that urban policy be judged according to its long-term, wide-ranging effects. Illustrating with case studies of three successful "social investment" programs, he argues that investing in youth can promote efficiency while redressing significant inequities.

Part III, "Planning for Justice," opens with Susan Fainstein's "Redevelopment Planning and Distributive Justice in the American Metropolis." Fainstein tackles head-on the shift in discourse and policy that motivates this volume. After examining historical shifts in the role that city planning played in shaping the development of the metropolis, she articulates principles for redevelopment oriented toward not order and growth but equity. Thad Williamson's "Justice, the Public Sector, and Cities: Relegitimating the Activist State" takes a different tack toward "planning for justice." Williamson makes the case that public leaders should actively promote "the public interest," defined not in purely procedural terms, but quasi-substantively as a shared interest in constructing and maintaining a flourishing and socially just polity. The author illustrates his normative argument with an original case study of efforts by Rachel Flynn, the Community Planning Director of Richmond, Virginia, to create and to implement a new downtown master plan.

The fourth and final section of our volume, "Justice and Institutions," begins with Gerald Frug's "Voting and Justice," which argues that injustice in the twenty-first-century metropolis is largely the product of our legal and institutional framework. Voting laws, Frug explains, enable some citizens to make decisions that profoundly affect other citizens, who have no political voice or effect. Expanding the franchise in local elections so that it includes many of those currently excluded, he suggests, would be an important step toward promoting justice. Like Frug's chapter, Richard Ford's "The Color of Territory: How Law and Borders Keep America Segregated" focuses on legal institutions. It returns to one of the central themes of this introductory chapter, drawing attention to the specifically *racial* dimensions of institutionally enabled injustice. Segregation in the American metropolis, Ford argues, is "*the primary* example of racism without racists because almost every other serious racial inequity in our society flows from it." Finally, in "Creating Justice for the Poor in the New Metropolis," Margaret Weir concludes our volume by returning to a theme Douglas Rae introduced in Part II. Place-based inequalities have increasingly moved outside central cities, Weir reminds us, to poor and working-class suburbs. She argues that locational disadvantages and weak institutional structures in poor suburbs produce "extrusion," a condition that renders poverty even more intractable, and less visible, than classic urban poverty. Social justice, according to Weir, requires federal policies that facilitate redistribution across metropolitan areas and at the same time amplify the voices of low-income people.

Rectifying the injustices that confront the residents of North St. Louis and of so many urban and suburban communities at the start of the twenty-first century, is no easy task. But the authors of this volume are united in their belief that it is an important task and one worth pursuing. A crucial first step is to change our political discourse about metropolitan America: to (re)direct it toward efforts to understand, criticize, and rectify *thick injustice*.

Notes

1. The quote is from the *New York Times* journalist John Herbers (1978), who observed, "St. Louis is not a typical city, but like a Eugene O'Neill play, it shows a general condition in stark and dramatic form."

2. Douglas Massey and Nancy Denton use five indices to estimate what they call "hypersegregation": (1) black isolation (i.e., the percentage of black individuals, on average, in the area where the average black person lives); (2) dissimilarity (the percentage of blacks who would need to move for the black population to be evenly distributed throughout a city); (3) the clustering of ghettoized areas near one another; (4) the concentration of blacks in relatively small areas; and (5) their centralization around an urban core. See Massey and Denton (1993, 74).

3. An important marker in this shift was Paul Peterson's influential *City Limits* (1981), which argued that cities must pursue economic growth to the exclusion of redistributive policies or suffer the consequences of massive disinvestment. The year before Peterson's book was published, the McGill Commission, appointed by President Carter, made the case that urban policy must adapt to the imperatives of economic restructuring, concluding that efforts to help ailing urban areas "are as unrealistic as they are nostalgic" (President's Commission 1980, 79). Although we respect the work of the Brookings Institution Metropolitan Policy Program, it reflects an economic approach to urban policy as well. The emphasis is on the need for new metropolitan policies to promote not justice but national economic growth. See, for example, the recent Brookings Report by Istrate, Rothwell, and Katz (2011).

4. For relevant exemplars of journalistic and scholarly work from this period, see Harrington (1962), Jacobs (1961), and Harvey (1973).

5. We are not alone in this endeavor. See especially Fainstein (2010) and Marcuse et al. (2009).

6. As this book goes to press, the Obama administration remains limited by the financial crisis in the funds it can commit to cities. Nevertheless, it has embarked on a series of initiatives, such as the Sustainable Communities Planning Grants

and the Promise Neighborhoods program, that approach urban issues from a metropolitan perspective and begin to push beyond a narrow economic calculus to focus on environmental and equity goals.

7. Logan and Molotch's (1987) important work on the city as growth machine was influenced by Marx but emphasized the central role of landowners in growth coalitions, which promote exchange values at the expense of use values. The growth machine, Logan and Molotch argued, sacrifices communal and environmental values in the name of promoting economic growth.

8. This is Rawls's famous "difference principle." For a detailed account of his two principles of justice and the method by which he derives them, see Stephen Macedo's chapter in the present volume.

9. Western Europe has far lower levels of economic segregation than the United States but is economically prosperous. Indeed, as Susan Fainstein has noted, Amsterdam is one of the most egalitarian cities in the world, but this has had no obvious negative effect on its economy (Fainstein 1997). See also Fainstein's defense of Amsterdam in response to critics (2010, ch. 5). Studies of regional differences within the United States suggest that spatial inequity retards economic growth. The greater the gap between the central cities and suburbs, the worse a regional economy performs. Various causal pathways have been hypothesized. A deteriorated central city may project a poor image for the region, for instance, or it may drive economic functions that benefit from clustering into less efficient suburban locations. For a synthesis of the research on spatial inequalities and regional economic competiveness, see Dreier, Mollenkopf, and Swanstrom (2004, 72–76).

10. We review evidence on the negative contextual effects of concentrated poverty in the section on "Thick Injustice and Place."

11. See, for example, MacIntyre (1981), Sandel (1982), and Walzer (1983). For useful overviews of the liberal–communitarian debate, see Gutmann (1985) and Buchanan (1989).

12. For many low-income St. Louisans, because the only affordable housing is within city limits, because public services are funded and distributed locally, and because the St. Louis municipality and school district have inadequate taxable resources to meet residents' needs, police protection, education, and other public services are inadequate.

13. Central-city neighborhoods like North St. Louis and older, inner-ring suburbs are often distant from good jobs—a "spatial mismatch" that translates inequalities of income and wealth into inequality of opportunity. Retail stores, moreover, are disproportionately clustered in middle-income and wealthy areas, even controlling for differential levels of consumer spending (Dreier, Mollenkopf, and Swanstrom 2004, 85–86).

14. We can imagine at least two significant libertarian rejoinders to this claim. A libertarian might argue, first, that racial discrimination is a thing of the past and that markets now operate freely and fairly in the contemporary metropolis. However, as we note in section two of this chapter, the capital whites accumulated in the form of equity in housing acquired during the heyday of state-sponsored

discrimination represents a nontrivial portion of the wealth held by white Americans. What is more, racial discrimination persists in the wake of fair housing legislation. Audits that pair subjects who are identical in every relevant way (except race) show nontrivial rates of discrimination (Cashin 2004; Turner, Struyk, and Yinger 1991; Wienk et al. 1979). Second, a libertarian might assert that welfare-state and affirmative action policies have already compensated for past injustices—perhaps even overcompensated, producing "reverse discrimination." This claim is difficult to support. Indeed, as we argue in this chapter, some welfare state policies (such as New Deal housing policies) exacerbated, rather than ameliorated, discrimination, and the inequalities built into metropolitan American institutions and spatial forms help reproduce and reinforce historical injustice. Fair-minded libertarians, we believe, will agree with Rawlsian liberals and communitarians on the need to address metropolitan injustice, even if they disagree on *how* they should be redressed (e.g., favoring vouchers, for instance, over state-led redistribution).

15. In Baltimore, for instance, between 1951 and 1964, 90 percent of families displaced by urban renewal and highway building were African-American (Frieden and Sagalyn 1989, 29).

16. See, for example, Jacobs (1961), Gans (1965), and more recently, Fullilove (2004). In *Village of Arlington Heights v. Metropolitan Housing Development Corp* (429 U.S. 252 [1977]) the U.S. Supreme Court ruled that a local zoning law could not be struck down because it discriminated against various socioeconomic or ethno-racial groups. Rather, plaintiffs must demonstrate that the law *intended* to discriminate against these groups. More recently, the Supreme Court ruled that citizens could not sue under Title VI the 1964 Civil Rights Act on the grounds that a federally funded program had a disparate impact on a racial group (*Alexander v. Sandoval*, 532 U.S. 275 [2001]). Disparate impacts are *presumed* to be unintentional and therefore not subject to civil rights law. The movement by conservative jurists to protect government actions that are not explicitly motivated by discriminatory intent, we argue, ignores thick injustice—the ways that historically grounded spatial relations render decisions made on economically rational and formally equal grounds profoundly unjust.

17. For an overview and critique, see Bell and Parchomovsky (2006).

18. At the time of the 2000 census, more than 92 percent of Wellston's residents were African-American, and more than 68 percent lived below the federal poverty level (U.S. Census Bureau, 2003). This suburb is anything but unique. Myron Orfield (2002) estimates that 40 percent of the metropolitan population in the United States lives in what he terms "at-risk" suburbs: suburbs with below average taxing capacity and above average spending demands. Indeed, by 2005, more poor people lived in suburbs than in central cities (Berube and Kneebone 2006), and the majority of immigrants settled not in cities but in suburbs (Singer, Hardwick, and Brettell 2008).

19. Community development corporations (CDCs), for instance, are much more common in central cities than in suburbs. The lack of CDCs accounts for the inability

of many suburban municipalities to respond effectively to the foreclosure crisis (Swanstrom, Chapple, and Immergluck 2009).

20. The black isolation index, which measures the degree to which people categorized as "black" are isolated in predominantly black areas, was only 5 percent in St. Louis in 1890 (Cutler, Glaeser, and Vigdor 1999). Typically, an isolation index must reach 30 percent before it is considered high. That same year, the index of dissimilarity, which measures the evenness of the distribution of people categorized as "black" throughout an area, was in St. Louis a moderate 33 percent. Generally, a dissimilarity index must reach 60 percent before it is considered high (Cutler, Glaeser, and Vigdor 1999). For detailed discussions of both measures, see Massey and Denton (1993, ch. 2) and Cutler, Glaeser, and Vigdor (1999). By 1970, the index of isolation in St. Louis had reached 73 percent, and the index of dissimilarity 85 percent (Cutler, Glaeser, and Vigdor 1999).

21. Another reason segregation persists at the start of the twenty-first century is that discrimination persists in private market transactions. Major housing audit studies conducted after the passage of fair housing legislation show consistent widespread discrimination against minority home buyers and renters (Cashin 2004; Turner, Struyk, and Yinger 1991; Wienk et al. 1979). Still another contributing factor is the *increase*, in recent years, in socioeconomic segregation (Dreier, Mollenkopf, and Swanstrom 2004, 54). With race and class so closely intertwined (for the reasons discussed previously), economic discrimination reproduces and reinforces the racial inequalities and hierarchies constructed during the pre–civil rights movement years.

22. The seminal work is Tiebout (1956). For an application of this view to the St. Louis metropolitan case, see Jones (2000, ch. 5).

23. This assumption is wrongheaded, not only because of the "spatial mismatch" discussed previously, but also because education, which is distributed according to place of residence, is a powerful determinant of income. See Mishel, Bernstein, and Allegretto (2007).

References

Alexander v. Sandoval, 532 U.S. 275 (2001).

Anderson, Martin. 1964. *The Federal Bulldozer: A Critical Analysis of Urban Renewal, 1949–1962*. Cambridge, Mass.: MIT Press.

Bell, Abraham, and Gideon Parchomovsky. 2006. "The Uselessness of Public Use." *Columbia Law Review* 106, no. 6: 1412–49.

Berube, Alan, and Elizabeth Kneebone. 2006. *Two Steps Back: City and Suburban Poverty Trends, 1999–2005*. Washington, D.C.: The Brookings Institution.

Buchanan, Allen. 1989. "Assessing the Communitarian Critique of Liberalism." *Ethics* 99, no. 4: 852–82.

Cashin, Sheryl L. 2004. *The Failures of Integration: How Race and Class Are Undermining the American Dream*. New York: Public Affairs.

Cutler, David, Edward Glaeser, and Jacob Vigdor. 1999. "The Rise and Decline of the American Ghetto." *Journal of Political Economy* 107, no. 3: 455–506.

Dreier, Peter, John Mollenkopf, and Todd Swanstrom. 2004. *Place Matters: Metropolitics for the Twenty-First Century*, rev. ed. Lawrence: University Press of Kansas.

Ellen, Ingrid Gould, and Margery Austin Turner. 2003. "Do Neighborhoods Matter and Why?" In *Choosing a Better Life: Evaluating the Moving to Opportunity Experiment*, ed. John Goering and Judith D. Feins. Washington, D.C.: Urban Institute Press.

Erie, Stephen. 1988. *Rainbow's End: Irish-Americans and the Dilemmas of Urban Machine Politics, 1840–1985*. Berkeley: University of California Press.

Fainstein, Susan S. 1997. "The Egalitarian City: The Restructuring of Amsterdam." *International Planning Studies* 2, no. 3: 295–314.

———. 2010. *The Just City*. Ithaca, N.Y.: Cornell University Press.

Faulkner, William. 1994. "Requiem for a Nun." In *Faulkner, Novels: 1942–1954*, ed. Joseph Bloom and Noel Park. New York: Library of America.

Foucault, Michel. 1986. "Of Other Spaces." *Diacritics* 16, no. 1: 22–27.

Frieden, Bernard J., and Lynne B. Sagalyn. 1989. *Downtown, Inc.: How America Builds Cities*. Cambridge, Mass.: MIT Press.

Fullilove, Mindy Thompon. 2004. *Root Shock: How Tearing Up City Neighborhoods Hurts America, and What We Can Do about It*. New York: One World.

Gans, Herbert. 1965. "The Failure of Urban Renewal: A Critique and Some Proposals." *Commentary* 39, no. 4: 29–37.

Gordon, Colin. 2008. *Mapping Decline: St. Louis and the Fate of the American City*. Philadelphia: University of Pennsylvania Press.

Gutmann, Amy. 1985. "Communitarian Critics of Liberalism." *Philosophy and Public Affairs* 14, no. 3: 308–22.

Harrington, Michael. 1962. *The Other America: Poverty in the United States*. New York: Simon and Schuster.

Harvey, David. 1973. *Social Justice and the City*. London: Edward Arnold.

———. 1989. *The Urban Experience*. Baltimore, Md.: The Johns Hopkins University Press.

———. 1996. *Justice, Nature, and the Geography of Difference*. Malden, Mass.: Blackwell.

———. 2000. *Spaces of Hope*. Berkeley: University of California Press.

Hayward, Clarissa. 2003. "The Difference States Make: Democracy, Identity, and the American City." *American Political Science Review* 97:501–14.

———. 2009. "Making Interest: On Representation and Democratic Legitimacy," In *Political Representation*, ed. Ian Shapiro, Susan Stokes, Elisabeth Wood, and Alexander Kirschner, 111–35. Cambridge, U.K.: Cambridge University Press.

Hayward, Clarissa, and Steven Lukes. 2008. "Nobody to Shoot? Power, Structure, and Agency: A Dialogue." *Journal of Power* 1, no. 1: 5–20.

Herbers, John. 1978. "Decade after Kerner Report: Division of Races Persists." *New York Times*, February 26. http://partners.nytimes.com/library/national/race/022678race-ra.html (accessed February 6, 2011).

Hochschild, Jennifer. 1995. *Facing Up to the American Dream: Race, Class, and the Soul of the Nation*. Princeton, N.J.: Princeton University Press.

Imbroscio, David. 2010. *Urban America Reconsidered: Alternatives for Governance and Policy*. Ithaca, N.Y.: Cornell University Press.

Istrate, Emilia, Jonathan Rothwell, and Bruce Katz. 2011. "Export Nation: How U.S. Metros Lead National Export Growth and Boost Competitiveness." http://www.brookings.edu/reports/2010/0726_exports_istrate_rothwell_katz.aspx.

Jacobs, Jane. 1961. *The Death and Life of Great American Cities*. New York: Vintage Books.

Jargowsky, Paul A. 2003. *Stunning Progress, Hidden Problems: The Dramatic Decline of Concentrated Poverty in the 1990s*. Washington, D.C.: The Brookings Institution.

Jones, E. Terrence. 2000. *Fragmented by Design: Why St. Louis Has So Many Governments*. St. Louis, Mo.: Palmerston & Reed.

Kelo v. City of New London et al., 545 U.S. 469 (2005).

Kerner Commission. 1968. *Report of the National Advisory Commission on Civil Disorders*. Washington, D.C.: U.S. Government Printing Office.

Lipsitz, George. 2006. *The Possessive Investment in Whiteness: How White People Profit from Identity Politics*, rev. ed. Philadelphia: Temple University Press.

Logan, John R., and Harvey L. Molotch. 1987. *Urban Fortunes: The Political Economy of Place*. Berkeley: University of California Press.

Marcuse, Peter, James Connolly, Johannes Novy, Ingrid Olivo, Cuz Potter, and Justin Stein. 2009. *Searching for the Just City: Debates in Urban Theory and Practice*. New York: Routledge.

Marx, Karl. 1978a. "The German Ideology: Part I." In *The Marx-Engels Reader*, ed. Robert Tucker, 146–200. New York: Norton.

———. 1978b. "Capital, Volume I." In *The Marx-Engels Reader*, ed. Robert Tucker, 294–438. New York: Norton.

Massey, Doreen. 1994. *Space, Place, and Gender*. Minneapolis: University of Minnesota Press.

Massey, Douglas S., and Nancy A. Denton. 1993. *American Apartheid: Segregation and the Making of the Underclass*. Cambridge, Mass.: Harvard University Press.

Milliken v. Bradley, 418 U.S. 717 (1974).

Mishel, Lawrence, Jared Bernstein, and Sylvia Allegretto. 2007. *The State of Working American 2006/2007*. Ithaca, N.Y.: Cornell University Press.

Nozick, Robert. 1974. *Anarchy, State, and Utopia*. New York: Basic Books.

Omi, Michael, and Howard Winant. 1994. *Racial Formation in the United States*. New York: Routledge.

Orfield, Myron. 2002. *American Metropolitics: The New Suburban Reality*. Washington, D.C.: The Brookings Institution.

Oxford English Dictionary, 2nd ed., s.v. "thick."

Peterson, Paul E. 1981. *City Limits*. Chicago: University of Chicago Press.

powell, j. 2009. "Reinterpreting Metropolitan Space as a Strategy for Social Justice." In *Breakthrough Communities: Sustainability and Justice in the Next American Metropolis*, ed. M. Paloma Pavel. Cambridge, Mass.: MIT Press.

President's Commission for a National Agenda for the Eighties. 1980. *Urban America in the Eighties*. Washington, D.C.: U.S. Government Printing Office.

Raphael, Steven, and Michael A. Stoll. 2002. *Modest Progress: The Narrowing Spatial*

Mismatch between Blacks and Jobs in the 1990s. Washington, D.C.: The Brookings Institution.

Rawls, John. 1971. *A Theory of Justice.* Cambridge, Mass.: Harvard University Press.

———. *Political Liberalism.* New York: Columbia University Press.

Rusk, David. 2008. "Housing Policy *Is* School Policy." In *Urban and Regional Policies for Metropolitan Livability,* ed. David K. Hamilton and Patricia S. Atkins, 204–31. Armonk, N.Y.: M. E. Sharpe.

Saito, Leland T. 2009. *The Politics of Exclusion: The Failure of Race-Neutral Policies in Urban America.* Stanford, Calif.: Stanford University Press.

Sandel, Michael. 1982. *Liberalism and the Limits of Justice* Cambridge, U.K.: Cambridge University Press.

Shapiro, Thomas M. 2004. *The Hidden Cost of Being African American: How Wealth Perpetuates Inequality.* New York: Oxford University Press.

Shelley v. Kraemer, 334 U.S. 1 (1948).

Singer, Audrey, Susan W. Hardwick, and Caroline Brettell, eds. 2008. *Twenty-First Century Gateways: Immigrant Incorporation in Suburban America.* Washington, D.C.: The Brookings Institution.

Soja, Edward. 1996. *Thirdspace: Journeys to Los Angeles and Other Real-and-Imagined Places.* Cambridge, U.K.: Blackwell.

———. 2010. *Seeking Spatial Justice.* Minneapolis: University of Minnesota Press.

Swanstrom, Todd, Karen Chapple, and Dan Immergluck. 2009. "Regional Resilience in the Face of Foreclosures: Evidence from Six Metropolitan Areas." Working paper 2009-05, MacArthur Foundation Research Network on Building Resilient Regions. Berkeley: Institute of Urban and Regional Development, University of California Berkeley.

Testa, Bill. 2006. "Manufacturing Exit Tough on Midwest Central Cities." Federal Reserve Bank of Chicago, July 6. http://midwest.chicagofedblogs.org/archives/2006/07/manufacturing_e_1.html (accessed September 1, 2010).

Tiebout, Charles. 1956. "A Pure Theory of Local Expenditures." *Journal of Political Economy* 64, no. 5: 416–24.

Turner, Margery, Raymond Struyk, and John Yinger. 1991. *Housing Discrimination Study: Synthesis.* Washington, D.C.: U.S. Department of Housing and Urban Development.

U.S. Census Bureau. 1980. *Statistical Abstract of the United States: 1980.* Washington, D.C.: U.S. Government Printing Office.

———. 2003. *2000 Census of Population and Housing.* http://factfinder.census.gov (accessed February 6, 2010).

U.S. Department of Housing and Urban Development. 2010. "Investing in People and Places: FY 2011 Budget." http://portal.hud.gov/portal/page/portal/HUD/documents/fy2011budget.pdf (accessed July 20, 2010).

Village of Arlington Heights v. Metropolitan Housing Development Corp, 429 U.S. 252 (1977).

Walzer, Michael. 1983. *Spheres of Justice: A Defense of Pluralism and Equality.* New York: Basic Books.

Wienk, Ronald, Clifford Reid, John Simonson, and Frederick Eggers. 1979. *Housing Markets Practices Survey*. Washington, D.C.: U.S. Department of Housing and Urban Development.

Young, Iris. 2000. *Inclusion and Democracy*. Oxford, U.K.: Oxford University Press.

———. 2004. "Responsibility and Global Labor Justice." *Journal of Political Philosophy* 12:365–88.

I

THE ROOTS OF INJUSTICE IN THE AMERICAN METROPOLIS

1 PROPERTY-OWNING PLUTOCRACY

Inequality and American Localism

STEPHEN MACEDO

THE AMERICAN DREAM IS A dream of liberty and opportunity. It promises reward and advancement to those who pursue it. The dream is pursued by families: parents seek it for themselves and their children. It involves owning a home and sending one's children to a good school. These ideals organize our lives and inform our institutions. Public policy promotes it in all sorts of ways: for example, by encouraging home ownership and by providing free public education for all. It is a dream that most of us pursue, and it is a dream that we believe—or want to believe—is available to all. But is the dream available to all?

This chapter argues that American local institutions are deeply flawed. Competition among local communities, homeowners, and school districts creates a race to the top for some, while leaving many behind. The nexus of home ownership, local funding and control of schools, and the power of local communities to zone to exclude the poor provides enormous positional advantages to those who can afford to live where the best schools are. It also, as we will see, builds perverse inegalitarian incentives into the motivational structures of ordinary citizens, who function as parents, property owners, and citizens.

Good Schools for All?

The website GreatSchools.org allows parents to search the country for the "best schools for your housing dollars." It reports that "every year millions of U.S. parents consider pulling up stakes to make a city and school upgrade," and many move "from city to city in search of educational excellence and affordable living." The website helpfully rates cities and towns across the country, sorted according to housing prices and the quality of the local schools. It combines research on school quality with analysis of the local housing market. The best school districts "recruit and retain, motivate, and develop great teachers." Other keys to success, according to the website, are small class sizes, low teacher–student ratios, constant innovation, access to "cutting-edge technology," and superintendents who approach their work with "unflagging intensity and creativity." The very best schools, in places like the wealthy suburbs around Boston, "offer students an enriching environment of artistic, athletic, and musical extracurriculars" (GreatSchools Inc. 2010).[1]

Not all the towns with excellent schools are superrich, and Great-Schools.org insists that it is possible to have excellent schools in places where homes are affordable. Tiny Harrison, Arkansas (population 13,000), has excellent schools and a median home price of only $99,800. Harrison also has a thriving business community and "an intensely committed parent body." The high school's booster club recently raised $7 million for a new sports facility. Generally, however, many of the very best schools are indeed in wealthy communities. There are medium-sized cities with good schools—such as Raleigh, North Carolina; Pittsburgh, Pennsylvania; and San Francisco, California—that, in fact, score much lower than top suburban and small-town schools. So while the website provides options for anyone who can afford to live in a wide range of places, it also candidly states, "Want a superior education? Follow the money."

GreatSchools.org is not a source of cutting-edge research on income and school achievement, but it is a window into the American dream and apparently, at least, a helpful guide for concerned parents with sufficient resources to be mobile. Across the country, suburban realty web pages boast of the quality of local schools. Home values are enhanced by the quality of the local schools. Ideally, every family, by choosing where to live, will be able to find a community with at least a decent school for their children. And the whole system of fragmented metropolitan areas with many local jurisdictions, each with their own local schools, competing for residents based on the relative quality of schools, and thereby helping to bid up home prices, should lead to educational improvements overall. And indeed there is some evidence that school quality increases, and the general cost of public services may be kept down, in metropolitan areas with multiple suburban and ex-urban jurisdictions.

Decentralization and Democracy

Decentralization of political power to the local level has long been seen as a key to the health of American democracy; it is one of the central themes of Alexis de Tocqueville's *Democracy in America*. Keeping power local and accessible rather than distant helps engage the interests of ordinary citizens in public affairs, which they then perceive to be connected with their immediate interests and capable of being influenced. Tocqueville also thought that widespread property ownership was a key to diffusing energy in society and promoting social equality. Some of the most astonishingly hopeful reflections in Tocqueville's influential book are connected with these themes and occur very early on (in a chapter called "The Social State of the Anglo-Americans"). In eloquent passages Tocqueville introduces his pivotal idea that the "social condition" of Americans is "essentially [or "eminently"] democratic" (Tocqueville 1988, 50). Tocqueville argues that "equality of conditions" is the central characteristic of democracy and that it was more highly developed in Jacksonian America than anywhere else on Earth: in America "men are nearer equality in wealth and mental endowments, or, in other words, more nearly equally powerful, than any other country of the world or in any other age of recorded history." "In America now," he says, "the aristocratic element, which was from the beginning weak, has been, if not destroyed, at least made the feebler still, so that one can hardly attribute to it any influence over the course of things," while "the democratic element" is "not merely preponderant but, one might say, exclusive" (56).

These are very strong statements. And it is worth recalling that for Tocqueville, the effects of equality of conditions are completely pervasive. Democracy is not merely an arrangement of political offices, based on political equality and accountability to the people; it is rather a "regime" in Aristotle's sense, where principles of political order shape and depend on a common way of life. The democratic way of life for Tocqueville was pervasively egalitarian and included distinctive forms of family life, literature, and even philosophy.

So what is it, Tocqueville asks, that gave rise to equality of conditions in America? Why is equality—and therefore democracy—so highly developed here? The reasons seem to be many and include distinctive patterns of immigration, plus American's wide open frontier. But one factor in particular is singled out for extended scrutiny. Tocqueville says that "the laws of inheritance . . . caused the final advance of equality." He meant in particular the end of the feudal property laws of primogeniture and entail, which required estates to pass intact to the eldest son. Once freed of these restrictions on the distribution of inheritance, property tends to be divided among children equally, and then, Tocqueville says, "the death of each owner causes a revolution in property" in which estates are "continually broken up into smaller fractions" (52). I will quote at length to give the flavor and emphasis:

> I am surprised that ancient and modern writers have not attributed greater importance to the laws of inheritance and their effect on the progress of human affairs. They are, it is true, civil laws, but they should head the list of all political institutions, for they have an unbelievable influence on the social state of peoples, and political laws are no more than the expression of that state. Moreover, their way of influencing society is both sure and uniform; in some sense they lay hands on each generation before it is born . . . The mechanism works by its own power and apparently spontaneously aims at the goal indicated beforehand. If it has been drafted in a certain way, it assembles, concentrates, and piles up property, and soon power too . . . ; in a sense it makes an aristocracy leap forth from the ground. Guided by other principles and directed toward other goals, its effect is even quicker; it divides, shares, and spreads property and power; then sometimes people get frightened at the speed of its progress; despairing of stopping its motion, men seek at least to put obstacles and difficulties in its way; there is an attempt to balance its action by measures of opposite tendency. But all in vain! It grinds up or smashes everything that stands in its way; with the continual rise and fall of its hammer strokes, everything is reduced to a fine, impalpable dust, and that dust is the foundation for democracy. (51–52)

The laws of property thus underwrite Tocqueville's master distinction between aristocracy and democracy. Under the rules of primogeniture and entail, "family feeling finds a sort of physical expression in the land," which perpetuate its "name, origin, glory, and virtue" (52). Under the democratic rules of equality of condition and divided inheritances, "a taste for every form of independence" is awakened (51). There is also a downside: as links across generations weaken, time horizons contract, and as connections across extended families wither, the family becomes "a vague, indeterminate, uncertain conception." Whereas once the heads of great families presided over far-flung dependents and thought in terms of centuries past and to come, democratic fathers think "about getting the next generation established in life, but nothing further" (53). This discussion is a microcosm of the argument of *Democracy in America* as a whole. Democracy diffuses liberty and opportunity widely—leveling the economic and social order and dissolving inherited social hierarchies—but it also shrinks the greatest ambitions and narrows social circles. In every respect it radically remakes the social, political, and intellectual worlds.

The Laws of Property and Local Government

Tocqueville was right about one thing (many things, actually): laws of local property ownership interact with local political institutions to shape and distribute privileges across generations, fostering a distinctive set of values and interests and coloring the political regime. But we hardly notice.

The laws of property deserve to be regarded as part of what John Rawls, a more recent theorist of American democracy, calls the "basic structure of society" (Rawls 1999, 6). The "basic structure" is composed of the major institutions of society: the political and legal system, including the Constitution and its specification of basic rights and liberties; laws regulating property, inheritance, employment, and taxation; and laws regulating the family. The basic structure is the main subject of reflections on justice for several obvious reasons. These major institutions have pervasive and deep effects on our lives: they shape our opportunities and expectations from cradle to grave. These institutions persist across generations and are crucial for stabilizing expectations and promoting reciprocal subscription to common principles: mutual expectations of fair cooperation based on principles of justice are far more realistic when they are embedded in institutions. Finally, these major institutions can have a profound *educative or formative effect*: our self-understandings and identities are shaped by the major social, political, and economic institutions within which we live. "Those who grow up in a well-ordered society will, in good part," says Rawls, "form their conception of themselves as citizens from the public culture and from the conceptions of person and society implicit in it" (Rawls 2001, 122). Our self-understandings and identities are equally shaped by flawed institutions.

Both Tocqueville and Rawls hope to lay bare the deep structure of liberal democracy for the sake of helping us to correct it via political science. The effects of local institutions and property arrangements are profound and pervasive: they shape our life prospects and standing relative to others. And they operate in advance, as it were, of our individual choices and transactions: local institutions and property arrangements become part of the background architecture of our social, political, and cultural lives, the effects of which are often preconscious and liable to be taken for granted. Local institutions of property ownership and political power ought to be given a much more prominent place among these formative institutions.[2]

What Does Justice Require?

What principles should guide the design of the basic institutions of society? While Tocqueville is mainly concerned with identifying the possibilities and pathologies of modern democracy, Rawls provides a more systematic account of the principles of political morality that should guide the design of our most basic institutions.

So what principles should guide our assessment and reform of our institutions? What principles give fair consideration to the well-being of all Americans? According to Rawls's thought experiment, we imagine ourselves behind a veil of ignorance, not knowing the circumstances of our birth, race, gender, talents, or genetic endowments, but knowing that all of these will differentiate people. We also put aside knowledge of our conception of "the good life" and religious views. The point of the veil of ignorance is to put aside knowledge that could lead us to favor ourselves. In order to think about principles of justice that are fairly acceptable to all, we should imagine ourselves occupying any social position—rich or poor; white, black or brown; man or woman. The moral aspiration at work here is the desire to discern principles of social justice that could be endorsed by all of our reasonable fellow citizens, with full information, and regarded as free and equal. We ask, which principles of social justice, were they adopted as a basis for institutional construction and reform, would make the political and social order acceptable from everyone's point of view, especially the least well off?

Rawls famously proposes three main principles. First, we should give priority to the protection of a list of familiar basic liberties, including freedoms of religion, expression, privacy, movement, choice of occupation, and so on. In addition, we should endorse two principles of distributive justice to guide the design of the basic structure for the system of property, taxation, inheritance, and the provision of public services, including education. First is *fair equality of opportunity*: systems of education and inheritance, taxation, and social provision should be organized so that all children—regardless of the circumstances of their birth—have a *fair chance* to compete for the best jobs or positions of leadership in society based on talent and effort.[3] Second is the *difference principle*: having satisfied the fair equality of opportunity principle, we should look at the inequalities that are subsequently generated from the position of the least well-off group in society and further arrange systems of property and taxation so that the inequalities tend to make the least well off as well off as possible. These three principles are "lexically ordered," meaning that the basic liberties should be fully provided for first, then fair equality, and finally the difference principle. We pursue collective well-being and the whole range of public goods subject to these principles. We allow people to garner unequal rewards to help call forth their free and willing effort, but only when we have done our best to design the background institutions of society to satisfy these three principles of justice.

Why does Rawls argue that these principles are required as a matter of justice? The core idea is that in a democratic society each and every citizen is ultimately responsible for the way power is exercised over others: political institutions belong to all of us, and we must justify their effects to one another or work to reform them. The principles of political justice should guide our political decisions and those of our leaders so that our politics tend to be justifiable to all. We want the whole social order to be freely acceptable or endorsable from everyone's point of view, with full information and on due reflection. When the institutions that generate economic inequalities tend to satisfy the two distributive principles, the system allows for unequal rewards but also expresses to the least well off that they matter as moral equals.[4]

How should property be organized in the just society?[5] Instructive for our purposes is Rawls's contrast between a "capitalist welfare state" (similar to what we have in the United States, though the "welfare" part is underdeveloped) and what Rawls calls a "property-owning democracy." Both of these allow "private property in productive assets." The capitalist welfare state "permits very large inequalities in the ownership of real property" so that "control of the economy and much of political life tend rests in a few hands." Welfare benefits provide a decent minimum and there are no *legal* bars to anyone competing for the best jobs and positions of leadership in society. But while capitalist welfare states may redistribute unequal gains downward, they fail to provide for fair equality of opportunity (Rawls 2001, 138).

Capitalist welfare states place too much emphasis on the redistribution of people's very unequal gains, via income and other taxes, at the end of the day. Even if high levels of redistribution are put in place, so as to satisfy the difference principle, the system would fail to provide a fair opportunity for all citizens from the beginning, and the redistributive commitments of such a system seem liable to be unstable. Participants in a redistributive welfare state, which generates large inequalities based not only on unequal talent but also on unequal family advantages, will tend to regard the least well-off as "objects of charity and compassion" (Rawls 2001, 139).

Far preferable, says Rawls, is a "property-owning democracy," which gives priority to fair equality of opportunity by putting "in the hands of citizens generally," and not only a few, productive means, including real and human capital, "knowledge and an understanding of institutions, educated abilities, and trained skills" (Rawls 2001, 140). A property-owning democracy seeks to insure that property and educational opportunities are sufficiently dispersed across each rising generation so that everyone starts off with a fair chance to compete for the best jobs and positions of leadership in society. The idea is to try to arrange things so that our equal standing is guaranteed from the get-go and not simply restored at the end of the day after great inequalities have been generated. Such a system should do a much better job of creating the conditions for all citizens to interact as equals. It is important that the principles of justice be institutionalized in the right way—that is, as part of a system that guarantees fair distribution of wealth, education, and other sources of opportunity and advantage from the start, and not simply as a *redistributive* system that generates great inequalities and then hopes to rearrange them.[6]

Like most political observers nowadays, Rawls's view is generally top-down: his vantage point is that of national institutions. But we need to look at the problem from the bottom up as well: from the frequently ignored standpoint of local political institutions and laws that shape home ownership and access to the best neighborhoods and schools, including taxing, spending, and zoning powers. If local background institutions operate so as to generate large and systematic inequalities from the start, especially ones that are inheritable and closely connected with family ties, then there may be very little chance that people—as citizens— will support the sort of redistributive system that would be necessary to correct for these mal-distributive effects. Indeed, if substantial inequalities are generated by background institutions, education, and market transactions, aren't we, as Rawls suggests, liable to come to regard the less well off not as moral and social equals and participants in a system of social cooperation whose fate is closely bound up with our own but as distant objects of charity?

So how does our current system of local institutions and laws of property measure up?

Local Engines of Inequality

If the rules of property continued to work in the way that Tocqueville described—grinding, smashing, and leveling estates and holdings from one generation to the next—then that would evidently be very good from the standpoint of equality of opportunity. Tocqueville's description is, however, very far from current realities. For one thing, it is widely acknowledged that wealth and income are distributed very unequally in the United States and that these inequalities have been growing over the last 30 years. So how should we update Tocqueville, keeping in mind his emphasis on the fundamental nature of the "laws of inheritance," broadly conceived: do local laws and institutions make opportunity available to all or do they, conversely, allow—even encourage—special advantages to be passed from one generation to the next?

In America today, home ownership and the ways we organize local jurisdictional boundaries, powers, and privileges play unique and central roles in concentrating and perpetuating relative advantages and disadvantages. Because these patterns of home owning and local community membership are so closely intertwined, they deserve to be regarded together as central features of our "laws of inheritance," in Tocqueville's terms. Local institutions are also certainly core features of what Rawls calls the "basic structure," the primary subject of justice. For their effects are pervasive and they shape citizens' understanding of their interests and identities.

In thinking about the nature of poverty and inequality in America— including why poverty persists, why it is so hard to ameliorate, and why intergenerational mobility is not nearly as great as Americans seem to believe—it is important to look to the laws that organize property locally and with it the distribution of relative advantages and disadvantages. The laws of property at the local level make us stakeholders in inequality, shaping our operative interests and values as parents, homeowners, and citizens, and distorting our conception of freedom.

Douglas Massey and Nancy L. Denton provide an excellent account of the ways in which local policies and institutions foster geography-based inequalities in their aptly titled *American Apartheid*. The high concentrations of rich versus poor across American metropolitan areas is not simply the consequence of individual market choices. Local laws and background institutions facilitate the sorting of Americans by race and class.[7] These deep pathologies result neither from political design nor private choice alone but rather from private choices within faulty institutional structures.

Local political structures—the way we organize local political institutions, draw their boundaries, and allocate powers among them—have contributed to the formation of communities marked by persistently high levels of racial segregation and high and increasing levels of class stratification. It is true enough that the old image of the "city–suburb doughnut"—with impoverished central cities and high concentrations of minority residents, and middle-class and overwhelmingly white outer rings—is outdated. Suburbs are diverse: many Asians, African-Americans, Hispanics, and immigrants live in suburbs (Macedo et al. 2005; Orfield 2002; Dreier, Mollenkopf, and Swanstrom 2004). Nevertheless, much of this diversity is *across* rather than *within* suburbs. Racial segregation has lessened somewhat, due partly to immigration, but segregation remains high. On average, as many as half of all blacks would need to move across census tracts to achieve an equal racial distribution (Massey and Denton, 1993; Glaeser and Vigdor 2003; Logan, 2000; Danielson, 1976). And economic *stratification*—the separation of rich and poor—continues to increase; *affluent people are ever more likely to live in the company of the privileged and poor people more likely to live in areas of concentrated poverty* (Macedo et al. 2005, 75; Massey and Fischer 2003).[8] A study of fifty metropolitan areas finds that the percentage of suburban residents living in middle-class suburbs declined from 74.9 percent to 60.8 percent between 1980 and 2000 (Swanstrom et al. 2004).[9] Most worrisome is the persistence of what Massey and Denton call "hyper segregated" inner-city areas marked by debilitating concentrations of disadvantage.

As my coauthors and I argued in another context, local and regional political structures and policy choices have profound effects on the composition and form of political communities—who lives where and with whom?—and this in turn has significant implications for Americans' interests as parents, homeowners, and citizens (Macedo et al. 2005).

The crux of the problem is the way we organize public and private choices and ownership at the local level. Several features of local governance are especially significant. American metropolitan areas are often quite fragmented—crazy quilts of municipalities, counties, districts, and authorities. The St. Louis metropolitan area, for example, is composed of nearly 800 units of local government, including 300 cities and townships (Dreier, Mollenkopf, and Swanstrom 2004; Macedo et al. 2005, 75). This fragmentation helps keep government close to the people, and access spurs participation; it appears that Tocqueville's observations on this score nearly 200 years ago remain true. However, our system decentralizes not only administration but also financing of local public services, including education, which is in significant measure supported by local property taxes. This creates a familiar and perverse local incentive to welcome higher-income residents whose contribution to the tax base and public service provision is high and whose draw on many public services is low and to exclude poorer people who depend on social services and pay less in taxes.

The local engines of inequality include more than public finance: the quality of schools is influenced by the available resources and also by the composition of the student body. Schools made up largely of children from better-off backgrounds have enormous educational advantages over schools composed predominantly of children from disadvantaged neighborhoods. Indeed, "peer effects" are significant in shaping student achievement levels (Burke and Sass 2008; Betts, Reuben, and Danenberg 2000), and better-resourced schools containing children from middle- or upper-class backgrounds have a host of other advantages. Teenage pregnancy rates are higher in schools containing mostly children from disadvantaged backgrounds, and high rates of pregnancy among peers influences individual behavior. And students attending schools in disadvantaged communities are much less likely to develop the social connections and networks that are important to finding employment (Kahlenberg 2001, 30–31).

As the designers of GreatSchools.org know, housing prices vary along with the relative quality of local schools, and homes represent the single largest investment—the largest wealth asset—of American families. As a consequence, *even those homeowners with egalitarian political and moral impulses have a powerful personal incentive to practice the politics of exclusion* (Danielson 1976; Macedo et al. 2005). Once again, local politics gives them the means to do so because local communities exercise a great deal of control over the composition of local housing via zoning laws (e.g., by specifying minimum lot sizes for homes) and other development decisions. Specifying a two-acre minimum lot size for homes is a very effective way of making sure that homes for the poor will not be constructed in one's community, and one has the satisfaction of telling oneself and one's neighbors that its really all about protecting the environment and preserving the character of the community.

The Liberty to Live Where One Wishes?

But what about liberty? Rawls made the protection of basic liberties the first principle of justice, giving it priority over equality (i.e., fair equality of opportunity and the difference principle). Does not that protect people's freedom of residence? Isn't deciding about the sort of community that one wants to live in, and raise one's family in, crucial to the autonomy of family life and the most basic liberties in our lives? But what understanding of liberty would we choose from behind the veil of ignorance and in the original position if we did not know into what family or class we might be born? The crucial question is not freedom of choice but how we would organize and structure the institutions within which people exercise their equal liberties.

Political and social scientists, economists, and law professors have celebrated the choices that metropolitan areas provide to citizens without adequately weighing the adverse consequences—that is, the ways that poorly structured choices in flawed institutions undermine an inclusive public sphere. In classic essays from the 1950s and 1960s, Charles Tiebout argued that metropolitan areas should be viewed as a kind of marketplace of jurisdictions in which "the consumer–voter may be viewed as picking that community which best satisfies his preference pattern for public goods" (Tiebout 1956, 418). From this perspective, metropolitan consolidation should be avoided because a multiplicity of local governments fosters greater choice and market efficiency (Ostrom, Tiebout, and Warren 1961). The basic premise of this public-choice approach to metropolitan governance is that citizens can "vote with their feet" on the particular bundle of local taxes and services that best meets their preferences. Fragmented local institutions would, it was thought, sort citizens according to their preferences for local public goods and reduce the need for traditional forms of participation. The exit option thus means that citizens can satisfy their policy preferences via private choices, making public participation far less significant. Citizens' abilities to "exit" a jurisdiction that have policies they disapprove of might, thus, be viewed as substitutes for other forms of political "voice" and citizen participation ("getting your way" by moving to a place with like-minded others rather than persuading fellow citizens to adopt your point of view; Hirschman 1970).

Obviously, the consequences of this way of structuring the interaction of public and private choices is not all bad. There is evidence, for example, that public school competition in highly fragmented metropolitan areas with many school districts improves overall school quality (via competition; Hoxby 2000; Rothstein 2007). More centralized education funding could lead to leveling down.

Nevertheless, this model of metropolitan governance is deeply flawed: it has very effectively promoted exclusion rather than inclusion and worsened political inequalities. Local governments compete not so much to satisfy different preferences as to attract residents and businesses that will contribute more in taxes than they cost in services. The greatest problems come when local control of schools and local funding is coupled with exclusionary devices such as control over land use via zoning. Minimum lot sizes for building or restrictions on construction of apartments and low-income housing transform local control into a very effective engine for excluding the less well-off and worsening their disadvantages. Narrow interests are constructed and empowered at the expense of fairness to the wider community. Most significantly, households vary a great deal in their capacities for exit and entry. The experience of poor residents of New Orleans in the face of Hurricane Katrina exposed this fact in brutal ways.

"Voting with your feet" is not a way that poor people can effectively hold governments accountable, but it is often a way that better-off people hold governments accountable to their interests at the expense of the poor. Voting with one's feet can communicate information about personal preferences to local governments, but that does not make it a form of political or civic engagement. The choice to move is often a flight from the need to deliberate with others about common problems: it is often in search of private benefit rather than an engagement in public activity. Stephen L. Elkin puts it well: action is "public" when "others have to be convinced, justification is essential. I must, that is, move beyond assertions of what is beneficial to me" (Elkin 1987, 149). Exit is often an alternative to political voice, and in today's metropolitan conditions, it undermines a sense of shared fate among richer and poorer citizens.

The laws of property in America today give all parents and homeowners as members of local communities, whatever their ideology or partisanship, an interest in and the capacity for zoning out the poor. The result is local communities and schools divided by class privilege. Stratification is especially harmful to those who live amid concentrated disadvantage. People's capacity to become involved in civic affairs, and their ability to develop human capital, is diminished greatly where inequalities are "cumulative rather than offsetting" (Rae 2003, 421). Disadvantaged areas are characterized by greater health problems, transportation difficulties, and crime and safety concerns. As Rae explains, "Too often, the end of urbanism has undermined [the democratic] experience by promoting social homogeneity within municipalities, leading to the evolution of regional hierarchies in which 'purified communities' [Richard Sennett's term] . . . bring likes together, safe from contact with persons different from themselves . . . The bottom rung more often than not lies in the formerly working-class neighborhoods of central cities, where opportunity is scarce, danger is commonplace, and democracy in any plausible sense seems out of reach" (Rae 2003, 421). Stratification by political subdivision thus encourages narrow and self-serving political activity. As Grant McConnell observed of narrow constituencies in general, "It often appears that the achievement and defense of particular status and privilege are the central goals of narrow and cohesive groups" (McConnell 1966, 12). Indeed, some would argue that such exclusionary appeals to localism often mask underlying racist motivations. It is hard to deny that the prospect of racial integration was among the factors that encouraged "white flight" to the suburbs. Local political structures and the ideal of local control (or "home rule") allow for the defense of what amounts to class-based and (to some degree) racial exclusion without explicit appeal to either class or race, as Thomas Byrne Edsall and Mary Edsall argue (1992).

Metropolitan regions carved into Balkanized pieces marked by concentrations of wealth or poverty, with few institutions capable of effectively addressing the larger problems of the region and with no adequate opportunities to hold political authorities accountable to all the citizens of the metropolitan region, suffer from serious democratic deficits. Such Balkanization impedes cross-class communication and intercourse, narrows citizens' interests and understandings, and sets them in competition with one another (Young 2000; McConnell 1966; Dreier, Mollenkopf, and Swanstrom 2004). The greatest problems are the ways in which local institutions concentrate disadvantage and facilitate the assembling of unfair advantage.

Redistribution and Opportunity in America?

But don't our public institutions work to some extent to correct for the inequalities generated by American property laws? While we tax incomes progressively and provide a variety of public services, including public schools, these do not suffice to counteract the inequality-generating institutions we have been discussing. In addition, redistributive institutions, inadequate as they are, are under increasing stress.

Far from operating so as to dissipate accumulated privileges and promote fair equality for all, inheritance taxes have come under attack. Called the "death tax" by its opponents who seek to kill it, the inheritance tax is deeply unpopular. Research suggests that this massive unpopularity is matched by equally profound public ignorance: people think their chances of having to pay the tax are much greater than they in fact are, and they also do not understand the extent to which income and wealth are skewed (Philips 2002; Bartels 2004; Graetz and Shapiro 2005). But let's leave aside the estate tax and focus on the local organization of property, power, and privilege.

Following Tocqueville, we might seek a contrast between the beliefs and patterns of life of "aristocratic" Europeans and "democratic" Americans. Many Americans would no doubt continue to see the world that way. There is indeed evidence of differences in worldviews and distributive outcomes, but it defies the stereotypes that reassure Americans. Roland Bénabou and Jean Tirole describe evidence of striking differences across countries in beliefs about "the causes of wealth and poverty, the extent to which individuals are responsible for their own fate, and the long term rewards to personal effort" (Bénabou and Tirole 2006, 700). Thus Americans continue to believe in the American dream according to which "hard work and good deeds will ultimately bring a better life," and "people generally get what they deserve and deserve what they get" (Bénabou and Tirole 2006, 700).

Europeans, on the other hand, tend to be less optimistic and more "realistic." Whereas only around 30 percent of Americans believe that the poor are trapped in poverty and that luck "rather than effort or education, determines income," the figures for Europeans are nearly double: 54 percent and 60 percent, respectively (Bénabou and Tirole 2006). Despite these differences in belief about the causes of poverty and the poor's prospects for emerging from it, upward mobility seems to be no greater in the United States as compared with Europe: "The actual evidence on intergenerational income or educational mobility . . . shows no significant difference with European welfare states" (Bénabou and Tirole 2006, 702–3). Bénabou and Tirole suggest that distinctive American belief patterns, while unsupported by what we know of the real extent of upward mobility, may serve to help rationalize and perpetuate a system of low social provision. The fact is that welfare for the poor, unemployment assistance, and other forms of redistribution are relatively generous in Europe and stingy in America: rich and poor alike in America may be better able to rationalize this situation by perpetuating a "myth" of unlimited opportunity for all. Bénabou and Tirole suggest, in effect, that the American dream according to which success is available to all who try—though no truer in the United States than Europe—plays an especially important motivational and ideological role in the United States.

We would, therefore, need to revise Tocqueville's estimation that democratic equality is most highly developed in America. Americans may still think this is the case, but it would appear that they are wrong. It is well known that the share of national wealth going to those in the top 1 percent, and even more so in the top one-tenth of 1 percent, increased considerably after 1980 (Philips 2002; Bartels 2008).[10] In America the top fifth earn eleven times more than the bottom fifth, and that ratio is considerably higher than other advanced countries (only the United Kingdom comes close; Philips 2002, 124).

A consequence of these trends is that birth seems increasingly to determine one's fate. A sign of this would be the fact that entry into elite universities is increasingly correlated with family income. Among members of the entering class at the University of Michigan in 2004, more freshmen came from families earning more than $200,000—the top 2 percent—than from families in the entire lower half of families earning less than the median national income of $53,000 (Leonhardt 2004, 21).

Education is widely regarded as the key to economic success in the new economy. The main moral problem respecting education policy in the United States is the grossly unequal and inadequate education received by the poor. In 75 percent of the public schools in America, as Richard Kahlenberg puts it, "a majority of the students are from middle-class households" and the schooling provided is generally fine. In the other 25 percent of schools, "a majority of the children are from low-income household, and those schools overwhelmingly fail to educate children to high levels of achievement" (Kahlenberg 2001, 1–2). As a consequence, Kahlenberg notes, "some 76 percent of high-income students complete bachelor's degrees, compared with a mere 4 percent of low-income students" (Kahlenberg 2001, 1–2). These assertions obviously refer not only to claims about educational inequality but also to a theory of causation: socioeconomic stratification across schools is a chief cause of highly unequal education opportunities and outcomes. The theory is very plausible. And obviously in the economy of the present and future, educational achievement is an important precondition of economic success.

So what do we say about all this from the standpoint of justice? Is this just a case of the old trade-off between equality and liberty, with important and basic values on both sides of the ledger? Nathan Glazer has suggested that it is: "To be sure, the case for both [racial] integration and equality of expenditure is powerful. But the chief obstacle to achieving these goals does not seem to be the indifference of whites and the non-poor to the education of white and the poor . . . Rather, other values, which are not simply shields for racism, stand in the way: the value of the neighborhood school; the value of local control of education and, above all, the value of freedom from state imposition when it affects matters so personal as the future of one's children" (Glazer 2005, 12–13). Glazer is mistaken to regard the operation of our current system simply as a matter of "freedom from state imposition": the system itself is a political imposition, with predictable winners and losers. Obviously, parents do have a right (across some range of activities) to help their own children and promote their interests. And people should have reasonable options to live where they want. But nobody has a right to the current system that *structures choice* in the ways I have described. There may be value in local schools but not in a system that makes the quality of different local schools so unequal, especially when the ramifying effects of increasing concentrations of advantage and disadvantage are likely to be so profound. The value of local control of education is instrumental. It may foster some good qualities—greater parental involvement and greater willingness to support educational funding—but it is an administrative device that ought to be designed with an eye toward basic principles of justice, including fair equality of opportunity. And so as Harry Brighouse and Adam Swift have pointed out, people have no basic liberty interest in—and so no moral right to—the pathological features of the current system (2008).

Political boundaries help shape citizens' interests and identities pre-ideologically: they demarcate communities of shared interests. When inequality is geographically concentrated, the poor are conveniently hidden from the view and purview of the better-off, and some shock or eruption is needed to force our attention. Hurricane Katrina was such an event. It drew public attention (temporarily) to the pervasively unequal life chances associated with place-based inequality: unequal vulnerability to crime; to dysfunctional schools; and to poor conditions for health, recreation, and raising families. Public institutions are supposed to guarantee every child an equal opportunity to succeed and to provide every child with an adequate preparation to participate in politics. Whatever the sins of the parents, children are not responsible for their disadvantaged circumstances, and allowing their life chances to be made grossly unequal by virtue of the circumstances of their birth is fundamentally unfair.

Local politics as currently organized make all of us into stakeholders in undemocratic exclusion and the perpetuation of inequality. The system works very effectively without our ever thinking about it. Those with greater advantages "naturally" tend to live among others similarly advantaged. All we need to do is pursue the American dream in the normal way for ourselves and our children. Because this system of local housing and educational stratification has such profound consequences for home values and the quality of education, it is not too much of a stretch to see them as similar to Tocqueville's "laws of inheritance," though their effects are anything but egalitarian and democratic. Because the effects of these institutions on children's life chances and prospects are so great, they ought also to be understood as central features of our capitalist welfare state: no amount of subsequent redistribution is going to undo their effects. And indeed, since geographical sorting allows the advantaged to dissociate themselves from the disadvantaged, it is hard to imagine that these patterns do not undermine the patterns of reciprocal cooperation that might otherwise sustain a sense of solidarity and shared fate.

The pathologies described so far are deeply entrenched on account of the extent to which the local politics of exclusion shapes citizens' personal interests as parents and homeowners. These structures underwrite families' wealth holdings, and therefore their economic security and well-being and their desire to help their children do as well as possible. It is hard not to be pessimistic about possibilities for fundamental change. But of course, there are several strategies for pushing against these tendencies. The problems we face at the local level are not altogether immutable.

What Is to Be Done?

While I have used the egalitarian theory of John Rawls to explicate the requirements of justice, one need not be a Rawlsian to regard the current organization of housing and schooling as deeply problematic. So what should we do about it? That is a hard question, and specific answers will not be found in the department of political theory. Importantly, policy proposals must address empirical questions of sustainability and likely effects. Policy and institutional design is importantly pragmatic: we must know what arrangements work best to advance our values and goals. Should we seek ways to integrate neighborhoods by class and race? How? Via litigation strategies or other political means? What forms of school choice might be designed to make a positive contribution to this most difficult and deeply entrenched problem, while also being politically sustainable? There are many things that might be done, but which are most plausibly efficacious and also capable of generating sufficient political support to be saleable and sustainable in our politics? These are not questions I can answer here.

We should find ways to reduce concentrations of rich and poor across metropolitan areas. Vigilant enforcement of fair housing laws already on the books would give some Americans a fairer shot at living in desirable neighborhoods. We need to encourage or require municipalities to provide a mix of housing that reflects the needs of the people who work and live in the area. Madison, Wisconsin, for example, several years ago passed an inclusionary zoning law that requires all new development to include low-income housing. Of course, Madison, Wisconsin, is a progressive enclave. State efforts—often driven by courts—to require fairer housing patterns have not been hugely successful.

An alternative to housing integration is the litigation has also sought to establish rights to more equitable education funding under state constitutions. Between 1972 and 1997, there were thirty-two serious constitutional challenges to state education-funding formulas, of which sixteen were at least partly successful, based on education provisions in state constitutions. Where litigation was successful, Douglas S. Reed argues that state court judges did secure somewhat higher and more equitable school funding (Reed 2001). The well-known case of *Campaign for Fiscal Equity vs. State of New York* has succeeded in pressuring the state legislature and governor to increase state aid to the poorest school districts. Such successes are to be applauded—they swim against the strong currents that I have described previously—but they seem to temper somewhat rather than reverse a problem; the underlying political dynamics are still in place.

School voucher programs could be designed so as to promote egalitarian reform. Publicly funded school-choice programs in the United Kingdom and elsewhere in Europe often do include equality-promoting design features, including larger vouchers for disadvantaged students (Reuter 2004). Children with special needs, children from disadvantaged backgrounds, and children whose first language is not English should receive larger vouchers so that schools have an incentive to include rather than exclude them (Bowls and Gintis 1976; Brighouse 2000). In addition, wealthier parents should not be allowed to "top up" the voucher in order to use it to send their children to an expensive school. The amount of the voucher itself should be fully adequate, and schools receiving vouchers should be barred from receiving additional payments from parents. If parents can "top up," then the subsidy will tend to flow to wealthy parents, making choices that are inaccessible to the rest.[11]

Richard Kahlenberg argues that every publicly funded school should be required to maintain a certain proportion of students from disadvantaged (less-than-middle-class) backgrounds: he suggests that qualifying for federally subsidized school lunch is a good (and workable) standard (Kahlenberg 2001). And he suggests that an appropriate target would be that schools should be expected to enroll approximately 40 percent of students from disadvantaged backgrounds: up to approximately this point, there is no evidence that attending economically integrated schools in any way harms the education of middle-class kids, and so the requirement should be saleable to middle-class parents. Further, if this target were reached, every child in America would attend a school with a majority of kids from middle-class households, which in turn tends strongly to insure that children receive a good education.

Kahlenberg's proposals are an attractive combination of idealism and realism. Reformers must consider how best to deal with highly nonideal circumstances given various practical political constraints. Class-based segregation across schools and school districts is the great underlying problem. Moral criticism helps to inform the critique, but, especially since the issue concerns far-reaching reform of highly visible and salient institutions, a crucial constraint is to devise proposals that have a chance of being politically feasible and sustainable. Criteria should not be prone to manipulation and data should be easily available. Moreover, if better-off people are going to support class-based integration of schools, then a crucial threshold is the point at which evidence suggests that the proportion of students from lower-class backgrounds will have a discernible negative impact on the education of children from middle-class families.

Other reformers advocate simply redrawing school district boundaries to create integrated public school districts (Levinson and Levinson 2004). The Supreme Court hit the brakes on school desegregation when it held, in *Millikin v. Bradley*, that suburban school districts could be included in desegregation plans only under limited circumstances (where a history of de jure segregation could be shown; *Millikin* 1974). In principle, this was a disaster for integration, though racial integration encompassing suburbs could have led to a wider flight from public education altogether.

The fragmentation of American metropolitan areas has facilitated a sorting of the population by race and, especially, class that now constitutes a deep problem for democracy; certainly it is a matter of "thick injustice" as the introduction to this volume suggests. Suburban homeowners are hugely invested in separate schooling and the other advantages that flow from class sorting. Property owners might need to be subsidized for the loss of value for some reform proposals to get off the ground. And of course, there would be dangers of a backlash in reforms imposed from above—if a highly egalitarian public-education regime were somehow imposed, better-off citizens might flee public schooling in favor of private schooling.

I raise these difficult questions not to answer them but to indicate some of the issues we must think about in moving from moral criticism to political reform. The first step is to redirect our attention and clearly identify the problems.

Local political institutions are too often neglected by scholars of American democracy and public policy and also by political theorists whose attention is typically drawn to national institutions. When local politics is addressed, it is usually to highlight local opportunities for civic participation. While the decentralized nature of many political functions does boost participation, the structure of local politics and property helps create an extremely unequal distribution of opportunities and rewards in our society.

Conclusion

Some of the most serious shortcomings of American statecraft reside at the local level. The organization of local political life and home ownership defy the requirements of justice. Local political boundaries allow the better-off to form defensive cartels against the worse-off (including, or especially, the worst-off). Real opportunities are highly unequally distributed as a result: privileges are passed along to the next generation, along with wealth, in the form of educational advantages. I have suggested that these features of local political organization and ownership are crucial features of our "capitalist welfare state": they preserve and even enhance the advantages of the well off while imposing no formal barriers to advancement. Because this alternative regime—I have called it "property owning plutocracy"—is so well established and deeply entrenched, it is not easy to say how to go about dismantling it. It is supported by many entrenched interests and the American dream itself.

If consciousness-raising experiences are about encountering unfamiliar, previously hidden perspectives and recognizing their previously unseen familiarity (Young 2000), local political institutions often function as consciousness-lowering devices: they widen differences while also insulating us from their impact, and they place the unpleasant realities of class disparity at a distance. If we do nothing, then the situation will continue to worsen all by itself: geographically concentrated inequalities feed on themselves. But the pathologies are containable, and in many respects, the whole system seems highly sustainable. Aside from considerations of justice, the better-off seem to have little incentive to do anything. Nevertheless, we must seek first to understand this regime and then to address its shortcomings if we are to have anything resembling a reasonably just political order.

Notes

1 The quoted passages are all from GreatSchools Inc. 2010. http://www.great schools.org (accessed April 24, 2010). Scholarly research on school achievement would place greater weight on parental education, which is closely related to parental income, however. Per-pupil spending alone is not a strong predictor of educational

achievement. See Hankla, Pate, Leech, and Grubbs (2007). See also the news report in Ohio that suggests that "the test score connection with income is more than twice as strong as with other state report card factors like race, teacher pay, teacher education or school district spending" (Scott Elliott, "Income, Test Scores Strongly Linked in Ohio Schools," *Dayton News*, September 5, 2006, http://www.daytondaily news.com/o/content/shared-gen/blogs/dayton/education/entries/2006/09/05/income_test_per.html).

2 The principles of justice, for Rawls, are designed to operate on the institutions of society that form the background and context of our individual choices and not, in the first instance at least, on individual choices themselves. This is a point that many mistake and fail to appreciate.

3 Given equal talent and effort, children should have a roughly equal chance of attaining the best jobs and positions of leadership in society.

4 This is a very quick, and I hope not entirely inaccurate, paraphrase of *A Theory of Justice* and what I take to be its core argument.

5 He allows for a liberal "democratic socialist" regime to be one just option. Here, ownership of productive capital is collectivized and organized for collective purposes in accordance with the principles of justice; it seems unlikely that the United States will embrace such a model anytime soon (see Rawls 2001, 135–36). There are still other alternatives: "laissez-faire capitalism" and "state socialism" are unacceptable, but "liberal (democratic) socialism" is a possible option for organizing economic institutions in accordance with principles of justice.

6 Obviously, in market systems, and given unequal talents and other differences among people, this will not be easy to arrange, and adjustments will, of course, need to take place after any system is established.

7 These policies included Federal Home Loan Association policies that "redlined" racially diverse inner-city neighborhoods and housing and transportation policies that encouraged middle-class flight and discouraged the renovation and rehabilitation of inner-city housing (see Massey and Denton 1993).

8 While the neighborhood of the average poor person was 13.6 percent poor in 1970, by 2000, the figure had risen to 24.6 percent (Macedo et al., 2005, 75).

9 Middle-class suburbs are defined as suburbs with per capita incomes between 75 and 125 percent of the regional per capita income. Swanstrom et al. (2004).

10 Philips reports that the share of the nation's wealth held by the top 1 percent increased from 22 percent to 39 percent between 1979 and 1989 (2002, xiii). He argues that "the essence of plutocracy, fulfilled by 2000, has been the determination and ability of wealth to reach beyond its own realm of money and control politics and government" (xv). For additional evidence, see Bartels (2008).

11 There would be other conditions on vouchers needed to protect children's freedom and to promote equal access: As in Milwaukee and Cleveland, schools that decide to admit children with vouchers should be limited in the criteria that they may employ in selecting children (especially, but not only, if they are oversubscribed). Giving preferences to siblings seems OK, as does preferring children from the local neighborhood (so long as the effect is not to segregate or stratify).

Religious schools should not be allowed to prefer coreligionists: schools that seem desirable to parents should be equally open to them without regard to their faith. Similarly, schools should not be allowed to require children attending with vouchers to pray or to attend mandatory religion classes. This reflects a reasonable concern that slots funded by the public should be open to all children and also that children should not be pressured into religious exercises within schools.

References

Bartels, Larry M. 2004. "Homer Gets a Tax Cut: Inequality and Public Policy in the American Mind." Unpublished working paper. http://www.princeton.edu/~bartels/homer.pdf.
———. 2008. *Unequal Democracy: The Political Economy of the New Gilded Age*. Princeton, N.J.: Princeton University Press.
Bénabou, Roland, and Jean Tirole. 2006. "Belief in a Just World and Redistributive Politics." *The Quarterly Journal of Economics* 121, no. 2: 699–746.
Betts, Julian R., Kim S. Reuben, and Anne Danenberg. 2000. *Equal Resources, Equal Outcomes? The Distribution of School Resources and Student Achievement in California*. San Francisco: The Public Policy Institute of California. http://www.ppic.org/content/pubs/rb/RB_200JBRB.pdf.
Brighouse, Harry. 2000. *School Choice and Social Justice*. New York: Oxford University Press.
Brighouse, Harry, and Adam Swift. 2008. "Putting Educational Equality in Its Place." *Education Finance and Policy* 3, no. 4: 444–66.
Burke, Mary A., and Tim Sass. 2008. "Classroom Peer Effects and Student Achievement." Working paper no. 18. Washington, D.C.: Urban Institute. http://www.urban.org/publications/1001190.html.
Campaign for Fiscal Equity, Inc. v. State of New York. Supreme Court of the State of New York, County of New York. 86 N.Y. 2d 307 (1995).
Danielson, Michael N. 1976. *The Politics of Exclusion*. New York: Columbia University Press.
Dreier, Peter, John Mollenkopf, and Todd Swanstrom. 2004. *Place Matters: Metropolitics for the Twenty-First Century*. 2nd rev. ed. Lawrence: University Press of Kansas.
Edsall, Thomas Byrne, and Mary Edsall. 1992. *Chain Reaction: The Impact of Race, Rights, and Taxes on American Politics*. New York: W. W. Norton.
Elkin, Stephen L. 1987. *City and Regime in the American Republic*. Chicago: University of Chicago Press.
Glaeser, Edward L., and Jacob L. Vigdor. 2003. "Racial Segregation: Promising News." In *Redefining Urban and Suburban America: Evidence from Census 2000*, ed. Bruce Katz and Robert E. Lang, 211–34. Washington, D.C.: The Brookings Institution.
Glazer, Nathan. 2005. "Separate and Unequal: Review of Jonathan Kozol, *The Shame of the Nation: The Restoration of Apartheid Schooling in America Random House*." *New York Times*, September 25, 12–13.

Graetz, Michael J., and Ian Shapiro. 2005. *Death by a Thousand Cuts: The Fight over Taxing Inherited Wealth.* New Haven, Conn.: Yale University Press.

Hankla, Steven, James L. Pate, Don Leech, and Scott Grubbs. 2007. "Academic Achievement and Money: The Debate Continues." *Journal of Research for Educational Leaders* 4: 29–43.

Hoxby, C. M. 2000. "Does Competition among Public Schools Benefit Students and Taxpayers?" *The American Economic Review* 90, no. 5: 1209–39.

Hirschman, Albert O. 1970. *Exit, Voice, and Loyalty.* Cambridge, Mass.: Harvard University Press.

Kahlenberg, Richard D. 2001. *All Together Now: Creating Middle-Class Schools through Public School Choice.* Washington, D.C.: The Brookings Institution.

Leonhardt, David. 2004. "As Wealthy Fill Top Colleges, Concerns Grow Over Fairness." *New York Times,* April 22, A1, A21. http://www.nytimes.com/2004/04/22/us/as-wealthy-fill-top-colleges-concerns-grow-over-fairness.html?n=Top/Reference/Times%20Topics/Organizations/U/University%20of%20Virginia&pagewanted=2.

Levinson, Meira, and Sanford Levinson. 2003. "'Getting Religion': Religion, Community, and Diversity in Public and Private Schools." In *School Choice: The Moral Debate,* ed. Alan Wolfe, 104–25. Princeton, N.J.: Princeton University Press.

Logan, John R. 2000. "Ethnic Diversity Grows, Neighborhood Integration Lags." In *Redefining Urban and Suburban America: Evidence from Census 2000,* ed. Bruce Katz and Robert Lang, 235–55. Washington, D.C.: The Brookings Institution.

Macedo, Stephen, Yvette Alex-Assensoh, Jeffrey M. Berry, Michael Brintnall, David E. Campbell, Luis Ricardo Fraga, Archon Fung, William A. Galston, Christopher F. Karpowitz, Margaret Levi, Meira Levinson, Keena Lipsitz, Richard G. Niemi, Robert D. Putnam, Wendy M. Rahn, Rob Reich, Robert R. Rodgers, Todd Swanstrom, and Katherine Cramer Walsh. 2005. *Democracy at Risk: How Political Choices Undermine Citizen Participation, and What We Can Do about It.* Washington, D.C.: The Brookings Institution.

Massey, Douglas S., and Nancy A. Denton. 1993. *American Apartheid: Segregation and the Making of the Underclass.* Cambridge, Mass.: Harvard University Press.

Massey, Douglas S., and Mary J. Fischer. 2003. "The Geography of Inequality in the United States, 1950–2000." In *Brookings-Wharton Papers on Urban Affairs 2003,* ed. William G. Gale and Janet Rothenberg Pack, 1–40. Washington, D.C.: The Brookings Institution.

McConnell, Grant. 1966. *Private Power and American Democracy.* Chicago: University of Chicago Press.

Millikin v. Bradley, 418 U.S. 717 (1974).

Orfield, Myron. 2002. *American Metropolitics: The New Suburban Reality.* Washington D.C.: The Brookings Institution.

Ostrom, Vincent A., Charles M. Tiebout, and Robert Warren. 1961. "The Organization of Government in Metropolitan Areas: A Theoretical Inquiry." *American Political Science Review* 55:831–42.

Philips, Kevin. 2002. *Wealth and Democracy: A Political History of the American Rich.* New York: Broadway Books.

Rae, Douglas W. 2003. *City: Urbanism and Its End.* New Haven, Conn.: Yale University Press.

Rawls, John. 1999. *A Theory of Justice.* Rev. ed. Cambridge, Mass.: Harvard University Press.

———. 2001 *Justice as Fairness: A Briefer Restatement.* Cambridge, Mass.: Harvard University Press.

Reed, Douglas S. 2001. *On Equal Terms: The Constitutional Politics of Educational Opportunity.* Princeton, N.J.: Princeton University Press.

Reuter, Lutz R. 2004. "School Choice and Civic Values in Germany." In *Educating Citizens: International Perspectives on Civic Values and School Choice,* ed. Patrick J. Wolf and Stephen Macedo, 213-37. Washington, D.C.: The Brookings Institution.

Rothstein, Jesse. 2007. "Does Competition among Public Schools Benefit Students and Taxpayers? A Comment on Hoxby (2000)." *American Economic Review* 97, no. 5: 2026–37.

Swanstrom, Todd, Colleen Casey, Robert Flack, and Peter Dreier. 2004. *Pulling Apart: Economic Segregation in the Top Fifty Metropolitan Areas, 1980–2000.* Washington, D.C.: The Brookings Institution.

Tiebout, Charles M. 1956. "A Pure Theory of Local Expenditure." *The Journal of Political Economy* 64, no. 5: 416–24.

Tocqueville, Alexis de. 1988. *Democracy in America.* Edited by J. P. Mayer. New York: Harper Collins.

Young, Iris Marion. 2000. "Residential Segregation and Regional Democracy." In *Inclusion and Democracy,* ed. I. M. Young, 196–228. Oxford, U.K.: Oxford University Press.

2   PUBLIC REASON
AND THE JUST CITY

LOREN KING

IN THIS CHAPTER I CONSIDER some problems of urban inequality
in light of a particular dimension of justice: the importance of good reasons for imposing burdens on others. This will require saying something
about what counts as a good reason, what sorts of burdens demand such
reasons, and what counts as imposing a burden on others (as distinct
from being blamelessly implicated in harm to others).

In their introduction to this volume, Clarissa Hayward and Todd
Swanstrom suggest that a recent lack of official public concern with issues
of justice in and around our cities may be rooted in the *thickness* of many
distinctly urban and more broadly metropolitan injustices: the complex-
ity and historical depth of these moral wrongs, and their rootedness in
particular locations, may "make it difficult to assign moral responsibility for injustice, and to motivate collective political action to change it"
(Hayward and Swanstrom 2010, 9). I agree, but there is at least one other
way in which both moral responsibility and political redress may be difficult to find. Attending to *public reason* in urban and metropolitan life
may help us distinguish cases of *thick injustice* from *reasonable disagreement* over the demands of justice.

Let me begin, however, with the first side of that distinction, by exploring a particularly distressing way in which inequality can be a moral
problem: a historical example of unequal voice implicated with unambiguously bad reasons for imposing burdens on others.

Race and Realty in St. Louis

Throughout the first half of the twentieth century and into the 1960s,
St. Louis realtors and their trade association, the St. Louis Real Estate

Exchange, engaged in explicitly racist practices, helping to sustain starkly segregated residential neighborhoods. In 1915, the Exchange lobbied aggressively for racial zoning, issuing pamphlets and mailings with racist language depicting the threat to property values and public safety of the "Negro invasion" of neighborhoods in the north and west of the city, and extending into incorporated municipalities such as Clayton and University City. The racial ordinances were short-lived—the practice was condemned as unconstitutional by the Supreme Court in 1917—but realtors and their exchange continued to be active in promoting racial restrictions in private-deed covenants (Gordon 2008, ch. 2).

St. Louis was hardly unique in these respects, but as Colin Gordon explains, the real estate industry here "played an unusually active and formal role in drafting and sustaining restrictive deed covenants" (2008, 79). The city was host to the named parties in the famous supreme court decision *Shelley v. Kraemer* (1948), which deemed state enforcement of racial restrictions in deed covenants a violation of equal protection guaranteed by the Fourteenth Amendment. That decision allowed such restrictions in private covenants between consenting parties, but state action was deemed unconstitutional.

Eventually the court did reject private racism as a grounds for restricting ownership in *Jones v. Mayer* (1968), appealing to the Thirteenth Amendment, which addresses the legacy of slavery and demands equal property rights for all citizens, regardless of race. Legislative efforts, such as the Fair Housing Act (1949), and subsequent Supreme Court decisions, such as *Hills v. Gautreaux* (1976), provoked modest and sporadic efforts at reform throughout the country, but the damage of almost a century of unbridled racism in urban and suburban housing markets had arguably been done. Subsequent efforts at racial integration in housing, on the one hand, and slum clearance and public housing, on the other, were, in St. Louis as in so many other cities, largely ineffective and often pernicious, involving heavy-handed and paternalistic efforts that did little to address either the complex legacies of racial injustice or the deeply inegalitarian vagaries of urban capitalism.

Local Politics and the Just City

Those of us concerned with justice in the city can cite, almost reflexively, a litany of well-studied problems evidenced by this example: dramatically unequal life chances along sharp divisions of race and class; racist attitudes and practices by both private citizens and commercial organizations; complicit government agencies at local, state, and federal levels; well-intentioned legislative and judicial interventions that ignore or misunderstand the complex—*thick*—sources of injustice in and around cities; and privileged interests leading to short-sighted urban renewal efforts with limited benefits, least of all to the worst-off in the city region.

Scholars who have argued explicitly for a normative approach to urban politics and planning (e.g., Smith 1994; Mitchell 2003) tend to understand justice in broadly egalitarian terms, emphasizing, as Susan Fainstein (2000) does, the distributional consequences of market processes and political practices. For Fainstein, drawing on John Rawls, Amartya Sen, and Martha Nussbaum, the *just city* is committed to residents having roughly equal means and opportunities to live meaningful lives (Fainstein 2001, 85). The challenge Fainstein poses is to meet this normative standard in ways that harness market forces and citizen participation toward more equitable outcomes.

Others—for instance, Colin Gordon in the case of St. Louis, and Gerald Frug and Steven Macedo, in this volume—point to how local politics structure property ownership and public service provision in urban regions, citing the fragmentation characteristic of so many U.S. metropolitan areas. Here again, St. Louis is a telling example: citing 1997 data, Gordon notes that the greater region boasted "789 distinct political units, an average of 12.5 'general purpose' (excluding school and other special districts) governments for every 100,000 residents, nearly three times the average (4.4 per 100,000) for the nation's largest metro areas" (2008, 45). The proliferation of so many independent jurisdictions seems to have undermined not only the revenue base and service-provision capacity of central cities but also the opportunities for residents to imagine themselves as urban *citizens*, sharing not only material benefits but also civic responsibilities beyond their enclaves of culture, race, and class.

If, as John Rawls (1971, 6–10; 2001, 10–12) argues, distributive justice applies to the basic structure of institutions that profoundly shape our life chances, then the structure of local politics in and around cities seems troubling, insofar as it determines, in complex ways, the quality of public services, especially education, that children grow up enjoying. For Macedo, such stark and unchosen inequalities in life chances, which impact so dramatically our equal standing as citizens and the worth of our liberties, are obviously problematic as matters of justice.[1]

For Fanstein, Macedo, and Frug, attractive solutions will likely involve moves toward regional coordination and integration, attempting to regulate urban markets and local public services to overcome what Margaret Weir (1994) has aptly termed the "defensive localism" characteristic of fragmented metropolitan regions. Some possible reforms include strengthened regional regulatory agencies enforcing socioeconomic and racial integration in housing markets and school districts (Fainstein, Macedo); regional voting schemes to supplement existing structures of political representation (Frug); or regulating market-inspired voucher schemes toward more egalitarian ends (Macedo).

I largely agree with the egalitarian understandings of justice behind these inclusive and integrative proposals, but I want to explore another facet of justice more closely tied to considerations of legitimacy than distribution, although obviously these two facets are intimately related. Indeed, just how they are related is clarified, I think, when we ask what justice demands by way of *reasons* for particular institutional forms and public policies. But a turn to *public reason* in the evaluation of urban inequalities comes at some cost and may reveal a tension between egalitarian concerns for distributive justice, on the one hand, and a commitment to diverse citizens living meaningful lives together, on the other.

The Just City: Distributive Fairness and Legitimate Reasons

When we ask about *the just city*, it is difficult to avoid the pull of egalitarian formulations of justice: how could a plausible story about justice in cities and their regions *not* focus on the dramatic inequalities—of resources, opportunities, political influence, and the varied sources of dignity and respect—that characterize urban and, more broadly, metropolitan life?[2] The market values that dominate our world today and that shape the forms of our cities so profoundly surely need the corrections that an account of justice can offer. Those market values, however, also suggest a story about justice, one grounded in the priority of market-related liberties and the importance of economic growth and efficiency. Advocates of this sort of story suspect that many unequal burdens we find in cities and their regions are largely blameless, often just (or at least not clearly unjust), and that reasons justifying state intervention in private choices must be weighty indeed.

Are these ultimately irreconcilable approaches to the just city? Certainly the hopes for any meaningful reconciliation seem slim at the extremes of libertarian and egalitarian conceptions of justice, but I think a concern with good reasons—justifications rendered in a morally attractive way—helps us take libertarian challenges seriously, without simply resigning ourselves to a neoliberal status quo. While John Rawls is often (quite reasonably) invoked to illustrate the unfairness of particular institutional arrangements and associated distributions (of rights, opportunities, resources), one of the striking features of Rawls's theory of justice, especially prominent in later formulations, is his attempt to balance deep and often conflicting moral commitments. By giving us a way to reason about distinct and conflicting moral principles (i.e., his method of *reflective equilibrium*) and to argue about burdens and benefits (i.e., the importance of *public reason*), Rawls's approach tries to find a principled reconciliation and ordering of liberty and equality not only with respect to one another but also against concerns for stability and the common good.

Justice as Fairness

Rawls takes liberty very seriously, granting it pride of place in his principles of justice. Yet his basic liberties are not the natural rights of, say, John Locke or Robert Nozick: Rawls emphasizes distinctly personal and civic liberties and includes a right to hold and control property only insofar as it is essential to the development and exercise of "our two moral powers": our capacities to affirm a sense of justice and to develop and pursue a conception of the good (2001, 18–19, 112–14). In Rawls's account, there is neither a right of self-ownership nor a right to maximal return from our assets on a free market. Furthermore, another facet of liberty—our political freedoms—must, Rawls argues, be more than formally ensured: they must be guaranteed *fair worth* (2001, 148–52). The fair worth of political liberties respects our equal standing as "self-authenticating sources of valid claims" (1993, 32) who are the willing authors of the laws we obey.[3]

Fair equality of opportunity is also critical for Rawls: those with roughly similar talents and motivation ought to face comparable life chances. And it is only once equal basic liberties (including the fair worth of political liberties) and fair equality of opportunity are satisfied that we turn to distributive concerns, regulated by his famous and controversial difference principle, which asks of remaining inequalities that they maximize the prospects (and thus the worth of liberties) faced by the least advantaged.

For Rawls, justice is about striking a satisfying balance and ordering of those moral commitments that survive not only our own deep intro-spection but also careful and informed debate in scholarship and the public sphere throughout modern history. Yet what (if anything) makes such a balancing act *satisfying* or *convincing*? Here Rawls advocates an intuitive (yet controversial) approach to thinking about justice: *reflective equilibrium*. This approach ultimately leads him to a theory that is as much about legitimate public justification as it is about criteria for a just distribution of resources and opportunities. I believe that this feature of Rawls's approach—the importance of justifications reached in a certain way—has implications for thinking about the just metropolis, although some of those implications may be frustrating and unsettling. Let me first explain the approach.

Reflective equilibrium asks us to move back and forth between (1) considered judgments that have survived careful, sincere, informed reflection and serious challenges and (2) formal statements and elabo-rations of principles and arguments for their strongest interpretations and relative priorities. We do this against (3) a background of reasonably settled understandings of facts and explanations, drawn from histori-cal analysis, on the one hand, and from the natural, life, and human sciences, on the other (which are themselves involved in a continuing process of clarification, challenge, and transformation associated with scientific reflective equilibrium seeking).[4]

In this way, we make a sustained effort to offer a principled interpre-tation and balancing of the core values that are to regulate a just basic structure. Again, central among these are personal freedom and some commitment to fair equality. This approach to thinking about justice is not without its critics, who variously accuse it of vicious circularity, capri-cious application, or bias toward the status quo.[5] Yet how else can our ethical reasoning take seriously the reality of not only ethnic and cul-tural but also moral and philosophical diversity that is so prevalent in the modern age, especially in and around cities?

The experiences of city life—both when it is dense, diverse, and cacophonous on the one hand, and when we find citizens dispersed and segregated into purified metropolitan enclaves on the other—buttress a strong suspicion that, even if we could achieve a just city and urban region with respect to distributive concerns and life chances, there will not be agreement on fundamental philosophical (i.e., spiritual, moral, metaphysical) questions or a uniquely plausible interpretation and ordering of distinctly political values that garner widespread support.[6] Some citizens will have good reasons for giving pride of place to liberty as a moral fixed point but then disagree about whether liberty ought to be understood as self-ownership, freedom of choice, or something else. Others will side with fairness, emphasizing equality as a moral primitive but then disagree about which dimensions of equality should take precedence (resources? opportunities? welfare? capabilities?). Still others will give priority to communal solidarity, identity-related concerns, or the tenets of their faith, perhaps favoring insular and homogenous communities. A vision of the just city will need to take seriously these deep philosophical disagreements, fostering reconciliation when possible, but offering principled grounds for asserting priorities when reconciliation seems unlikely.

There is no comprehensive view of city (or society) that can reconcile any and all moral values and associated regulative principles. But the hope implicit in Rawls's approach is that we might at least find ways that many citizens could nonetheless hold some shared political principles as legitimate, even as they disagree—often profoundly—on deep spiritual, moral, and metaphysical questions of truth and goodness. This is how the method of reflective equilibrium in moral reasoning leads naturally to the ideal of public reason as central to public justification and to the associated ideas of reasonableness and reasonable disagreement.

Public reason describes the character of acceptable reasons for public authority claims and especially for the uses of coercion to enforce those claims. The *ideal* of public reason is satisfied to the extent that citizens and public officials offer each other such reasons in support of their public claims.[7] We suppose that citizens, by and large, are able to argue sincerely when justifying their public claims to others, respecting one another as bearers of valid (but not uncontestable) moral claims and legitimate (but not unquestionable) aspirations, deserving our honest and informed consideration. We suppose that, while citizens have distinctive ends they wish to pursue and recognize others as having ends also, they wish to pursue their aims in accord with mutually shared principles of justice. This is the sense in which they are, or can be, reasonable; insofar as they still disagree on public matters, such disagreement is reasonable.

An oft-cited way of fleshing out this idea is to follow Rawls's discussion of civility and reciprocity (1993, 217), as Amy Gutmann and Dennis

Thomson (1996) do: when we argue within public reason, we offer sincere assertions, appeal to shared evidence, apply plausible rules of inference, and eschew controversial foundations as best we can. The difficulty with this formulation is in finding widespread agreement on what counts as an objectionably controversial premise or interpretation. Our assumptions and interpretive practices will have consequences for what we take to be unproblematic evidence; thus the criteria of shared rules of inference and bodies of evidence will in turn be controversial.

A better way to define what counts as a controversial assumption and interpretation is to reject those that fail to respect (1) citizens' fundamental interests and (2) their status as free and equal authors of the laws they obey. This links the standard of reasonableness directly with Rawls's emphasis on fair equality of opportunity and the fair worth of political liberties: in justifying our claims on others as expressed through coercive public institutions, we must respect the capacity of citizens to develop their moral powers and their equal standing as fellow citizens who are in some meaningful sense the collective authors of coercive public authority.

Obviously we typically fail to live up to any such ideal in practice: many disagreements in public life, and especially in urban and municipal politics, are better described as unreasonable outcomes of unreflective power politics. Certainly the example of St. Louis realtors wielding both social and political influence toward racist ends seems more typical of what we find in cities. Yet if we think that citizens have fundamental interests in developing and exercising their moral powers and that they are moral equals with respect to public authority, then we need to justify exercises of that authority in terms that treat citizens with sufficient respect as moral equals, willing to abide by shared principles of justice in pursuing their distinctive beliefs and aspirations. Demanding that citizens accept some policy or regulation—about store closures, street signage, or zoning restrictions—merely because a majority believes in a certain religious view or a stringent interpretation of property rights is not a respectful stance.

If we accept this line of argument, then we must affirm reasonableness as an attractive, if demanding, ideal. Yet even if the ideal is satisfied, reasonable parties thus understood will still disagree. Reasonableness does not ensure any sort of practical consensus; it only ensures that disagreements are consistent with respect for the moral equality of free citizens as both authors and subjects of the law.

Revisiting our opening example, I would say that, from the point of view of public reason, what is striking about the actions of the St. Louis Real Estate Exchange is not merely the evidence of disproportionate political influence or the enduring consequences of that disproportionate influence with respect to unequal opportunities (for access by black residents to particular neighborhoods and reliable public services). In addition to the *thickness* of this injustice, what is surely striking is the *unreasonableness* of those racist activities and the public influence their proponents enjoyed: both private motives and public reasons did not respect the fundamental interests or equal standing of a class of citizens.

I think the Supreme Court's judgment in *Shelley v. Kraemer* has some suggestive implications with respect to public reason thus understood, although I claim this due to the very feature of the decision that has been criticized: subsequent lower court decisions have generally not accepted *Shelley*'s implication that the state cannot enforce private agreements that would, if legislated, be unconstitutional. As Mark Rosen (2007) notes, courts routinely enforce nondisclosure agreements among private parties that would violate First Amendment guarantees if legislated. Rosen argues that *Shelley* should have been decided, as *Jones* was some two decades later, on Thirteenth Amendment grounds.

Yet I think the *Shelley* Court was on the right track, *morally speaking*, in the following respect: if private contracts have significant and adverse public implications, or if they promise to provoke new or strengthen existing legislation that seriously threatens the fundamental interests and equal standing of some class of citizens, then those private agreements are suspect. And a plausible test of such impact is the rule suggested by the *Shelley* Court: if a private agreement has significant public consequences yet would not pass constitutional muster as legislation, then it is at the very least suspect.

Now obviously the matter of setting a threshold for objectionable public impact by private agreements is in practice difficult and contentious; as a matter of constitutional law, the *Shelley* rule is problematic for the reasons Rosen has detailed. Yet as a *moral criterion* for the admissibility of private reasons as public justifications, this strikes me as a good test. Indeed, we should be—and often are—deeply concerned when enforceable nondisclosure agreements (e.g., between a corporation and its employees) conceal information vital to public health and safety.

The question of whether subsequent urban-renewal and public-housing efforts, in St. Louis and elsewhere, meet the test of public reason is complex. Certainly these efforts emerged from Supreme Court judgments and legislative efforts that acknowledged the injustices of racial segregation in the first half of the twentieth century. The reasons offered for urban-renewal efforts were arguably responsive to the fundamental interests of citizens as moral and political equals: the 1949 Federal Housing Act (FHA) addressed inadequate housing stock, calling for the "realization as soon as feasible of the goal of a decent home and a suitable living environment for every American family, thus contributing to the development and redevelopment of communities" (qtd. in Halpern 1995, 65).

Shortly after the FHA, the Supreme Court paved the way, in *Berman v. Parker* (1954), for states and city governments to expropriate private property not for public *uses*, narrowly understood, but for uses promising *public benefit*. This decision remains somewhat controversial on both the political Left and Right in the United States, as it has allowed cities and municipalities to run roughshod over urban communities, declaring blight on cavalier grounds and taking private property not for public uses per se (as in a park, port, or public right-of-way), but for other private parties, if the transaction is part of a plan promising potential gains in, say, employment opportunities and tax revenues. But while the consequences of *Berman* have been controversial, the interpretive shift itself does not seem unreasonable: interpreting "public use" as "in the public interest" arguably allows for creative approaches that can tap local knowledge while trying to improve the lives of residents.

Of course, any such hope has rarely played out in practice. What clearly violates reasonableness in retrospect has been the implementation of so many of these programs. One problem, consistent with the concerns expressed by advocates of regional reforms, was that most programs were to be implemented by local governments to better tailor projects to particular circumstances—not an unreasonable stance in principle, but in practice, and paired with the looser understanding of the Fifth Amendment's "Takings Clause," this has allowed municipalities to expropriate property and implement fair-housing ideals in ways that have been anything but fair and broadly public minded.

An example: an ambitious redevelopment project in the north end of Flint, Michigan, during the 1960s provides a striking illustration of how reasonable hopes that hold at least some promise of being broadly responsive to citizen interests—and that garner significant support across differences in race, class, and effective political power—can nonetheless fail dramatically when unreasonable methods of implementation are adopted. The St. John neighborhood plan involved clearing part of the heavily polluted north end of the city for industrial expansion, highway extension, and commercial development. Residents were mostly poor and predominantly black, but some of them, and several community groups, were guardedly optimistic that the plan, although favored by influential industrial elites (especially General Motors, whose Buick foundry contributed much to polluting the surrounding neighborhoods), would nonetheless improve housing conditions in the city (Highsmith 2009, 354–56).

The city, however, announced these plans well in advance of more detailed planning and funding and then contracted (predominantly white) realtors to assess the value of (predominantly black-owned) residential properties. Assessments were to be of "fair market value"—not simply relocation costs—and relied heavily on roadside visual inspections, often with realtors never leaving their cars. During this time, the city also refused to issue permits for property improvement in the condemned neighborhood and was largely unsympathetic to the subsequent complaints of resident homeowners, who maintained their properties as best they were able but were presented with "fair market" prices for their properties that seemed unreasonably low (Highsmith 2009, 357–59). Andrew Highsmith concludes that ultimately "all but a few black families from St. John Street moved to either segregated public housing or segregated private rental housing in the racially transitional neighborhoods bordering the North End. Only a handful of the five hundred black families who owned property in St. John prior to 1960 could afford to purchase homes in their new neighborhoods. By the 1980s, the Interstate 475 and St. John projects once supported by black residents in the 1950s came to represent two of the most crushing defeats ever suffered by Flint's civil rights activists" (2009, 360).

Now clearly this is an example of legacies of racial injustice and profound deficits in political influence for poor residents and community groups, and any plausible account of justice would give us ample critical resources to condemn these legacies and deficits and recommend more just institutions and practices. It is also consistent with Clarissa Hayward's (2003) concerns that we attend to how state policies constitute and sustain group difference, especially along the lines of race and class. Yet attention to public reason supplements such critical analyses of this and related cases, drawing into relief the contrast between reasonable statements of principle and policy ends, on the one hand, and morally insufficient or contemptible strategies of implementation, on the other.

Moving beyond this particular example, the pathologies associated with "home rule" and municipal fragmentation also seem to be largely failures of implementation and not necessarily intrinsic to municipal independence and fragmentation per se. That much, of course, is understood by advocates of strengthened regional institutions: no one simply proposes adding another layer of stifling, unresponsive bureaucracy between cities and states. But what matters, from the perspective of public reason, is that such regional innovations and reforms explicitly attend to the often-glaring gap between reasonable hopes and unreasonable implementation. In this light, we have grounds for endorsing various institutions not because they enhance participation, are more equitable, or are more efficient, but rather because (and insofar as) participation, equity, and efficiency are vital to protecting citizens' fundamental interests and treating them as moral equals, ensuring fair equality of opportunity and the fair worth of political liberty. Municipal fragmentation is pernicious insofar as it perpetuates and insulates bad reasons for various privileges that play out along lines of race and class in and around our cities.

Public Reason, Regional Planning, and Metropolitan Governance

Consider now, then, in light of public reason, some prevalent policy and planning approaches in recent U.S. debates: growth-oriented "competitive city" recommendations, community-oriented "new urbanist" approaches, and aggressive "regionalism" approaches.

The first two positions have been powerfully critiqued by Harvey (2000, 164–73), Fanstein (2000), and others: growth-oriented solutions are either naïve or dishonest given the mounting evidence of how growth-oriented urban development exacerbates inequalities, marginalizes vulnerable residents, and largely excludes from political influence a range of residents and organizations. By contrast, communitarian initiatives such as new urbanism tend not to question the growth-oriented priority on market-related rights and concerns, leaning instead toward a simplistic spatial determinism according to which certain spatial and aesthetic features (mixed uses, short blocks) will somehow generate the class, ethnic, and economic diversity and dynamism that Jane Jacobs (1961) famously praised. These are damning criticisms, but another problematic feature of these approaches is that they fail to take seriously the reasonable claims of those who dispute the priority of market-related rights and imperatives, as well as the dominant formulations of those rights.

Take the case of communitarian "utopias of spatial form" (Harvey 2000, 164), such as the new urbanist movement. Here, attention to public reason provides something these movements do not possess: critical self-awareness of exclusionary impulses that inevitably accompany any call to solidarity *in place*. On this point, David Harvey complains that "in its practical materialization, the new urbanism builds an image of community and rhetoric of place-based civic pride and consciousness for those who do not need it, while abandoning those that do to their 'underclass' fate" (2000, 170).

What public reason provides, I suggest, is a standard for assessing place-based claims of entitlement and a right to exclude, requiring that place-bound solidarity only impose burdens on citizens—both within and outside relevant boundaries—supported by reasons that respect their basic interests and fundamental equality with respect to public authority.

The third recent tendency involves calls for stronger regional institutions, often citing—as we saw at the outset—the extraordinary fragmentation of so many U.S. metropolitan regions. Critics of municipal fragmentation and divisive localism find mixed empirical support, however. Some studies claim to find a correlation between fragmentation and more-efficient local government, but others identify inefficiencies relating to jurisdictional overlap (Berry 2008). Still others, controlling for the historical trend toward more-centralized state government in the United States, find that more integrated, centralized metropolitan regions are more economically competitive than fragmented regions (Hamilton, Miller, and Paytas 2004). The relationship between regional economic disparities and the number and density of municipal governments is also unclear, with a recent study finding no clear association (Post and Stein 2000). Residential segregation, by income and race across relevant jurisdictions, seems to be significantly associated with fragmentation (Morgan and Mareschal 1999; Dawkins 2005; Bischoff 2008) and in what is by far the most rigorous and plausible of these studies, Alesina,

Baqir, and Hoxby (2004) find a trade-off in U.S. county-level data, where some potential economic gains from municipal consolidation seem to be forgone when the result would be increased income and racial heterogeneity.

All of these findings are sensitive to a range of measurement and scaling issues, and several fail, sometimes quite seriously, to resolve thorny issues of appropriate statistical estimation procedures and model specification. Furthermore, none tests the difficult questions of whether and how citizens experience and adapt to racial and class diversity over time, at various spatial scales, and mediated by specific institutional arrangements. Indeed, the statistical measures of fragmentation typically used—jurisdictions per capita, jurisdictional density, and probability measures—are insensitive to different kinds of institutional arrangements and fail to capture specific modes of interaction within and between institutions.

But these empirical complexities aside, a concern with urban public reason suggests two questions to ask of proposals for regional coordination and integration. First, are the proposed reforms or innovations consistent with the ideal of citizens as free moral equals with respect to public authority, even when citizens reasonably disagree? Second, do the reforms or innovations promise to foster reasonable arguments and identify unreasonable claims? If, as an empirical matter, some proposed institutional innovation—whether integrative or fragmenting—promises to perform well on these two moral standards, moderating reasonable disagreements in ways responsive to all citizens' reasonable claims and that respect their moral authority as citizens, then we ought to favor that proposal.

Frustrating Implications

I hinted early on that the turn toward public reason in evaluating urban inequalities comes with a cost and may be in some respects be frustrating and unsettling. How? Consider again our opening St. Louis example of racial residential segregation emerging through a convergence of racist preferences among homeowners, racist practices by realtors, undue influence by their commercial organization, and complicit or ineffectual local and federal political efforts. The turn to public reason gives us one way to identify an underlying commonality linking these diverse causal factors: each features unreasonable beliefs and actions that have public consequences. But whereas egalitarian or libertarian approaches to urban justice give us a clear criterion to evaluate outcomes in terms of consequences (e.g., for liberty, for equality), urban public reason pulls us to find what is reasonable in the positions we reject, and that has consequences for how we approach, for instance, the problem of residential segregation. After all, not all segregation reflects grave injustices perpetrated by the lucky, powerful, or simply racist upon the less affluent or those who appear different. Some spatial patterns of race, ethnicity, culture, and class in urban regions surely reflect reasonable choices to associate along lines of shared interests and identities. Beyond the most obvious and egregious instances of racial and class exclusion, citizens and scholars will reasonably disagree over how to weigh the value of free association in residential choices against public values of civic engagement and fair equality of life chances that may be undermined by certain patterns of spatial sorting in and around cities. Thus while many of us believe that boundaries of class and race, produced and sustained across urban space, demand careful moral scrutiny and serious efforts at reform (e.g., Fiss 2003; Kohn 2004), such a belief runs headlong into a conflicting intuition that many forms of separation and regulation, in spaces both territorial and imaginative, are an inevitable consequence of free choices and reasonably efficient exchange mechanisms that we have no good grounds for restricting, even if some (perhaps dramatic) inequalities in wealth and opportunities result (e.g., Beito, Gordon, and Tabarrok 2002).

To be sure, some, perhaps many, locational preferences held by middle-class prospective homeowners are either strategic concessions to existing realities (adaptive preferences) or shaped by prevailing norms in consumer society (false consciousness). Here a concern with urban public reason invites two sorts of questions: first, how might we structure institutions better to interrogate such preferences? Second, how should we best accommodate reasonable conflicts that persist after such interrogation? Once unreflective and merely self-serving claims are exposed, there is likely to be a residue of sincere, informed, and reasonably justified moral convictions and material demands. Citizens advancing such claims sincerely care about the common good, and they want to justify their public claims to others, on terms that respect their fundamental interests and equal standing as citizens and are not hopelessly partisan and controversial. The challenge is to take these claims seriously.

Similarly, citizens and planners may reasonably disagree about the virtues of density and suburban development, and related questions surrounding municipal fragmentation and tax bases. Such disputes make clear policy recommendations difficult. Consider debates over suburban sprawl. Many critics condemn low-density suburban development as wasteful, unsustainable, aesthetically bland, outright ugly, and injurious to the social fabric of communities and the civic engagement of residents. Others reply that sprawl reflects widespread preferences and that critics seek to impose their elitist aesthetic ideals, and their narrowly class-based interests, in preserving urban forms and lifestyles that distinctly favor affluent, university-educated residents.

The temptation here is to imagine that there are facts that will decide the debate: existing market incentives create sprawl and are implicated in the preferences that sustain it; suburbia depends critically on cheap petroleum and implicit subsidies on vital services. These are empirical claims that can be corroborated.[8] Factual claims, however, are also at stake in rejoining arguments that something like suburban life can adapt to alternative energy sources and different provision strategies for a range of public services and that the preference for big lots, a house and yard of one's own, and quiet residential streets is not merely a product of our consumer society but rather of legitimate preferences of autonomous citizen–consumers.

I do not think the defense of suburbia as it exists today can in fact be sustained on reasonable grounds: the car-based, low-density lifestyle is simply too burdensome on resources and civic attitudes (e.g., Williamson 2010) to be sustained in the longer term. Suppose, however, that in addition to what we already know (i.e., cheap petroleum and implicit subsidies foster unsustainable sprawl), some locational preferences for suburban lifestyles really are considered and sincere. Suppose further that we discover plausible ways to adapt at least some forms of suburban and exurban life to alternative energy sources, transportation technologies, and public-service provision strategies (perhaps by reimagining large metropolitan regions as dispersed networks of moderately dense but largely residential towns). Would the popular preference among planners and urbanists (and latte-sipping architects and professors) for high density and mixed uses then be largely an aesthetic conceit? I do not know—and I am nervous about the answer because the conceit is one I strongly share—but I do not think the matter will ultimately turn on factual claims, and it is not obvious that questions of distributive justice would select specific policies about the spatial structure of urban regions: we could imagine comparably just arrangements with dramatically different spatial forms and aesthetic elements.

We are faced, then, with the possibility that, even if we could achieve a just city with respect to fundamental interests, distributive fairness, and the equal standing of citizens, dramatic disagreements over institutions, spatial forms, and aesthetic ideals would likely persist. The turn to public reason illuminates (and at best helps regulate) these sorts of disagreements rather than pointing to a favored solution.

Metropolitan Governance within Public Reason

We might conclude here that, conditional on justice, fair representative politics is an acceptable way to resolve reasonable disagreements over such matters. If every citizen enjoys the fruits of justice—basic liberties of conscience, expression, and association; a sufficient command over resources to ensure a meaningful life; effective means to give voice to their political preferences and judgments, to vote for candidates and referenda, and to pursue public office if they desire—then the play of majoritarian politics can generate policies within the space of reasonable options (i.e., policies supported by reasonable arguments).

Alternatively, we might explore institutional arrangements that not only are as open as possible to citizen involvement, ensuring the fair worth of political liberties, but also leave considerable space and opportunity for groups of like-minded citizens to realize their reasonable aspirations, even if they are persistently in an out-voted electoral minority.

I favor the latter approach to the institutional structure of the just city and region, and it goes some way to addressing a serious worry about invoking public reason to evaluate urban and regional inequalities: reasonableness is, almost by definition, a conservative standard for evaluating contending values, interests, and arguments. Yet a common strand running through all the examples cited so far is that class and racial inequalities are difficult to correct once entrenched, and nowhere is this clearer than in the spatial forms and political realities of our cities. A just city would surely demand transformations—of attitudes, preferences, and legal structures of ownership and entitlement—that would count as controversial to entrenched interests. Wouldn't reflective equilibrium-seeking within public reason tend to lead us away from precisely the (controversial) solutions required to tackle entrenched injustice?

The force of this worry is lessened, I believe, by understanding reasonableness in terms of respect for the fundamental interests of citizens and their equal standing vis-à-vis public authority. Most entrenched injustices will be recognized within public reason, even if the more radical ways of addressing them will likely be rejected as unreasonable. The worry is further diminished, I believe, if we understand that the aim of just institutions is not only to ensure for all citizens the bases of a meaningful life with equal standing as citizens but also to minimize, so far as possible, the burdens imposed by public policies on reasonable ways of life. In the urban context, and given an emphasis on the basic structure of institutions, an obvious and fundamental concern of justice is, then, how to formulate policies and regulate activities in ways that maximize the options available for diverse land uses and transportation choices that undergird urban life?

Citizens may reasonably disagree on precisely this point, of course. They may accept that we owe fellow citizens duties of justice, involving the satisfaction of their basic interests in living a meaningful life and being treated as moral equals with respect to the laws, the force of which we collectively authorize. But they may dispute that we have further obligations to ensure that all reasonable ways of life can be meaningfully pursued. If most urban residents are not, say, vegan cyclists living in downtown housing cooperatives, then why should that minority lifestyle—however reasonable—be subsidized by the (also reasonable) majority?

Fair enough, and I do not want to make the strong claim that *maximal* opportunities for reasonable ways of life is a *demand* of justice.[9] I instead offer the weaker requirement—of increased space and reduced burdens for alternative ways of living in cities—as a reasonable way to structure institutions in accordance with public reason and sensitive to the worry that the standard of reasonableness is objectionably conservative.

Let me take up that worry further by offering what may seem a perverse assertion at first blush: on matters of justifying state coercion through legislation or police action, we should, I think, desire a status quo bias, even if that status quo is largely unjust in key respects!

To see why, consider the well-studied bias in urban politics toward commercial interests. This is clearly unjust on my favored approach: citizens do not have equal standing as authors of the laws if their voices are persistently discounted not because of the persuasiveness of their claims but rather because of the structures of property ownership tied to great wealth, paired with uncritical deference to historical standards in building codes and urban planning (Ben-Joseph 2005). Yet addressing these biases directly and aggressively would involve dramatic changes in the definition of property, systematic (and expensive) overhaul of influential building code standards, and the orientation of urban zoning and rede-velopment efforts toward diverse uses, rather than privileging ownership and expected revenues. Such transformations threaten to replace infor-mal and often private forms of coercion (the neoliberal status quo) with direct public coercion.

Perhaps what our cities really need is revolution of this sort. But as a matter of gaining political support for proposals consistent with justice, that seems to me to be a nonstarter. I agree with Susan Fainstein that, how-ever we understand the just city, we must "incorporate an entrepreneurial state that not only provides welfare but also generates increased wealth; moreover, it needs to project a future embodying a middle-class society rather than only empowering the poor and disfranchised" (2000, 468).

In contrast to selling dramatic revolution from below, I suspect it would be far easier to convince skeptical affluent citizens that they ought to support unpopular but reasonable ways of life. In urban settings this may be an easier sell than at the national level, targetting, say, religion or culture—think of the recurring conservative fury in the United States over federal government endowments supporting controversial art or the recurring debate in Canada over public funding for religious schools. This is because, in urban regions, support for alternative, reasonable ways of life will often more clearly involve infrastructure investments that have broader public appeal, such as diverse transportation alternatives (e.g., pitched not only to commuters but also to users of a range of interlinked recreational sites) or alternative ownership structures for housing (some of which may appeal not only to low-income housing advocates but also to smaller, commercial lessors and investors). In this way, a commitment to reasonableness still allows subtle and gradual challenges to status-quo interests and practices, if we design institutions to foster more contesta-tory politics within public reason.

Notes

1 The precise definition of a *basic structure* is a matter of considerable ongoing debate in political philosophy, especially whether it is the generality and scope of institutions that makes them basic, or the degree of their influence, or their fun-damentally coercive nature. Even if we reject the basic structure restriction, we still have good reasons to think of these local political structures as problems of justice. For instance, we might think, with Cohen (2008, ch. 3), that justice applies not only to institutions but also to individual actions yet still argue that, if private

choices about home ownership and our children's education reinforce harmful inequalities of access and opportunity, then they are at the very least morally suspect. Macedo notes this particular point of likely convergence among versions of egalitarian justice, on the one hand, and Rawlsian attention to the basic structure and how local institutions threaten fair equality of opportunity, the fair worth of liberties, and the equal standing of citizens, on the other.

2 Here I have in mind three related but spatially distinctive forms of inequality: first, the stark and spatially regimented inequalities infamously characteristic of twentieth-century U.S. cities; second, more recent forms of resource inequality within sprawling metropolitan regions, which generate disputes between revenue-strapped central cities and more affluent surrounding municipalities; and third, the sort of disparities between metropolitan regions that inspire some scholars to rethink the familiar jurisdictional authorities and divisions of powers in the U.S. federal system—again, see Frug in this volume and (2002).

3 This Rousseauian current in Rawls has been explored recently by Corey Brettschneider (2007).

4 This formulation of Rawlsian reflective equilibria is largely due to Daniels (1979).

5 For example, Haslett (1987), Cohen (2008, chs. 6–7), and compare Brower (1994). This is not the place to delve into these rich philosophical debates, but I will note that the critics have faced powerful replies: in particular, philosophers have shown ways in which the apparent circularity of reflective equilibrium is, or can be rendered, benign (e.g., McKinnon 2002; compare Estlund 2007; Cohen 2009). The problem of status quo bias is real, but as I will argue later, there are good reasons to desire such bias in some settings and plausible grounds for hope that the bias can be corrected when it sustains unjust power differentials.

6 These are the currency, Rawls thinks, of "freestanding" conceptions of justice likely to win widespread support among free and equal citizens with diverse and conflicting comprehensive doctrines. For Rawls, a political conception of justice elaborates, organizes, and justifies distinctly public concepts and values and thus is not merely an application of some more comprehensive and foundational moral theory; nor does it require for acceptance that we first believe in some elaborate metaphysical or religious worldview.

7 The standard elaborations are Rawls (1993, lecture 6; 1997).

8 The latter claims are almost trivially true, but the evidence relevant to the former claim—about market forces and sprawl—is interestingly complex: see Levine (2006), who makes the case that some restrictive zoning practices exacerbate sprawl and undermine more compact and sustainable urban forms that markets might in fact sustain. More generally, see Lewis (1996) on how local governance structures affect patterns of suburban development.

9 I do, however, think that something like this conclusion about institutional structure falls very easily out of an influential way of arguing about justice; see King (2005). With Rawls, I believe that "certain institutional forms are embedded within the conception of justice" (Rawls 1971, 231).

References

Alesina, Alberto, Reza Baqir, and Caroline Hoxby. 2004. "Political Jurisdictions in Heterogeneous Communities." *Journal of Political Economy* 112, no. 2: 348–96.

Beito, David T., Peter Gordon, and Alexander Tabarrok, eds. 2002. *The Voluntary City: Choice, Community, and Civil Society.* Ann Arbor: University of Michigan Press.

Ben-Joseph, Eran. 2005. *The Code of the City: Standards and the Hidden Language of Place Making.* Cambridge, Mass.: MIT Press.

Berry, Christopher. 2008. "Piling On: Multilevel Government and the Fiscal Common-Pool." *American Journal of Political Science* 52, no. 4: 802–20.

Bischoff, Kendra. 2008. "School District Fragmentation and Racial Residential Segregation: How Do Boundaries Matter?" *Urban Affairs Review* 44, no. 2: 182–217.

Brettschneider, Corey. 2007. *Democratic Rights: The Substance of Self-Government.* Princeton, N.J.: Princeton University Press.

Brower, Bruce. 1994. "The Limits of Public Reason." *Journal of Philosophy* 91:5–26.

Cohen, Gerald A. 2008. *Rescuing Justice and Equality.* Cambridge, Mass.: Harvard University Press.

Cohen, Joshua. 2009. "Truth and Public Reason." *Philosophy and Public Affairs* 37:2–42.

Dawkins, Casey J. 2005. "Tiebout Choice and Residential Segregation by Race in U.S. Metropolitan Areas, 1980–2000." *Regional Science and Urban Economics* 35:734–55.

Daniels, Norman. 1979. "Wide Reflective Equilibrium and Theory Acceptance in Ethics." *Journal of Philosophy* 76, no. 5: 256–82.

Estlund, David. 2007. *Democratic Authority.* Princeton, N.J.: Princeton University Press.

Fainstein, Susan. 2000. "New Directions in Planning Theory." *Urban Affairs Review* 35, no. 4: 451–78.

———. 2001. "Competitiveness, Cohesion, and Governance: Their Implications for Social Justice." *International Journal of Urban and Regional Research* 25, no. 4: 884–88.

Fiss, Owen. 2003. *A Way Out: America's Ghettos and the Legacy of Racism.* Princeton, N.J.: Princeton University Press.

Frug, Gerald E. 2002. "Beyond Regional Government." *Harvard Law Review* 115, no. 7: 1764–1836.

Gordon, Colin. 2008. *Mapping Urban Decline: St. Louis and the Fate of the American City.* Philadelphia: University of Pennsylvania Press.

Gutmann, Amy, and Dennis Thompson. 1996. *Democracy and Disagreement.* Cambridge, Mass.: Harvard University Press.

Halpern, Robert. 1995. *Rebuilding the Inner City: A History of Neighborhood Initiatives to Address Poverty in the United States.* New York: Columbia University Press.

Hamilton, David K., David Y. Miller, and Jerry Paytas. 2004. "Exploring the Horizontal and Vertical Dimensions of the Governing of Metropolitan Regions." *Urban Affairs Review* 40, no. 2: 147–82.

Harvey, David. 2000. *Spaces of Hope.* Berkeley: University of California Press.

Haslett, D. W. 1987. "What Is Wrong with Reflective Equilibria?" *Philosophical Quarterly* 37, no. 148: 305–11.

Hayward, Clarissa. 2003. "The Difference States Make: Democracy, Identity, and the American City." *American Political Science Review* 97, no. 4: 501–14.

Highsmith, Andrew R. 2009. "Demolition Means Progress: Urban Renewal, Local Politics, and State-Sanctioned Ghetto Formation in Flint, Michigan." *Journal of Urban History* 35, no. 3: 348–68.

Jacobs, Jane. 1961. *The Death and Life of Great American Cities*. New York: Vintage Random House.

King, Loren A. 2005. "The Federal Structure of a Republic of Reasons." *Political Theory* 33, no. 5: 629–53.

Kohn, Margaret. 2004. *Brave New Neighborhoods*. New York: Routledge.

Lewis, Paul G. 1996. *Shaping Suburbia: How Political Institutions Organize Urban Development*. Pittsburgh, Pa.: University of Pittsburg Press.

Levine, Jonathan. 2006. *Zoned Out: Regulation, Markets, and Choices in Transportation and Metropolitan Land-Use*. Washington, D.C.: Resources for the Future Press.

McKinnon, Catriona. 2002. *Liberalism and the Defence of Political Constructivism*. New York: Palgrave Macmillan.

Mitchell, Don. 2003. *The Right to the City: Social Justice and the Fight for Public Space*. New York: Guilford.

Morgan, David R., and Patrice Mareschal. 1999. "Central-City/Suburban Inequality and Metropolitan Political Fragmentation." *Urban Affairs Review* 34, no. 4: 578–95.

Post, Stephanie Shirley, and Robert M. Stein. 2000. "State Economies, Metropolitan Governance, and Urban–Suburban Dependence." *Urban Affairs Review* 36, no. 1: 46–60.

Rawls, John. 1971. *A Theory of Justice*. Rev. ed. Cambridge, Mass.: Belknap Press.

———. 1993. *Political Liberalism*. Exp. ed. New York: Columbia University Press.

———. 1997. "The Idea of Public Reason Revisited." *University of Chicago Law Review* 64, no. 3: 765–807.

———. 2001. *Justice as Fairness: A Restatement*. Edited by Erin Kelly. Cambridge, Mass.: Harvard University Press.

Rosen, Mark D. 2007. "Was *Shelley v. Kraemer* Incorrectly Decided? Some New Answers." *California Law Review* 95:451–512.

Smith, David M. 1994. *Geography and Social Justice*. Oxford: Blackwell.

Weir, Margaret. 1994. "Urban Poverty and Defensive Localism." *Dissent* 41, no. 3: 337–42.

Williamson, Thaddeus. 2010. *Sprawl, Justice, and Citizenship: The Civic Costs of the American Way of Life*. Cambridge, U.K.: Cambridge University Press.

United States Supreme Court Decisions

Berman v. Parker, 348 U.S. 26 (1954).

Hills v. Gautreaux, 425 U.S. 284 (1976).

Jones v. Alfred H. Mayer Co., 392 U.S. 409 (1968).

Shelley v. Kraemer, 334 U.S. 1 (1948).

3 PUBLIC SPACE

IN THE PROGRESSIVE ERA

MARGARET KOHN

THE FIRST ENDURING DISCUSSION OF justice, Plato's *Republic*, is also one of the few works that explores the connection between justice and the city (Plato 1992). *The Republic* does not lend itself to any simple interpretation, but one of the most prominent arguments is Socrates's claim that the just city is organized hierarchically, with each class performing the task it is suited for. Today, under the influence of John Rawls, most political theorists hold the opposite view (1999, 2001). A just society is one that maximizes equality while protecting basic freedom. But what about the just city? This question has received little attention. There are two different ways of explaining why "justice and the metropolis" has been a relatively marginal concern. One reason has to do with the metropolis itself: its highly segregated and stratified character has rendered its injustices invisible to the privileged. Friedrich Engels made this point in his book *The Condition of the Working Class in England* (2009) and his concern was underscored by American progressives in the early twentieth century. A second reason is that many theorists tend to assume that inequality is best remedied through economic redistribution. This approach has the advantage of respecting individuals' autonomy and their ability to pursue their own concept of the good life. One implication of this approach, however, is the assumption that urban problems should disappear after economic equality is achieved and that those problems that remain can be solved through planning and technical expertise.

Contemporary political theory provides little guidance for thinking about justice and the American metropolis. For example, in his seminal work *City of Quartz*, Mike Davis exposes the exclusions and inequities that are concealed and intensified by the projects of "starchitects", downtown boosters, and ex-urban developers but writes very little about the alternative that he would like to promote. He does, however, provide one clue. In the chapter titled "Fortress Los Angeles," Davis mourns the passing of the "Olmstedian vision of public space" (Davis 1992, 226). What is this Olmstedian vision, and is it relevant today? This chapter will show that the Olmstedian approach to public space is paradoxical; it is both disciplinary and democratic, and it romanticizes nature while also recognizing the dynamism of urban life. These tensions were addressed, but perhaps not entirely resolved, by Progressive era thinkers who shared his concerns about the challenges and inequalities of city life.

In early twentieth-century America, urbanization was still a new phenomenon; its injustices were extreme but had not yet thickened. They had not yet been rendered invisible by geography and habit. Progressives like Jane Addams and John Dewey were concerned not only with freedom and material deprivation but also with democratic citizenship. They criticized the American metropolis not for its injustice but for undermining the democratic institutions and ethos necessary to fight injustice. They suggested that public space could help secure the promise of democracy in three ways: (1) public spaces could be sites of empowerment for the disenfranchised, (2) they could promote acculturation into the dominant society, and (3) they could foster sympathy and mutual understanding between members of different social classes. Progressives envisioned public space as a site of both freedom and social order, integration and transformation. This chapter is a critical intellectual history of this strand of democratic theory. It reconstructs the development of the democratic theory of public space by focusing on the work of Olmsted and Addams and also evaluates its relevance for contemporary debates.

The Olmstedian Vision

Today Olmsted is fondly remembered as the founding father of Central Park, America's most prominent public space, but his original vision was controversial in his own day. Olmsted was a strong proponent of the idea that parks should try to recreate a natural, pastoral landscape. He criticized both the highly ornamental gardens of European estates and commercial amusement parks. According to Olmsted, public parks were supposed to strengthen the social fabric of big cities by approximating the beneficial aspects of country living in an urban environment. Public parks should provide the quiet, relaxation, beauty, and serenity of the countryside in the middle of the city (Rybczynski 2000). Olmsted also argued that a large park would benefit the public by improving the health and well-being of all urban dwellers (1971, 15).

Olmsted was not an opponent of urban life. He recognized that concentrations of population made both commerce and culture possible, and he argued that the division of labor in the city made domestic work less burdensome. Nevertheless, he noted that the intense concentration of buildings and people caused crowding, turbulence, disease, and disorder (Olmsted 1971, 30). The solution was to create an antidote within the city. The urban park could prevent disease by improving the quality of air in the city, but its main effect on public health was indirect; by providing opportunities for recreation and relaxation, it functioned as a safety valve that helped dispel the tensions, anxiety, and anger experienced by urban dwellers. Olmsted believed that this was especially important for people from the lower and middle classes who had little access to the seaside or country retreats.

Olmsted recognized that creating a beautiful pastoral landscape on wastelands in the middle of a large city required a great deal of artifice. Olmsted saw the park as a work of art and expected park visitors to treat it as such. This meant that conduct was highly regulated and strictly enforced by a special park police force. Olmsted hired twenty-four uniformed officers; their personal appearance was regulated by a strict code similar to the rules governing military recruits, and the park police officers were even forbidden from drinking in taverns when off duty. The police enforced rules that forbade visitors from walking on the grass, picking flowers, speeding on the carriage ways, gambling, selling goods, or using indecent language. Olmsted consistently emphasized the difference between a commons and a park. A park should not be mistaken for an unregulated space that was accessible to all for any purpose; it was a carefully crafted work of art that could contribute to the well-being of visitors, especially if they were trained to appreciate it. One year after Central Park was opened to the public, the commissioners passed additional ordinances forbidding swimming, fishing, playing musical instruments, and posting notices or parading for civic or military purposes (Rosenzweig and Blackmar 1992). It would be over one hundred years before the restrictions on political activity were lifted.

Contemporary scholars have pointed out that these rules of conduct were an attempt to enforce middle-class standards of behavior on the rest of the population (Rosenzweig and Blackmar 1992). Olmsted was quite explicit that one goal of Central Park was the moral improvement of the working classes. He thought that democratic culture had a tendency to produce "rowdyism, ruffianism, want of high honorable sentiment and chivalry" (cited in Rosenzweig and Blackmar 1992, 138). Elites had an obligation to help improve the character of democratic society through educational and cultural institutions. According to Olmsted, the park could contribute in two ways: the natural scenery had a "harmonizing and refining influence upon the most unfortunate and most lawless classes of the city" (Olmsted 1971, 96), and the design of the park would encourage appropriate leisure activities such as contemplation, conversation, promenading, and family time. Not surprisingly, middle- and upper-class New Yorkers were much more likely than workers to frequent Central Park (Rosenzweig and Blackmar 1992, 211–18). Part of the reason was probably the cost of transportation to the park and the small amount of leisure time that workers had at their disposal. But another explanation is that many workers preferred other destinations such as Jones Wood, a private park that allowed more boisterous recreation, including spectacles, beer tents, games of chance, popular music performances, competitive sports, dancing, and large picnics (Rosenzweig and Blackmar 1992, 233). Many of the leisure activities favored by the working classes were outlawed in Central Park.

Olmsted wanted Central Park to be a pastoral landscape that would foster refinement and create a highly regulated environment that would help inculcate standards of decent behavior. Why then would Mike Davis, the foremost critic of contemporary disciplinary space, invoke Olmsted in positive terms? I think the key is found in the following passage from Olmsted's lecture "Public Parks and the Enlargement of Towns":

> Consider that the New York Park and the Brooklyn Park are the only places in those associated cities where, in this eighteen hundred and seventieth year after Christ, you will find a body of Christians coming together, and with an evident glee in the prospect of coming together, all classes largely represented, with a common purpose, not at all intellectual, competitive with none, disposing to jealousy and spiritual or intellectual pride toward none, each individual adding by his mere presence to the pleasure of all others, all helping to the greater happiness of each. You may thus often see vast numbers of persons brought closely together, poor and rich, young and old, Jew and Gentile. (1971, 75)

In this passage Olmsted celebrates the intrinsic pleasures of public life. Earlier in the same lecture, he noted that city life tends to encourage an instrumental and disinterested attitude toward other human beings. It also fosters an acquisitive and materialist ethos. For Olmsted, parks were supposed to be a respite from the materialism of the city, which is why most commercial enterprises were restricted. He argues that public parks provide a setting in which it is possible to encounter other people not as competitors or instruments of gain but rather as fellow citizens. Olmsted also emphasizes that the diversity of the crowd is a positive attribute. The park is the site of a distinctively democratic type of sociability based not on interaction but rather on copresence and imitation. The aesthetic effect of the park comes not only from the experience of nature but also from the visual tableau of the democratic public.

Olmsted's vision is a profoundly ambivalent one. The diversity, intensity, and conflict of urban life forced Olmsted and other Mugwumps to think about the challenges of democracy. They tried to find ways of incorporating immigrants and workers into the demos by creating civil citizens, but they did not consider that democracy might involve dismantling existing structures of power and sources of inequality. Elites such as Olmsted felt that they had an obligation to serve the interests of the common people, but they neither expected that the people themselves would be able to articulate their own interests nor recognized that these interests might legitimately differ from the ones defined as the public interest. The tensions between inclusion and exclusion, equality and hierarchy, and nature and culture run throughout Olmsted's writings on public space but are not ultimately resolved. Instead of invoking the Olmstedian vision of public space, Davis would have been better off turning to the ideas of the next generation of reformers: the Progressives.[1]

The Progressives' Argument for Public Space

In the late nineteenth century, intellectuals witnessed a massive social and economic transformation as the United States became an urban society. At the same time, immigration from Eastern and Southern Europe was changing the demographic makeup of urban America, and reformers were concerned about how to integrate newcomers and foster civic identification and solidarity across the broader polity.[2] In the Progressive era, a second generation of urban reformers wanted to supplement the park system with local, neighborhood-based social spaces. Influenced by the German sociologist Alfred Toennies, they were worried about the alienating, isolating features of urban life. According to Toennies, in small towns, social norms were established and reinforced by face-to-face relations between neighbors and acquaintances. Local institutions cemented social relations that provided the benefits of sociability and solidarity to those who conformed to expected standards of behavior (1988). Furthermore, these institutions, at least in theory, brought together old and young, rich and poor, local and newcomer—groups that were permanently separated by the centrifugal tendencies of urban life. In the big city, the social and institutional structures that supported the moral order were weakened. With ample opportunities for friendships and amusement, there were fewer stable relationships and the threat of censure could no longer guarantee conformity. According to the conventional wisdom of the period, female virtue and male responsibility were both in jeopardy. The solution was to recreate a stable, face-to-face community within the broader urban fabric of the city (Goist 1971; White and White 1962).

Jane Addams's Hull House was emblematic of this ambition. Founded in 1889, it was an attempt to reestablish "social intercourse" between people from different social classes and backgrounds. Although Addams emphasized the need to improve the material conditions of the urban poor, she felt their struggles were exacerbated by the fact that "the social organism" had broken down in crowded parts of American cities. The spatial segregation of urban areas contributed to feelings of powerlessness and anomie, making it more difficult to create the social organizations that would help remedy the problems of transportation, overcrowding, and sanitation. She noted that the poor had little access to "clubhouses, libraries, galleries, and semi-public conveniences" because these amenities were located in the part of the city where people with resources and education lived (Addams 1965). Hull House was an attempt to remedy this situation. It provided idealistic, middle-class people with an opportunity to live among the poor in order to understand their plight and help solve urban problems by formulating public policies, fundraising, engaging in social work, or influencing public opinion. It also provided workers with opportunities to come together to deliberate, coordinate, and solve their own problems. Hull House offered space for child care, play groups, English lessons, art, theater, vocational training, political debates, reading newspapers and books, listening to lectures, and informal socializing. Although Hull House was privately owned and supported by philanthropy, it reflected public values of inclusiveness and diversity and served as a model for the municipal provision of social and recreational facilities like playgrounds, community centers, and libraries in cities (Addams 1912).

The settlement houses were part of a broader movement that tried to rebuild a democratic public under conditions of growing diversity and industrialization. Other important figures in this movement included Charles Zublin, who worked with Addams in Chicago and founded two settlement houses. Having seen the Social Science Club and public lectures at Hull House, Zublin became a proponent of the University Extension program at the University of Chicago. His own lectures on topics such as "The Structure of Society" were widely attended. Zublin also became a leading figure in the City Beautiful movement and played an instrumental role in establishing parks and museums. In his writings as a public intellectual, Zublin challenged the antiurbanism in American political ideology and celebrated the city as the apex of civilization. His vision of the city, however, was democratic and participatory. He is famous for promoting monumental public spaces, but he also fostered intimate forums for debate, deliberation, education, and sociability (Mattson 1998).

Frederic Howe promoted a similar vision of participatory democracy rooted in public deliberation and debate. Under his leadership, the People's Institute in New York City expanded its mandate beyond hosting public lectures and began to serve as a popular political forum where participants debated social issues before voting on resolutions that were sent to the city council. It became a model for similar forums in other parts of New York City and across the country (Mattson 1998). Participatory democracy, however, requires public space—places where citizens can come together to discuss their views not only with friends and family members but also with strangers, experts, officials, and opponents. The church serves as the nodal point of religious life, but there was no equivalent for democratic life. John Dewey promoted the idea that public schools should serve as community centers, which could become nodal points for democratic participation. At Hull House, Dewey saw working class immigrants come together to discuss solutions to local problems ranging from inadequate sanitation to dangerous conditions in factories, and this experience influenced his theories of participatory democracy (Dewey 1976; Westbrook 1991).

In addition to her practical work at Hull House, Addams was also a public intellectual who made a political case in favor of the public provision of social space. She argued that citizens who were unmoved by the spirit of altruism or Christian humanitarianism still had pragmatic reasons for supporting government projects to provide public space in urban areas. Addams thought public space could prevent social disorder and fostering a civic identity on the part of new immigrants. Like Olmsted, she felt that a system of urban parks could improve the living conditions of the urban poor, but she emphasized the value of recreation and play rather than the aesthetic pleasure of pastoral scenery. The problem was that large families lived in crowded, run-down tenements, and children had nowhere to play except the streets. Since real tenement reform would have required massive government funding, Progressive-era reformers focused on something more feasible. They created public amenities—mostly parks and playgrounds—where children and adults could enjoy the benefits of leisure and play.

Progressive-era reformers believed that public spaces could help solve urban social problems and prevent vice. Paul Boyer called this rationale "positive environmentalism" (Boyer 1978). Jane Addams argued that "a group of boys will not continue to stand upon the street corners and to seek illicit pleasures in alleys and poolrooms when all the fascinating apparatus of a recreation field is at their disposal" (Addams 1912, 617). She even suggested that public recreational facilities could help undermine the rampant bossism and political corruption of urban political machines by undermining the power of the youth gangs that served as training grounds for clientelistic relationships. She concluded optimistically that "the opportunity which the athletic field provides for . . . comradeship founded upon the establishment of just relationships is the basis for a new citizenship and in the end will overthrow the corrupt politician" (Addams 1912, 618). The playground movement was motivated by altruism combined with an interest in developing benign forms of social control (Addams 1990). The basic premise of the movement was that society was like an organism, and therefore the living conditions of one group affected the others. Jane Addams argued that improving the mental and physical health of the largely immigrant working class would benefit everyone by decreasing crime and disorder. According to the ideology of "positive environmentalism," public spaces could encourage virtues and temper vices while fostering identification with the polity.

Like Olmsted a generation earlier, the people promoting the playground movement wanted to socialize working-class children into middle-class habits (Rosenzweig 1983; Muraskin 1976; Jones 1977), but it was not simply a disciplinary project. It was also motivated by a critique of the disciplinary nature of factory labor and the regimented structure of urban life. Addams, for example, was concerned that urban youths did not have the opportunity to fulfill their natural desire for self-organization and creative play. The urban environment was not designed with these needs in mind; therefore they were repressed, channeled into vice (e.g., gambling, stealing), or expressed in dangerous places (e.g., busy streets). She felt that the need for play was especially urgent in modern society because of the extreme monotony of factory labor (Addams 1909).

Discipline and Democracy

Progressives made arguments for public space that drew on a range of traditions, including Christian humanism, philanthropy, and even social Darwinism, but they also advanced a distinctively political analysis of the issue. They explicitly linked public space to the challenges and opportunities of a democratic society. According to Jane Addams, the primary motive for creating Hull House was to expand democracy beyond the ballot box and make "the entire social organism democratic" (Addams 1965, 29). She recognized that political democracy would be an illusion if it were not supported by a more democratic society. In order for political democracy to flourish in a large, diverse polity, two things had to happen: (1) the dispossessed had to become integrated into the polity and (2) elites had to become accountable to the people. Thinkers like Addams, Dewey, and Howe felt that community centers, open universities, libraries, and public parks could help the poor increase their power and help the elites learn to listen.

However, this democratic rationale for public space is not particularly popular today. The Right has opted for a combination of laissez-faire and the carceral state. On the Left, the ideology of positive environmentalism has fallen out of vogue. There is no longer much confidence in the power of charity or government to improve the lives or lifestyles of individuals. Furthermore, the disciplinary character of some of these efforts—the playgrounds with trained supervisors, stringent rules, and tight schedules—is now perceived as a paternalistic attempt to encourage working-class children to adopt middle-class behavior and abandon their own, more exuberant styles of play. The political rationale behind the expansion of public spaces in the early twentieth century has been discredited (Kohn 2004).

The legacy of the Progressive era, however, is still with us in the physical form of public parks, community centers, and libraries that flourish in many North American cities. It is worth asking whether the theoretical rationale behind this movement to create public space should be reanimated. In order to answer this question, we need to consider the criticism that the progressive approach to public space had an excessively disciplinary character. There is certainly considerable evidence for this view. Social histories document the way that public spaces were highly regulated to inculcate middle-class norms of behavior, and the theoretical literature is quite explicit about the aim of "improving" the working classes.

In "The Objective Value of a Social Settlement" (1892), Jane Addams describes newly arrived immigrants as "densely ignorant of civic duties" (1965, 46) and characterizes the owners of tenement houses as "sordid and ignorant immigrants" with no understanding that wealth should bring responsibility and refinement. She concludes that for Italian immigrants, wealth doesn't encourage cleanliness, self-improvement, or education. According to Addams, working-class immigrants needed improvement, and one way to do this was to expose them to models of correct (elite) behavior. She emphasized that one goal of Hull House was "to bring them [new immigrants] into contact with a better type of Americans" (1965, 50). She felt that the scholarship, linguistic attainment, and beautiful surroundings featured at Hull House could benefit the neighborhood just as much as its day care, social activities, advocacy, and legal advice.

As we will see shortly, Addams's understanding of both Hull House and the surrounding community changed over the course of her career, but even in her essays, there were democratic as well as disciplinary dimensions. First, she emphasized that Hull House was not a charitable institution with a mission to help the poor but rather a social center for the whole community, including all ages, ethnicities, and classes. The goal of Hull House was to strengthen democracy by building solidarity through social, educational, humanitarian, and civic endeavors. The educational programs provided training in skills that were helpful for professional advancement, but they also functioned as schools of citizenship where students could explore contemporary political issues in depth. Nor were the working classes positioned simply as consumers of knowledge. Through institutions like the Working People's Social Science Club, workers had the opportunity to present their distinctive analyses of economic and political issues. Hull House was not a social welfare organization but rather a cooperative self-help organization; most of the projects were initiated and staffed by neighborhood volunteers.

In her writings, Addams analyzes the paternalism of elites and the way that such attitudes undermine the possibility of mutual understanding among different groups. In "Democracy and Social Ethics" (1902), Addams addresses her peers (and perhaps her own earlier self), challenging misconceptions about the behavior and attitudes of the poor and the working class (1965, 62–83). She argues that these misconceptions not only are barriers to social intercourse between classes but also can make it more difficult to formulate and adopt appropriate social policies. Addams points out how the key elements of middle-class ideology such as thrift, modesty, and temperance may not be appropriate for urban workers. Thrift, she realizes, may seem like mean-spirited miserliness when friends and family are hungry or lack necessities. Similarly, the saloon, which middle class reformers saw as a den of iniquity, was experienced by workers as one of the few sites of sociability and solidarity. The flashy clothes of a poor working girl may actually be a rational investment in self-presentation that is her only hope to overcome the prejudices against her class. The tenor of these comments is very different from Addams's contemptuous description of "sordid" immigrants written ten years earlier. I take this shift to be an illustration of the type of social learning that Hull House was designed to foster. By facilitating meaningful interaction between people of different backgrounds, Hull House provided opportunities for dismantling prejudices.

Addams's critique of paternalism is developed in more detail in her essay "A Modern Lear" (1965). The essay is a reflection on the lessons of the contentious strike at the Pullman Palace Car Company. The essay remained unpublished until 1912 because its criticisms of George Pullman were extremely controversial. Pullman was widely admired by the middle classes as an example of the type of benevolent industrialist that they hoped could heal the rift between capital and labor. Workers, on the other hand, felt that his much-praised company town was a particularly sophisticated form of exploitation. Both rents and retail prices were significantly higher than those charged in nearby communities, and when an economic downturn lead to a steep cut in hours and wages, there was no corresponding decrease in rent.

Initially, "A Modern Lear" seems like a further illustration of the paternalism that some scholars associate with the Progressive movement. Addams opens the essay with a critique of the "barbaric instinct to kill" unleashed by the strike and insists that "rage and riot" are never justified in a civilized community (1965, 107). Although she emphasizes that both sides of the strike were guilty of barbarism, she seems more concerned with the brutality of the strike itself than the oppressive working conditions that inspired it. She also sympathizes with the "ingratitude suffered by an indulgent employer" (Pullman). Yet the point of the analogy between King Lear and Pullman is clearly a critical one. According to Addams, the problem with Pullman's elaborate company town was that it did not really meet the needs of its inhabitants. The beautiful theater was too costly for performances that depended on the patronage of workers, and even the church was "too expensive to be rented continuously" (1965, 112). According to Addams, Pullman was unable to understand the needs of the workers, and without democratic institutions, there was no mechanism to ensure that the town was responsive to the residents' concerns: "The president of the Pullman company thought out within his own mind a beautiful town. He had power with which to build this town, but he did not appeal to nor obtain the consent of the men who were living in it. The most unambitious reform, recognizing the necessity for this consent, makes for slow but sane and strenuous progress, while the most ambitious of social plans and experiments, ignoring this, is prone to the failure of the model town of Pullman" (1965, 122). This passage makes it clear that Addams was no technocrat; she did not agree with Progressives who assumed that the solution to class conflict was more efficient social engineering. She insisted that workers, too, had legitimate desires for autonomy and self-determination. In fact, the residents of Pullman's model town had a much keener insight into the way the town functioned to mystify relations of economic power. "A Modern Lear" employs a not-too-subtle literary analogy to make a strong argument in favor of democratic participation, rather than benevolent paternalism, as the solution to the problems of industrial society.

Hull House was very different from Pullman's model town and also quite different from Olmsted's park. Unlike Pullman's town, Hull House was built with, rather than for, the residents of the neighborhood. Like Central Park, Hull House was imagined as a site of social interaction and a cultural venue that could improve the lives of the working population in the neighborhood. But at Hull House the social learning went in both directions. Workers might benefit from the education, refinement, and legal advice provided by the middle-class residents, but the middle-class residents could also learn a great deal about the lives of workers and the social conditions of the city. They also learned to understand and respect the strategies that workers adopted to survive in the industrial metropolis. The progressive approach to public space differed from the Olmstedian vision in at least two respects. First, there was more emphasis on the self-organization, mobilization, and empowerment of the disenfranchised. Second, the benefits of class mixing were understood to extend to the elite, as well as the poor.

Contact, Sympathy, and Solidarity

Jane Addams's urban theory and practice rested on the assumption that public space enlarges our sympathy by increasing the opportunities to encounter difference. Ralph Waldo Emerson, not usually someone to write paeans to urban life, argued that visiting the city was beneficial because it helped people expand their sympathies by mixing with different classes of society in the streets and squares (1903–1904, 149). Emerson emphasized that this type of encounter was beneficial to elites, not just the poorer classes. In a sense this is "positive environmentalism" turned upside-down. Rather than building monuments and playgrounds that encourage the urban poor to assimilate middle-class values, the goal is also to create public places where the middle classes may also question their own values.

To use a more contemporary idiom, we could say that the individual is constituted as a subject through interactions with other people. The built environment facilitates interactions with certain people and limits contact with others. The most frequent interactions are with family and friends—people who usually look and act very much like we do. In public space, the individual encounters a more diverse range of others, which potentially expands the community of people with whom she identifies. By encountering the unfamiliar, she may become more comfortable with difference (Young 1986; Bickford 2000). Yet some commentators have pointed out that theorists who expect this positive outcome rely on a naïve understanding of social psychology (Hayward 2007). In fact, exposure to difference can often elicit fear, anxiety, indifference, disgust, and even hatred. William James recognized this possibility and explored its significance in his influential essay "On a Certain Blindness in Human Beings." Far from assuming that exposure to difference results in sympathy, he argued that sympathy is a precarious achievement. He noted that each individual feels his own duties and needs with intensity but has trouble recognizing the same concerns in others. James added that we vainly look to others for sympathy: "Others are too much absorbed in their own vital secrets to take an interest in ours. Hence the stupidity and injustice of our opinions, so far as they deal with the significance of alien lives" (1899, 116). James was also skeptical that the gulf between the perspective of someone embedded in a certain way of life and the spectator can be easily bridged. He noted that "the spectator's judgment is sure to miss the root of the matter, and to possess no truth" because the judging spectator has access only to outward appearance when the real significance (for the subject) is determined by personal experiences or an interpretive framework which is not visible (1899, 117).[3]

It seems as if James is suggesting some sort of radical solipsism or subjectivity. His examples, however, highlight the way that misunderstanding results from the fact that people live in distinct interpretive communities. This becomes apparent in a passage that recounts his reaction to clear-cutting in the mountains of North Carolina. Viewing the activity from an aesthetic point of view, he saw the bare hillsides as "hideous, a sort of ulcer" (James 1899, 117). But the farmers swinging their axes saw the destruction as a significant improvement—the first step toward bringing wild land under cultivation. For James this illustrates "a certain blindness in human beings" (1899, 116)—that is, the tendency to see things from our own limited point of view. But his conversation with the Carolina mountain men also illustrates that this blindness is neither complete nor irrevocable. It suggests that exposure to a different point of view can make the subject aware of the limited and partial nature of his own judgments. The rest of the essay belies the claim that the spectator can have no insight into the experiences of another person. He introduces the reader to different ways of thinking and knowing and concludes that "even prisons and sick-rooms have their special revelations" (1899, 130). One implication of this comment is that the only way to improve our judgment is to remain open to the partial insights that come from diverse places and unexpected encounters.

James's essay influenced his students, including John Dewey and the urban sociologist Robert Park, who taught at the University of Chicago and knew Jane Addams. Some of James's concerns emerge in Addams's writing, where they are reworked to explain the value of public space. Addams notes that public space is the place where members of different classes, cultures, and backgrounds come into contact with one another. She argues that as long as different groups remain segregated from one another, they cannot develop the mutual sympathy and understanding that motivate public spiritedness. The slum street corner and the settlement house are, in a sense, like the prison or sickroom—places that many dismiss with instinctual revulsion but that actually provide privileged insight into the meaning of America. This insight, however, is not available to the casual spectator. It comes by way of the arduous work of understanding that takes place through social relations that cut across existing divides.

Yet there is an obvious objection to this strand of the Progressive era theory of public space; notwithstanding James's nuanced formulation, it still seems to depend on the questionable assumption that exposure to difference fosters mutual understanding. In the idiom of contemporary social science, this theory rests on the "contact hypothesis," the controversial claim that contact between members of different groups increases respect or solidarity. Although some contemporary theorists have argued that inclusive public space fosters democratic citizenship (Young 1986; Bickford 2000), others (Hayward 2007, 196) have cautioned that the empirical evidence is thin and that the underlying model of subjectivity is problematic. According to Clarissa Hayward, exposure does not necessarily produce cognitive or affective change because we perceive others through the lenses of social identities that encourage us to distance ourselves from strangers and to select evidence that confirms stereotypes (2007, 194). Moreover, racial prejudices are not only a matter of cognitive error but also ways of fixing racial hierarchies that confer benefits on members (Bobo 1999). In a similar vein, Ash Amin argues that the transformative affect of "the powers of visibility and encounter between strangers in the open spaces of the city" has been overstated: "The depressing reality, however, is that these spaces tend to be territorialized by particular groups . . . or they are spaces of transit with very little contact between strangers. The city's public spaces are not natural servants of multicultural engagement" (Amin 2002, 12–13). A number of empirical studies have also cast doubt on the contact hypothesis (Costa and Kahn 2003; for an overview of others see Putnam 2007, 142–43).[4] Most recently, Robert Putnam's *E Pluribus Unum* (2007) presented data showing that people living in racially, socioeconomically, and ethnically diverse neighborhoods are less likely to trust their neighbors and less likely to have regular social contact with one another. Relying on both behavioral and attitudinal measures, Putnam, to his dismay, found that exposure to difference seems to lead to distrust and anomie rather than understanding and solidarity.

Before we dismiss the contact hypothesis entirely, however, it is worth examining the empirical evidence more closely. In his classic social psychology experiment, Gordon Allport found that intergroup contact *did* decrease racial prejudice when four key conditions were met: shared goals, equal status within the relevant setting, a task requiring cooperation, and support from authority, law, or custom (1954). Since this landmark study, dozens of scholars have tested his model in real-world settings, including schools, military units, public housing projects, and work environments. Most of these studies have shown that integration, especially when it results in sustained interactions, does decrease racial prejudice (see Pettigrew 1998). One recent overview of the vast literature concluded, "Most studies report positive contact effects, even in situations lacking key conditions" (Pettigrew 1998, 68). Statistical analyses of large data sets have pointed in the same direction (Oliver and Wong 2003). For example, one study examining national survey data on racial attitudes found that several incidences of interracial contact resulted in more positive racial attitudes (Sigelman and Welch 1993).

How can we account for these apparently contradictory results? The empirical record may be mixed, in part, because different studies are testing different things. Some of the studies cited to refute the contact hypothesis actually show that more homogeneous groups have higher levels of trust and cooperation than do heterogeneous ones. This may be true, but it says very little about how we should structure public life in a diverse society. Apartheid-style separation has a bad track record, and ethnic cleansing raises obvious moral objections; therefore, the choice is not between homogeneity and heterogeneity but rather between exclusion and inclusion, between bridging and balkanization. The question then becomes how best to design institutions, norms, and spaces so that exposure to difference becomes an opportunity for dismantling prejudice rather than reinforcing it.

Academic research has provided some answers to this question. Allport's criteria have held up well in different settings. The fourth criteria (support from law, custom, or authority) is particularly important because it reminds us that encounters take place in social contexts, and their outcomes depend, to a large degree, on how we interpret those we perceive as different. Herein lies at least part of the importance of the "democratic aesthetic"—that is, of an interpretive framework in which diversity and difference can be seen in a positive light. Many people do react to difference with anxiety and hostility, but they are much less likely to do so when cultural cues remind them that there is little to fear and much to appreciate.

The structure of the interaction is also important. In a recent report responding to the race riots in 2001 in Britain, Ash Amin emphasized the importance of what he calls "sites of banal transgression" (2002, 16): multiethnic spaces such as community gardens, art projects, recreation centers, and child care facilities where shared interests can transgress entrenched identities. This suggestion is very similar to the program of the Progressives. Jane Addams realized that simple exposure does little to undermine prejudice and stereotypes. Misunderstanding is a common reaction to difference, especially when difference is associated with inequality or culturally coded as threatening, alien, or hostile. This is one of the reasons that Jane Addams founded Hull House. She realized that the charity workers who visited the slums understood nothing of the lives of the poor. These brief encounters reinforced prejudices and hostility on both sides. Only by living together and engaging in joint projects as equals over a sustained period of time would the two different groups come to recognize one another as fellow citizens. It is this insight that distinguishes the Olmstedian vision from the Progressive theory of public space.

Conclusion

On June 24, 1876, Chauncey Schultz gave a speech celebrating the opening of Forest Park in St. Louis, Missouri. He used Olmstedian language to celebrate a park inspired by Olmsted's ideas: "I present to you, the people of St. Louis, your own, this large and beautiful Forest Park for enjoyment of yourselves, your children and your children's children forever . . . The rich and poor, the merchant and mechanic, the professional man and day laborer, each with his family and lunch basket, can come here and enjoy his own . . . all without stint or hindrance."[5] This democratic aesthetic was naïve because it rested on the assumption that copresence alone was enough to create a *demos*, and perhaps it also expressed the hope that this performative equality could substitute for the much more arduous and dangerous work of equalizing political power. Yet the urban park was also a symbolic expression of equality and diversity at a time when these values were deeply contested. Mike Davis was probably drawn to the

Olmstedian vision because it celebrated public space for its inclusivity and diversity. It reflected a nascent democratic ethos—one that is almost forgotten today. In the twenty-first century, when civic leaders propose a new park or plaza the main goal is usually to attract tourist dollars.

Jane Addams argued that "there is no doubt that the future patriotism of America must depend not so much upon conformity as upon respect for variety, and nowhere can this be inculcated as it can in the public recreation centers" (1912, 616). This sounds hyperbolic until we think about the great degree of conformity demanded in the workplace, particularly the factory. Leisure time provides opportunities for people to express their individuality and cultural diversity. In a heterogeneous city, solidarity must be built out of an appreciation for this diversity. A sense of solidarity or respect is most likely to emerge when exposure to diversity takes place in the context of shared goals, mutual interdependence, and equal status—conditions that are met in recreational activities. Addams also noted that old city-states such as Athens or Florence were made up of citizens who were very similar to one another, and their unity was reinforced through shared experiences ("the area of government corresponded to the area of acquaintance"; Addams 1912, 616). Even in the larger nation-states of Europe, solidarity was possible to achieve through imagined communities made up of citizens with language, history, and memories in common. But in the diverse, heterogeneous cities of modern America, no such commonality was readily apparent. Community centers, parks, and playgrounds could establish this sense of commonality not by demanding conformity to one uniform standard on conduct but by providing opportunities for learning to respect difference. These public spaces do not forge a homogeneous citizenry but instead provide opportunities for the type of encounters that William James experienced in the North Carolina mountains: encounters that help individuals recognize the partiality of their own viewpoint and, perhaps, experience a connection that helps them understand "the inner significance" of things that they had previously realized "in a dead external way" (1899, 127).

Notes

1 The term "progressive" is a broad and contested label. In this chapter I use it to describe the movement that emerged in the late nineteenth and early twentieth century that promoted a series of political reforms (e.g., professional civil service, the initiative and referendum system, regulation of corporations, municipal

ownership of utilities) and social initiatives (e.g., public education, recreational amenities, and community services).

2 The population of Chicago almost doubled from 1890 to 1900 (from 1 million to 1.7 million). Most of the diversity, however, was due to immigration from Europe. The black population of Chicago in 1900 was 1.8 percent. See http://www.census.gov/ population/www/documentation/twps0076/twps0076.html (accessed March 17, 2009).

3 This section on James and the concluding paragraphs draw on passages from my book *Brave New Neighborhoods* (Kohn 2004).

4 Putnam cites a dozen studies that he claims show that diversity and solidarity are negatively correlated. A close examination of these studies, however, shows that some actually support the contact hypothesis. For example, in "Beyond the Optimal Contact Strategy: A Reality Check for the Contact Hypothesis," the authors "support the contact hypothesis in principle" but argue that this research needs to be more attentive to the way that the dynamics function in real-world settings rather than under experimental conditions (Dixon, Durrheim, and Tredoux 2005, 697).

5 http://stlouis.missouri.org/citygov/parks/forestpark/history/early.html (accessed February 3, 2011)

References

Addams, Jane. 1909. *The Spirit of Youth and the City Streets.* New York: The Macmillan Company.

———. 1912. "Recreation as a Public Function in Urban Communities." *American Journal of Sociology* 17, no. 5: 615–19.

———. 1965. *The Social Thought of Jane Addams.* Edited by Christopher Lasch. Indianapolis: The Bobbs-Merrill Company.

———. 1990. *Twenty Years at Hull-House.* Urbana: University of Illinois Press.

Allport, G. W. 1954. *The Nature of Prejudice.* Cambridge, Mass.: Addison-Wesley.

Amin, Ash. 2002. *Ethnicity and the Multicultural City: Living with Diversity.* Report for the ESRC CITIES Programme, www.aulaintercultural.org/IMG/pdf/ash_amin.pdf.

Bickford, Susan. 2000. "Constructing Inequality: City Spaces and the Architecture of Citizenship." *Political Theory* 28, no. 3: 355–76.

Bobo, L. D. 1999. "Prejudice as Group Position: Microfoundations of a Sociological Approach to Racism and Race Relations." *Journal of Social Issues* 55:445–72.

Boyer, Paul. 1978. *Urban Masses and Moral Order in America, 1820–1920.* Cambridge, Mass.: Harvard University Press.

Costa, D. L., and M. E. Kahn. 2003. "Civic Engagement and Community Heterogeneity: An Economist's Perspective." *Perspectives on Politics,* no. 1: 103–11

Davis, Mike. 1992. *City of Quartz: Excavating the Future of Los Angeles.* London: Verso.

Dewey, John. 1976. "The School as Social Centre." In *John Dewey: The Middle Works, 1899–1924,* ed. Jo Ann Boydston, 80–93. Carbondale: Southern Illinois University Press.

Dixon, John, Kevin Durrheim, and Colin Tredoux. 2005. "Beyond the Optimal Contact Strategy: A Reality Check for the Contact Hypothesis." *American Psychologist* 60, no. 7: 697–711.

Emerson, Ralph Waldo. 1903–1904. *The Complete Works of Ralph Waldo Emerson.* Vol. 6. Boston: Houghton Mifflin and Company.

Engels, Friedrich. 2009. *The Condition of the Working Class in England.* New York: Oxford University Press.

Goist, Park Dixon. 1971. "City and 'Community': The Urban Theory of Robert Park." *American Quarterly* 23, no. 1: 46–59.

Hayward, Clarissa. 2007. "Binding Problems, Boundary Problems: The Trouble with 'Democratic Citizenship.'" In *Identities, Affiliations, and Allegiances,* ed. Seyla Benhabib, Ian Shapiro, and Danilo Petranovic, 181–205. Cambridge: Cambridge University Press.

James, William. 1899. *Talks to Teachers on Psychology and to Students on Some of Life's Ideals.* London: Longman, Green, and Company.

Jones, Gareth Stedman. 1977. "Class Expression versus Social Control? A Critique of Recent Trends in the Social History of 'Leisure.'" *History Workshop* 4:163–70.

Kohn, Margaret. 2004. *Brave New Neighborhoods: The Privatization of Public Space.* New York: Routledge.

Mattson, Kevin. 1998. *Creating a Democratic Public: The Struggle for Urban Participatory Democracy during the Progressive Era.* University Park: Pennsylvania University Press.

Muraskin, William A. 1976. "The Social-Control Theory in American History: A Critique." *Journal of Social History* 9:559–80.

Oliver, J. Eric, and Janelle Wong. 2003. "Intergroup Prejudice in Multiethnic Settings." *American Journal of Political Science* 47, no. 4: 567–82.

Olmsted, Frederick Law. 1971. *Civilizing American Cities: A Selection of Frederick Law Olmsted's Writings on City Landscapes.* Cambridge, Mass.: MIT Press.

Pettigrew, Thomas. 1998. "Intergroup Contact Theory." *Annual Review of Psychology* 49:65–85.

Plato. 1992. *The Republic.* Translated by G. M. A. Grube. Indianapolis, Ind.: Hackett Publishing Company.

Putnam, Robert. 2007. "E Pluribus Unum: Diversity and Community in the Twenty-First Century." *Scandinavian Political Studies* 30, no. 2: 137–74.

Rawls, John. 1999. *A Theory of Justice.* Rev. ed. Cambridge, Mass.: Harvard University Press.

———. 2001. *Justice as Fairness: A Restatement.* Edited by Erin Kelly. Cambridge, Mass.: Harvard University Press.

Rosenzweig, Roy. 1993. *Eight Hours for What We Will: Workers and Leisure in an Industrial City, 1870–1920.* Cambridge: Cambridge University Press.

Rosenzweig, Roy, and Elizabeth Blackmar. 1992. *The Park and the People: A History of Central Park.* Ithaca, N.Y.: Cornell University Press.

Rybczynski, Witold. 2000. *A Clearing in the Distance: Frederick Law Olmsted and America in the 19th Century.* New York: Schribner.

Sigelman, Lee, and Susan Welch. 1993. "The Contact Hypothesis Revisited: Black–White Interaction and Positive Social Attitudes." *Social Forces* 71, no. 3: 781–95.

Toennies, Ferdinand. 1988. *Community and Society*. New Brunswick, N.J.: Transaction Books.

Westbrook, Robert. 1991. *John Dewey and American Democracy*. Ithaca, N.Y.: Cornell University Press.

White, Morton, and Lucia White. 1962. *The Intellectual versus the City: From Thomas Jefferson to Frank Lloyd Wright*. Cambridge, Mass.: Harvard University Press.

Young, Iris Marion. 1986. "The Ideal of Community and the Politics of Difference." *Social Theory and Practice* 12, no. 1: 1–26.

II

RETHINKING METROPOLITAN
INEQUALITY

4 TWO CHEERS FOR VERY UNEQUAL INCOMES

Toward Social Justice in Central Cities

DOUGLAS W. RAE

UPON THE RELEASE OF A RECENT United Nations (U.N.) study, the *Times of India* proffered, "In what could be thoroughly embarrassing for the U.S., its cities have been found to have levels of inequality as high as those of African and Latin American cities . . . Major U.S. cities, like Atlanta, New Orleans, Washington D.C., Miami, and New York have the highest levels of inequality in the country, similar to those of Nairobi, Buenos Aires, and Santiago." Other newspapers around the world offered similar interpretations. The embarrassment identified in these writings is evidently the social injustice of bare-knuckle capitalism, punched out in the commercial streets of the world's largest and (arguably) least-regulated advanced market society.

I will argue the contrary here: a relatively high degree of income inequality in central cities is in two important respects a *good* thing. First, given the historical flow of American urbanization, a low degree of central-city income inequality almost always arises because the high end of the distribution has melted away. This has happened as upper- and middle-income strata depart for the suburbs at high rates, leaving the poor to fend for themselves in the urban core. Indeed, as documented by Tables 4.2, 4.3, and 4.4, only nine U.S. central cities escape the broad sweep of this generalization.[1] The healthiest central city economies—New York, Los Angeles, Chicago, Dallas, Boston, and Atlanta, for instance—turn out to have *very* unequal income structures by overrepresenting both the highest and lowest strata. Second, it is good to have inequality *within* the central city because it will otherwise fall *between* that central city and the suburban penumbra. This second of my two cheers for central-city inequality forms the principal thread of the chapter.

In what follows, I take as given the fairly high degree of income inequality that typifies the United States. I also take as given the national rise in that inequality experienced since the early 1970s. The United States is in fact a middle-tier player in the Gini coefficient league that measures inequality (1.0 being the upper bound of inequality so measured). The most recent World Bank figure for the United States nationally is 0.408— well above many other advanced economies such as France (0.321), Japan (0.249), and Sweden (0.250), and only a little below Nigeria (0.437), Singapore (0.425), and China (0.469). Most of the remarkably high-inequality cases are postcolonial places like Panama (0.561), Columbia (0.586), and Namibia (0.743). If one works the question of urban inequality through carefully, as I hope to show in this paper, then the far more embarrassing pattern for the United States is actually one of *relatively high equality within municipalities, linked to great inequality between them.* In what follows, I will advance two main claims:

1. Given a fairly high degree of income inequality in America's overall system of cities and towns, there is a normative case favoring the capture of that inequality within cities, especially central cities.

2. Those of us who want better life chances for low-earning households in major cities should set out to increase inequality by attracting and keeping high earners, now greatly underrepresented in central city populations.

Both of these points are made with the understanding that social justice hinges substantially on the provision of benefits and opportunities to the least advantaged strata in a city or society at large. Without rigorous philosophizing, I conceive of urban social justice as a goal nicely captured by the difference principle in John Rawls's *Theory of Justice* (1971). While the difference principle is complex, and the argument for it even more so, the intuition boils down to the proposition that inequality is a good thing only insofar as it benefits its victims. In Rawls's words, "The inequality in expectations is permissible only if lowering it would make the working class even worse off" (Rawls 1971, 78).

How Equality in Each City or Suburb Relates to Inequality between Cities or Suburbs

High levels of equality within individual municipalities are apt to signal systematic patterns of social *in*justice in the larger system of which those municipalities are parts. Conversely, inequality within municipalities signals important elements of social justice and provides some of the basis on which social justice might be fostered within central cities that host large numbers of relatively disadvantaged people.

Here is the nub of the issue. Begin by taking the quite-unequal national income distribution as a fact. Note as well that the degree of inequality within U.S. metropolitan regions has increased since 1980 in all but one of 242 cases (Glaeser, Resseger, and Tobio 2009). In Figure 4.1 we have a stylized Paretian income distribution similar to that of the U.S. and most market economies. It has a bulky lower end and a long, thin, right-side tail representing the haves, the have-mores, and the seriously wealthy. Think now about a single region featuring one central city and a halo of suburbs. For simplicity, suppose we have three municipalities: A, B, and C. One (call it C for "central") is a central city, the other two (A and B) are its suburbs. Internally homogeneous (i.e., egalitarian) populations in each city or town imply a pattern of systematic sorting in the system as a whole. Those with great earning power are placed together in one municipality or tier of municipalities (like A in Figure 4.1). Those with middling earning power are lumped together in another municipality (B). Those with little or no earning power are brought together in yet another municipality (C). Considered singly, each of the three is economically homogeneous—displaying much less inequality than the

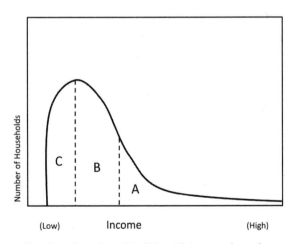

Figure 4.1. Three hypothetical municipalities with incomes drawn from one regional distribution

region as a whole. But inequality *between* A, B, and C is very great precisely because each is so homogeneous within itself. The result might well be called *income apartheid.*

There may well be a strong case for changing that overall national distribution by making it more egalitarian. But our topic, and the topic faced by our country's urban leaders in actuality, takes that national pattern as a fact of life. We can then decide what portion of the country's inequality to place *within* cities and what portion to place *between* cities. In Figure 4.1, we have a highly simplified example of letting most of the inequality fall between places, leaving relatively homogeneous municipalities in which people are drawn from a single tier. Instead, suppose we drew the inhabitants of each municipality in more or less equal pro rata shares from each income tier. Now each town's income curve would be a tiny replica of the national or regional one. Cities created using this second method would be very much like one another in income structure, but each would encompass the full range of inequality presented by the overall income curve. These would be very unequal cities, but the system of cities they imply would be far more egalitarian.

By having each municipality specialize in one income stratum, we distance affluent households from poor ones and give resources that are most needed by towns housing poor people to towns that exclude them. The A-tier municipality in Figure 4.1 would have a very low (highly egalitarian) Gini coefficient, something like the tiny town of Huntleigh, Missouri. Alone among towns in the St. Louis region, its median income exceeds $200,000. Of 111 owner-occupied properties with available estimated market values, 100 exceed $1,000,000 and none fall below $750,000. The 2000 census reports a median owner-occupied home value of $896,400 (compared to $119,600 nationally). Huntleigh is a very homogeneous community in other respects besides income: 99 percent white, 2 percent of Hispanic origin, and 0 percent black. More than 70 percent of its adult citizens hold college degrees, and more than 30 percent hold advanced degrees. About 95 percent of homes are owner occupied. Huntleigh's genial mayor, Gil Bickel III, tells me that the town has no need for a city hall. Its board of aldermen meets in Mayor Bickel's spacious home. Neither he nor the other elected officials takes a salary. Taxes are so low that a mansion selling for $4.7 million pays less than $30,000. Police, fire, and education are contracted out to other larger yet affluent towns (nearby Kirkwood, Ladue, and Frontenac). Busy Lindbergh Boulevard runs through town, but it is a state road maintained by Missouri. The remaining streets are private and are maintained by each of the town's several homeowners' associations. The town payroll has just one line—for the part-time services of an attorney.

As Gil Bickel freely admits, Huntleigh is a town long on resources and short on problems. It is also possesses one of the most egalitarian income distributions in the greater St. Louis region. Table 4.1 displays household incomes for Huntleigh and compares them with corresponding percentages for the St. Louis region at large. Since 76 percent of the incomes are above $100,000 and fewer than 4 percent are below $35,000, it is hardly surprising that the Gini coefficient is very low—0.300 to be exact. If Huntleigh were a microcosm of greater St. Louis, its percentage representation of each income tier would equal the regional ones shown in column D. Column C is important for our purposes because it shows the extent to which Huntleigh differs from the larger region. More exactly, it takes the percentage representation of each income stratum from column B in Huntleigh and divides by the regional number from column D. So for instance, the 51 percent representation of high-earning households on the bottom line is divided by the 2.5 percent regional figure to yield a ratio of 20.4 to 1 as shown in the last cell of column C. This is a startlingly high ratio, as are the ratios (ranging from 0.0 to 0.2) for all the income tiers below $50,000.

Table 4.1. Income class selection bias for Huntleigh, Missouri

A	B	C	D
INCOME STRATA (CENSUS 2000)	PERCENTAGE OF HUNTLEIGH'S HOUSEHOLDS	PERCENTAGE OF REGION'S HOUSEHOLDS	HUNTLEIGH SELECTION RATIO TO REGION (= B/D)
Under $10K	1.9	9.8	0.20
$10–15K	1.0	6.2	0.16
$15–25K	1.0	13.1	0.07
$25–35K	0.0	13.0	0.00
$35–50K	2.9	16.4	0.18
$50–75K	8.7	19.5	0.44
$75–100K	8.7	10.0	0.87
$100–150K	13.5	7.4	1.82
$150–200K	11.5	2.1	5.43
>$200K	51.0	2.5	20.40

It is obvious that powerful exclusionary mechanisms are at work in filtering the people who move into a town like Huntleigh. As Mayor Bickel notes, the town zoning ordinance makes no room for commercial or mixed-use properties. It likewise makes no place for affordable or lower-cost housing. Most of its properties are zoned at three acres, some at one acre, and a very small number at one-half acre. The economic engine that is St. Louis provides the stream of high-earning professionals and executives who chose Huntleigh and whom Huntleigh gladly welcomes. According to 2000 census data, about 90 percent drove alone to jobs in management, the professions, and sales, with just 2 percent working in the public sector. This is a town for those who are connected on the most favorable terms—for them, not for others—to the national market economy.

This pattern is repeated across America, from Glen Rock to Greenwich, from Tiburon to Scottsdale. It is the subject of a vast urban studies literature. Just as Greenwich has its Bridgeport, Huntleigh has low-income counterparts throughout the St. Louis region; in the 2000 census data, we find forty-eight municipalities with median incomes south of $30,000 and a handful below $20,000. For every Huntleigh that sops up twenty times its pro rata share of affluent households, there must be an East St. Louis or Brooklyn, Illinois, to absorb the surplus of low-income households. Where these turn out to be inner-ring suburbs, they share in a widespread pattern of fiscal and social distress notably chronicled by Myron Orfield and his colleagues (Orfield 1997).

A somewhat too-rosy way to envision a regional sorting process like this one is to think of each town as providing a particular bundle of amenities to which prices are attached and behind which structural filters are laid out. Each household picks the best it can afford, and something like an efficient market results. Indeed, a standard model in regional economics does just that (Tiebout 1956). A less optimistic view emphasizes the coercive aspects of differential access to the most desirable communities. As I have written elsewhere, "Such access is an instrument for the creation and perpetuation of advantage. The chain of connections to jobs, investment opportunities, credit, credibility, and many other valuable but hard-to-measure things is linked to place in [this] way . . . Although it is possible to argue about the specifics, it is difficult to deny the general role of income-determined differences in spatial mobility, which lead circularly to further differences of income, tending to precipitate further differences of mobility, and so on" (Rae 2001,

432). We are now back to the point where the discussion began. Using the extreme case of Huntleigh (and the obverse example of, say, East St. Louis), we have seen how income equality within municipalities has a link to income inequality between them. As one paper summarizes, "Increasing equality at the local level, while leaving national inequality untouched, requires the sorting of likes with likes. Segregation by income is another word for this kind of local equality" (Glaeser, Resseger, and Tobio 2009, 1). This may signal unjust mechanisms of selection that confine lower-income groups to limited opportunities and allow higher-income groups to escape the obligation to help meet common needs of a region. The importance of this arises from its implication for the welfare and life chances of individuals and families and also from the resulting inequality in the resource base from which communities can draw in addressing their problems. If a disproportionate share of the St. Louis region's income stream goes to a place like Huntleigh, then it is in that measure unavailable to less-fortunate places with longer and stronger lists of problems to address. As municipalities seek taxing power, a region following the pattern under discussion will find an inverse relationship between the legitimate demand for dollars and the actual collectible supply of revenue. This is, one might suppose, an instance of social injustice in the American metropolis. And having a region of municipalities, each with higher degrees of income inequality within its boundaries, might be part of a more satisfactory pattern.

Left-Biased Class-Selection Bias in Central Cities

In previous section, I focused for illustrative purposes on suburban towns. Much of what concerns this volume—social justice in the metropolis—includes attention to central cities, so I now turn to those. In Figure 4.2, we see the selection ratios for central-city St. Louis (the municipality itself) charted against the 230 municipality region surrounding (and including) St. Louis. This is a classic central-city class selection profile to which we might give the name "left biased." The term is not meant to imply Leftish politics, but just a leftward bias in the curve shown in Figure 4.2. Central-city St. Louis has roughly twice its pro rata share of the very poor. It has roughly its pro rata share of middling income strata and just under one-third its pro rata share of the highest earning strata. This means it faces far more than its share of challenges in critical sectors such as public education, public safety, and public finance. The strategic

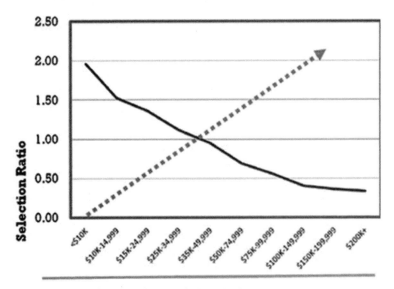

Figure 4.2. Selection bias curve for central-city St. Louis

path to improving the city's ability to meet these challenges runs toward attracting and keeping a higher share of high earners. And that path implies increasing inequality within city limits. A useful long-term analysis of St. Louis's predicament is provided by Gordon (2008). The difficulty, of course, lies in the wider opportunity range available to higher earners. The dotted arrow in Figure 4.2 is meant to approximate the number of municipalities in the greater St. Louis region that are within economic reach for each income stratum. High earners on the right in Figure 4.2 can live wherever they please. Low earners, on the left in Figure 4.2, can live only in a very few places offering very cheap housing. The competition to *retain* the limited number of high earners already living in the central city is as important, and almost as challenging, as is the competition to draw in new high-earning households.

Two key works in social science are especially pertinent in understanding the dilemma faced by leaders of a city like St. Louis. The first is Albert O. Hirschman's classic *Exit, Voice, and Loyalty* (1970). This interpretive essay charts the implications of the trade-off between trying to improve the functioning of a firm or government (voice) and the recognition of weak performance as a motive to leave (exit). In an era preceding the dominance of automobiles, central cities like St. Louis enjoyed a great deal of leverage over dissatisfied residents working at centrally located workplaces: leaving the central municipality while keeping a job greatly increased the cost and inconvenience of getting to and from work. One could either just take urban conditions as facts of life (loyalty) or engage in trying to improve them (voice). As the trolley, and more forcefully the car, diminished those costs, the switch from loyalty and voice to exit became more attractive to all economic strata but differentially more attractive to the strongest earning households (Fishman 1987; Rae 2001). This has a good deal to do with the depression of the income selection ratio on the right-hand side of Figure 4.2.

Paul Peterson's 1981 *City Limits* uses a set of ideas rooted in public finance to sketch the major tensions confronting urban leaders who concern themselves with social justice (e.g., see Musgrave 1959). If the leaders of a municipality initiate policies implying downward redistribution, then they should expect more low-income households to stay or arrive, while fewer high-income households stay or arrive. Thus a left-biased selection curve like the one in Figure 4.2 will tilt more sharply up on the left and down on the right—possibly initiating a sort of death spiral, stretching resources thinner and thinner until intervention from state government is required (e.g., receivership of the sort Buffalo, Bridgeport, and Springfield, among others, have experienced in recent years). Peterson's analysis goes through only if the redistributive policies are financed from local taxes and only if most people are driven by economic self-interest when making locational choices. All of us can find fault with so mechanical an analysis in one way or another. But Peterson and his ancestors in public finance have a point of considerable importance to the goal of social justice to which this volume is devoted. In Peterson's words, "City politics is limited politics." More generally, the resource base for social justice of a kind broadly responsive to Rawls's difference principle must be taken mainly from wide, not narrow, taxation geographies: federal over state, big state over little state, any state over its municipalities, and big (or elastic) municipality over small (or inelastic) municipality. Elasticity here refers to David Rusk's notion about the ability of a central city to annex its suburbs (Rusk 1995). This point is especially pertinent where very progressive candidates win city municipal office in largely conservative states. In my own days as chief administrative officer of New Haven, this lesson was summed up in the generalization that progressive city politics very quickly becomes progressive state politics—or dies. A useful generalization for social justice in American cities, and regional systems of cities, would probably be that *successful efforts to help poor people will invariably draw resources from levels of government higher than local government.* Only by pulling together resources from federal and state programs are materially based city and progressive initiatives apt to find traction. Absent a major shift in the behavior of the U.S. Congress, this doubtlessly implies a near-total reliance on state governments. There are several patterned coalitions that accomplish this, and none are easy at all to construct (Weir, Wollman, and Swanstrom 2005).

Table 4.2 shows sixty-three cities with populations over 100,000 with left-biased income structures based on 2000 census data. The entries are ranked by the ratio of the lowest income stratum's representation ratio divided by that of the highest stratum. This is a shorthand way of expressing the steepness of the left–right slope. The top of the ranking includes many notoriously hard-to-govern central cities—like Cleveland, Springfield, Newark, Buffalo, Rochester, Hartford, St. Louis, Milwaukee, Flint, Philadelphia, New Haven, and Louisville—with ratios of 3.0 or more. One would predict that these cities would frequently elect progressive mayors, but that they would be very limited in their abilities to mobilize resources at the municipal level. On anecdotal evidence one would predict strong public-sector union organizing of local government with sharp controversy when budget crises arise (e.g., Philadelphia under Rendell).

Right-Biased and Polarized Selection Curves in Some Central Cities

With few exceptions, these left-biased cities were and remain centers of a region. Their mirror images, slanted toward high income strata, are often major satellites of such cities but do not command a central position themselves. Here are some examples of such satellites: Scottsdale, Arlington, Irving, Pasadena, Sunnyvale, and Stamford. In Table 4.3, where only populations above 250,000 show up, we have central or quasi-central cities with right-biased selection ratios. Compared with left-biased cities, these are nice places to manage, as I am reminded by a New School panel I moderates some years ago. Philadelphia, Pittsburgh, and San Francisco were represented by their mayors. I asked each to talk about important goals that were hard or impossible to achieve, getting good answers from two mayors. Smiling, San Francisco's Gavin Newsom purported to have no such experience to report. The important advantage enjoyed by these cities is the retention of substantial high and upper-middle income strata. These strata not only increase taxable property rolls but also provide

Table 4.2. Left-biased cities, ranked by lowest/highest ratio (limited to cities above 100,000)

CITY	POPULATION	SELECTION RATIOS, CENSUS 2000							LOWEST/HIGHEST
		< $15K	$15–50K	$50–75K	$75–100K	$100–150K	$150–200K	> $200K	
Dayton	166,179	1.781	1.131	0.742	0.553	0.392	0.172	0.244	7.31
Cleveland	478,403	1.938	1.129	0.689	0.478	0.294	0.195	0.291	6.65
Brownsville	139,722	2.045	1.100	0.615	0.502	0.371	0.215	0.317	6.45
Toledo	313,619	1.434	1.103	0.925	0.743	0.506	0.320	0.227	6.32
Springfield	152,082	1.659	1.056	0.874	0.702	0.483	0.259	0.283	5.86
Newark	273,546	2.045	0.983	0.734	0.647	0.470	0.363	0.349	5.85
Buffalo	292,648	2.052	1.088	0.632	0.503	0.350	0.270	0.354	5.80
Kansas City	146,866	1.318	1.172	0.896	0.743	0.468	0.229	0.231	5.71
Erie	103,717	1.618	1.208	0.789	0.486	0.257	0.187	0.290	5.58
Rochester	219,773	1.830	1.111	0.702	0.571	0.413	0.310	0.330	5.55
Gary	102,746	1.891	1.041	0.726	0.650	0.508	0.267	0.351	5.38
Hartford	121,578	2.114	1.072	0.635	0.480	0.320	0.287	0.398	5.31
Portsmouth	100,565	1.246	1.189	0.944	0.677	0.446	0.360	0.236	5.29
Syracuse	147,306	2.013	1.078	0.621	0.544	0.441	0.305	0.382	5.28
St. Louis	348,189	1.813	1.133	0.687	0.539	0.387	0.346	0.353	5.13
Milwaukee	596,974	1.389	1.167	0.873	0.689	0.434	0.313	0.286	4.86
Allentown	106,632	1.334	1.196	0.894	0.601	0.489	0.196	0.276	4.84
San Bernardino	185,401	1.551	1.109	0.814	0.723	0.526	0.261	0.327	4.75
Lansing	119,128	1.208	1.173	0.963	0.778	0.444	0.284	0.263	4.60
Tucson	486,699	1.372	1.228	0.785	0.605	0.439	0.404	0.302	4.55
Detroit	951,270	1.729	1.051	0.770	0.681	0.589	0.390	0.388	4.45
Birmingham	242,820	1.879	1.130	0.678	0.475	0.371	0.293	0.424	4.43
Waterbury	107,271	1.402	1.060	0.913	0.804	0.698	0.433	0.323	4.34

(continued on next page)

Table 4.2. Left-biased cities, ranked by lowest/highest ratio (limited to cities above 100,000) (continued)

CITY	POPULATION	SELECTION RATIOS, CENSUS 2000							LOWEST/HIGHEST
		< $15K	$15–50K	$50–75K	$75–100K	$100–150K	$150–200K	> $200K	
Flint	124,943	1.761	1.065	0.769	0.654	0.493	0.323	0.420	4.20
Bridgeport	139,529	1.444	1.056	0.895	0.768	0.695	0.501	0.360	4.01
Philadelphia	1,517,550	1.692	1.046	0.804	0.704	0.551	0.434	0.442	3.83
Laredo	176,576	1.640	1.117	0.743	0.593	0.530	0.563	0.439	3.74
Waco	113,726	1.948	1.096	0.638	0.501	0.425	0.393	0.522	3.74
Pueblo	102,121	1.505	1.212	0.741	0.566	0.396	0.359	0.405	3.71
Lowell	105,167	1.261	0.998	1.047	0.923	0.770	0.613	0.343	3.68
Akron	217,074	1.388	1.163	0.899	0.626	0.437	0.343	0.394	3.52
Knoxville	173,890	1.775	1.130	0.677	0.522	0.455	0.419	0.532	3.34
Newport News	180,150	1.115	1.152	1.010	0.799	0.563	0.353	0.337	3.31
New Haven	123,626	1.843	1.002	0.754	0.686	0.563	0.540	0.558	3.30
Louisville	256,231	1.700	1.125	0.702	0.584	0.464	0.487	0.557	3.05
Green Bay	102,313	1.013	1.139	1.113	0.754	0.590	0.525	0.344	2.94
Baltimore	651,154	1.711	1.066	0.772	0.641	0.505	0.474	0.591	2.90
Topeka	122,377	1.117	1.173	0.973	0.724	0.599	0.418	0.392	2.85
Grand Rapids	197,800	1.096	1.133	0.998	0.864	0.581	0.535	0.390	2.81
Worcester	172,648	1.399	1.023	0.916	0.841	0.759	0.542	0.502	2.78
Athens-Clarke County (balance)	100,266	1.901	1.006	0.701	0.545	0.693	0.579	0.690	2.76
Fort Wayne	205,727	1.026	1.201	1.003	0.736	0.574	0.332	0.376	2.73
Spokane	195,629	1.348	1.158	0.858	0.647	0.562	0.423	0.501	2.69
Tallahassee	150,624	1.718	0.999	0.766	0.760	0.666	0.581	0.660	2.60

Stockton	243,771	1.348	1.044	0.900	0.868	0.719	0.630	0.534	2.52
Abilene (part)	110,442	1.238	1.227	0.815	0.670	0.467	0.508	0.496	2.50
Tacoma	193,556	1.147	1.090	0.997	0.873	0.689	0.495	0.462	2.48
El Paso	563,662	1.418	1.130	0.826	0.675	0.578	0.485	0.573	2.47
Columbus	711,470	1.079	1.097	1.036	0.891	0.669	0.530	0.437	2.47
Fresno	427,652	1.429	1.101	0.831	0.698	0.647	0.553	0.587	2.43
Sacramento	407,018	1.230	1.053	0.955	0.795	0.850	0.697	0.548	2.24
Lancaster	118,718	1.056	1.010	1.054	1.021	0.941	0.585	0.492	2.15
Fayetteville	121,015	1.153	1.164	0.901	0.734	0.639	0.580	0.586	1.97
Bakersfield	247,057	1.141	1.011	0.968	1.017	0.919	0.684	0.603	1.89
San Antonio	1,144,646	1.159	1.118	0.914	0.788	0.742	0.665	0.614	1.89
Montgomery	201,568	1.292	1.067	0.871	0.780	0.825	0.712	0.697	1.85
Albuquerque	448,607	1.059	1.092	0.934	0.910	0.861	0.729	0.601	1.76
St. Paul	287,151	1.060	1.073	1.004	0.889	0.804	0.732	0.627	1.69
Modesto	188,856	1.015	1.061	1.010	0.971	0.876	0.634	0.604	1.68
Jersey City	240,055	1.367	0.957	0.889	0.901	0.953	0.949	0.848	1.61
Madison	208,054	0.985	1.015	1.056	1.015	0.949	0.830	0.644	1.53
Columbia	116,278	1.585	1.077	0.701	0.617	0.657	0.823	1.122	1.41
Durham	187,035	1.060	0.994	1.009	0.977	0.989	0.890	0.869	1.22

Table 4.3. Right-biased central cities (limited to populations over 250,000)

NAME	POPULATION	SELECTION RATIOS, CENSUS 2000							
		< $15K	$15–50K	$50–75K	$75–100K	$100–150K	$150–200K	> $200K	LOWEST/HIGHEST
San Jose	894,943	0.492	0.609	1.031	1.532	2.407	3.259	2.126	0.23
San Francisco	776,733	0.931	0.730	0.908	1.184	1.710	2.427	2.590	0.36
Charlotte	540,828	0.722	0.980	1.051	1.069	1.140	1.349	1.723	0.42
Virginia Beach	425,257	0.489	1.038	1.260	1.161	1.057	0.821	0.897	0.54
Seattle	563,374	0.916	0.933	0.971	1.110	1.223	1.339	1.469	0.62
San Diego	1,223,400	0.887	0.945	0.991	1.094	1.248	1.366	1.262	0.70
Anaheim	328,014	0.687	0.992	1.073	1.163	1.265	1.166	0.917	0.75
Raleigh	276,093	0.743	0.983	1.049	1.150	1.246	1.242	0.954	0.78
Austin	656,562	0.934	0.997	0.987	1.014	1.068	1.154	1.171	0.80

valuable linkage to major corporations and to technical elites in every sector of the economy. In contradiction to Richard Florida, these are arguably the real "creative class" in cities lucky enough to have them (Florida 2002).

The right-biased cities add higher incomes to the distribution primarily at the expense of low-income groups, presenting a rough mirror-image of left-biased cities.

A quite distinct and especially important kind of income-selection bias curve is polarizing. These overrepresent *both* the top and the bottom strata at the expense of middle-income groups. These dynamic cities are often magnets for immigration, as with Los Angeles and New York. They are generally homes to one or another growth plate in the national economy, as with business services in New York and Atlanta; energy in Houston, Dallas, and Denver; and technology or advanced education in Boston, Cambridge, Berkeley, and Pasadena. These cities are champions of economic inequality—in some instances, they are the very cities that so concerned the world press as reported in the opening paragraph of this chapter. They are also, invariably, highly differentiated internally, with enclaves of gentrification and places that must in truth be called slums. They are also, nevertheless, far better equipped to achieve specific success in pursuit of social justice than are cities that have failed to retain the residential loyalty of their highest earning households. One might suppose that cities of this variety would be especially fertile grounds for the development of elaborate regime structures of the sort described for, among others, Atlanta by Clarence Stone (1989). I would also proffer the guess that they are better equipped to manage the city-suburban coalitions so important to legislative success at the state level.

Government, Governance, and the Possibility of Social Justice

This chapter began with the revulsion of some overseas journalists at reports of great income inequality inside some leading central cities of the United States—New York, Atlanta, Miami, and New Orleans. I have sought to suggest that this revulsion is misplaced, even if one begins with a concern for its victims—that is, for John Rawls's least-advantaged stratum, consisting of less-skilled workers in ordinary trades. In particular:

1. Given a fairly high degree of income inequality in America's overall system of cities and towns, there is a normative case favoring the capture of that inequality within cities, especially central cities.

Table 4.4. Polar cities (limited to populations over 100,000)

NAME	POPULATION	<$15K	$15–50K	$50–75K	$75–100K	$100–150K	$150–200K	>$200K
					SELECTION RATIOS, CENSUS 2000			
New York	8,008,278	1.461	0.888	0.856	0.884	1.005	1.137	1.448
Los Angeles	3,694,820	1.314	0.987	0.797	0.821	0.959	1.154	1.552
Chicago	2,896,016	1.291	0.976	0.913	0.876	0.924	0.937	1.034
Houston	1,953,631	1.163	1.082	0.832	0.780	0.891	1.038	1.098
Dallas	1,188,580	1.044	1.106	0.843	0.779	0.845	1.096	1.477
Boston	589,141	1.396	0.898	0.890	0.970	1.000	1.042	1.169
Washington	572,059	1.308	0.900	0.818	0.882	1.083	1.516	1.974
Denver	554,636	1.040	1.058	0.938	0.891	0.901	0.933	1.063
Atlanta	416,474	1.535	0.920	0.727	0.747	0.954	1.208	2.143
Oakland	399,484	1.245	0.941	0.862	0.910	1.112	1.336	1.249
Tampa	303,447	1.340	1.083	0.811	0.663	0.703	0.943	1.284
Lexington-Fayette	260,512	1.091	1.023	0.951	0.932	0.899	0.934	1.058
Winston-Salem	185,776	1.197	1.063	0.901	0.785	0.756	0.879	1.215
Little Rock	183,133	1.114	1.071	0.874	0.843	0.834	1.009	1.221
Fort Lauderdale	152,397	1.190	1.017	0.840	0.738	0.893	1.374	1.861
Pasadena	133,936	1.030	0.872	0.858	1.038	1.345	1.696	2.306
Columbia	116,278	1.585	1.077	0.701	0.617	0.657	0.823	1.122
Ann Arbor	114,024	1.003	0.881	0.904	1.073	1.452	1.584	1.564
Berkeley	102,743	1.338	0.773	0.813	0.938	1.388	2.165	2.236
Cambridge	101,355	1.039	0.828	0.881	1.156	1.356	1.777	2.208

2. The political challenge of achieving social justice in central cities presently lacking high levels of inequality may justify efforts to increase inequality by attracting and keeping high earners now greatly underrepresented in their populations.

In conclusion, it may be useful to return to these two contentions in a more specific way. The normative case for capturing inequality in central cities is, at its core, the case for capturing higher-earning households inside city limits. Left-biased central cities in the American context represent the erosive effect of suburban competition with uneven mobility among economic strata. Vastly disproportionate numbers of low-earning households are left in the core city, isolated in considerable measure from higher income groups. The isolation occurs both across neighborhoods and, most important for this discussion, across municipal lines. It has been encouraged by federal policies related to low-income family housing, interest deductibility under the IRC code, and failures to fund public transportation, combined with the enormous emphasis on accommodating the automobile.

If you think back to the era when "community power" studies compelled our scholarly interest, they were about cities where competing voices sought to control city hall. Such control was a big part of how groups—notably immigrant nationalities—got on in American life. City hall mattered a lot. Indeed, a critical feature of Robert Dahl's pluralism was that the private power exerted by, say, bankers over borrowers was ruled out of the analysis (Dahl 1961). Only if bankers controlled mayors, or edited their political agendas, did they register as powerful players in city life. In the first half, perhaps two-thirds, of the twentieth century, this picture made some sense because those modalities of power that turned on initiating, imposing, or vetoing government policies at the city level seemed relevant and even pivotal to the way people lived their lives. The academic debate was always whether higher strata of wealth and income monopolized or otherwise manipulated this struggle. People like Floyd Hunters, C. Wright Mills, and William Domhoff said, yes, these economically and socially advantaged strata did, mostly, control the agenda and the outcomes of local government. Dahl, Polsby, and other pluralists said no or at least that the issue was more complex. Keeping that view in mind momentarily, imagine suggesting to Floyd Hunter or C. Wright Mills that we would resolve these battles by means of economic segregation. The poor would be left to compete with one another in central cities while more advantaged groups would decamp for nicer places in which they could compete with one another for control of city hall or for the ear of a city manager. Where left-biased central cities are surrounded by right-biased suburbs, catering Tiebout style to several styles and strata of city leavers, this is pretty much what history has given us. City governments of central cities may never have been as potent as some scholars supposed them to be, but they were doubtless more potent then than they have become in the last generation.

Once class separation becomes a dominant mechanism, as it long since has, less desirable municipalities become less powerful. There was a brief era in which federal legislation—justified very often as a way to make up for the exit of middle-class families—funded major projects on behalf of central cities. As often as not, those projects did major social harm while doing at most some sort of photogenic good. The underlying political economy frequently profited development firms, the principals of which had long since left central city residences. If centrally located land-use questions are important economically to private capital, then central-city government has great leverage. Once this economic leverage erodes, the political and sociological leverage erodes with it. As population surges toward the periphery of region after region, the center of gravity in state legislatures goes with it (Weir, Wolman, and Swanstrom 2005). Where a ladder of places develops, with acute need concentrated toward the bottom rung and resources to meet those needs concentrated at or near the top rung, the resulting structure is the very epitome of injustice.

Looked at from within central cities located near the bottom, such a mismatch between needs and resources becomes an utterly central problem. Major internal redistribution leads, as Peterson suggests, nowhere good. On the other hand, achieving soft-tissue objectives like respect toward people living in ghettos is facilitated by the presence of people with resources and wide vision within central city politics. As Loren King's research suggests, "If cities are diverse places, they are also always sites of dramatic inequality of wealth and life chances, and so our concerns with freedom for bearers of diverse values and interests ought to be tempered with a concern for fairness, and especially attention to the ways in which the brute material and social circumstances we are born into can dramatically constrain our life chances" (King 2009). Following King's reasoning further, the inclusion of privileged strata within the same inner-city municipality as the least favored strata becomes a matter of "*the basic structure* of institutions that profoundly shape the character and life chances of those born into them." Another conference paper brings this thought closer to ground level when it calls attention to "the inegalitarian nature of institutions of local government and property in American society, understood broadly to include the powers of local political communities to zone out the poor and control local property taxes, garnering enormous positional advantages, not least through the local control of public education" (Macedo 2009). Susan Fainstein's very useful periodization of planning history finishes with an era of privatized thinking, which she sees beginning in 1982 or so and continuing well into the future. The clash between social justice and this line of planning, driven solely by markets and consumer preference, and the possibility of having whole cities that include all economic strata within one polity formulates our choice clearly. It will be important for central cities to reach out to both those with acute needs and those who bring great resources to the table. It will also be necessary to plan for regions and states to limit the public powers of exclusion available to local government.

Note

1 These are San Jose, San Francisco, Charlotte, Virginia Beach, Seattle, San Diego, Anaheim, Raleigh, and Austin. As can be seen, these are mainly Left-coast places with developmental histories atypical of the national story.

References

Dahl, Robert. 1961. *Who Governs?* New Haven, Conn.: Yale University Press.

Domhoff, G. William. 1978. *Who Really Rules? New Haven and Community Power Reexamined.* New Brunswick, N.J.: Transactions Books.

Dreir, Peter, J. Mollenkopf, and T. Swanstrom. 2001. *Place Matters: Metropolitics for the 21st Century.* Lawrence, University of Kansas Press.

Fainstein, 2009. "Planning and Distributive Justice in the American Metropolis." Paper presented at St. Louis, Mo., May.

Fishman, Robert. 1987. *Bourgeois Utopias: The Rise and Fall of Suburbia.* New York: Basic Books.

Florida, Richard. 2002. *The Rise of the Creative Class: And How It's Transforming Work, Leisure, Community, and Everyday Life.* New York: Basic Books.

Glaeser, Edward L., M. Resseger, and K. Tobio. 2009. "Urban Inequality." *Harvard Taubman Center Policy Brief.*

Gordon, Colin. 2008, *Mapping Decline: St. Louis and the Fate of the American City.* Philadelphia: University of Pennsylvania Press.

Hirschman, Albert O. 1970. *Exit, Voice, and Loyalty.* Cambridge, Mass.: Harvard University Press.

Hunter, Floyd. 1953. *Community Power Structure.* Chapel Hill: University of North Carolina Press.

King, Loren. 2009. "Liberal Justice and the City." Paper presented at St. Louis, Mo., May.

Macedo, Steven. 2009. "The Stakeholder Structure of American Localism: Property-Owning Plutocracy?" Paper presented at St. Louis, Mo., May.

McKenzie, Evan. 1994. *Privatopia: Homeowner Associations and the Rise of Residential Private Government.* New Haven, Conn.: Yale University Press.

Mills, C. Wright. 1956. *The Power Elite.* New York: Oxford University Press.

Orfield, Myron. 1997. *Metropolitics: A Regional Agenda for Community and Stability.* Washington, D.C.: The Brookings Institution.

———. 2002. *American Metropolitics: The New Suburban Reality.* Washington, D.C.: The Brookings Institution.

Peterson, Paul. 1981. *City Limits.* Chicago: University of Chicago Press.

Polsby, Nelson. 1980. *Community Power & Political Theory: A Further Look at Problems of Evidence and Inference.*

Rae, Douglas. 2001. "Viacratic America: *Plessy* on Foot v. *Brown* on Wheels." *American Review of Political Science* 4:417–38.

Rae, Douglas, et al. 1981. *Equalities.* Cambridge, Mass.: Harvard University Press.

Rusk, David. 1993. *Cities without Suburbs.* Washington, D.C.: Woodrow Wilson Center Press.

———. 1999. *Inside Game/Outside Game: Winning Strategies for Saving Urban America.* Washington, D.C.: The Brookings Institution.

Rawls, John. 1971. *A Theory of Justice.* Cambridge, Mass.: Harvard University Press.

Stone, Clarence. 1989. *Regime Politics: Governing Atlanta.* Lawrence: University of Kansas Press.

Tiebout, Charles M. 1956. "A Pure Theory of Local Expenditures." *The Journal of Political Economy* 64.

Weir, Margaret, H. Wolman, and T. Swanstrom. 2005. "The Calculus of Coalitions: Cities, Suburbs, and the Metropolitan Agenda." *Urban Affairs Review* 40:730–60.

5 BEYOND THE EQUALITY–EFFICIENCY TRADEOFF

CLARENCE N. STONE

FOR HIS 1974 GODKIN LECTURE, economist Arthur Okun chose as his topic "Equality and Efficiency: The Big Tradeoff" (1975). Okun put his thesis this way: "We can't have our cake of market efficiency and share it equally" (1975, 2). His lecture was a harbinger of a profound shift in public policy. California's Proposition 13, a keystone in the tax revolt movement, won approval in 1978, and that was followed by Ronald Reagan's election to the presidency in 1980 on an antigovernment platform. Equality concerns largely faded away.

The years following have seen the rise of supply-side economics with its accompanying notion of trickle-down as the meager concession to equity. In the field of urban politics, Paul Peterson's *City Limits* (1981) argued that in our federal system, with its inattention to fiscal equalization among localities, pursuit of economic growth necessarily governs local politics. As if in response to Okun's lecture, Peterson's treatment of local politics showed how redistribution easily becomes a nonissue. If it comes to a showdown, Okun's efficiency generally trumps equality in local political practice. Today it is generally taken as a given that localities accord economic development the top position on their agendas and minimize equality promotion.

Yet the equality–efficiency trade-off is hardly the whole picture. In this chapter, I pose social investment as an alternative to the equality–efficiency trade-off and then take a preliminary look at the subnational politics of social investment. As used here, social investment refers to programs for children and youths, ranging from prenatal care and early childhood education to after-school and youth-development programs.

Social Investment

Too often it is assumed that the only path to greater equality is redistribution, but I propose that we put aside the simple dichotomy between economic growth and redistribution and consider the social investment challenge. A word like "redistribution" indicates a zero-sum situation. One person's gain is deemed to be another's loss. Fixing on such a relationship encourages an antitax mentality—a view that "it's my money and I have a right to keep it." However, zero-sum thinking presupposes an atomized society; it has little to say about cross-generational responsibility.

Ours is a society in which the individual household is increasingly inadequate as a source of preparation for the rising generation's ability to assume a productive role. For nonwealthy households, society becomes a necessary contributor. The postindustrial society of the information age is profoundly different from the now-distant society that shaped much of our policy thinking—a society of farmers, fishing families, and craftspeople who had individual responsibilities and opportunities to inculcate in their children the work and other skills needed as an adult. However, the household is less and less a unit that provides for the development of cross-generational skills (both hard and soft).

With formal credentials assuming a greater role and with adjustment to rapid change of expanding importance, social investment can fill a vacuum left by the inadequacy of household-level capacity. Nonwealthy families lack the full gamut of resources needed to shoulder for society the responsibility of tutoring the younger generation for adult life in a world of fast-changing technology. If we assume that, for future well-being, society needs to provide for an increasingly complex form of education for everyone, then placing this responsibility on individual households runs the risk that a decreasing portion of the younger generation will be able to assume their place as productive members of society. In a society with a highly skewed distribution of private wealth, the tide of opportunity runs heavily against the nonaffluent (see Macedo, this volume). Serious underinvestment in future generations becomes increasingly likely, and social investment grows in urgency.

Politically, the term "social investment" points to something quite complex. Social investment is in itself a form of trade-off, one between the benefits of consumption now versus potential gain in the future. It involves both future time and a capacity to act as a community. Social investment holds the promise of a more prosperous and peaceful society in the future. An absence of social investment, or its presence in an anemic form, makes for a future that is less likely to be prosperous and peaceful.

Social investment means that a current civic generation provides for coming generations through some form of collective action. First, this means politically that public and civic effort has to prevail over free-rider calculations. Second, it involves deferring to a future outcome that may be less than certain. The politics of social investment thus means something quite different from reliance on market efficiency to meet our needs. It calls for the construction of a set of political relationships capable of dealing with both a need for collective support and the risk of future uncertainty.

Part of that construction calls for a sense of civic obligation to care about the future. It also means making the case that even childless couples, tax-paying businesses, and empty-nest households have an identifiable stake in providing opportunity for a rising generation.[1] Hence the case does not rest on altruism or purely an appeal to fairness for the young. After all, policy scholars Anne Schneider and Helen Ingram have observed that America's values "favor instrumental goals over justice-oriented goals" (1993, 340). That tendency to favor the instrumental may be a reason why Okun's trade-off has held such a prominent place in policy discourse. It puts the spotlight on the instrumental and directs attention away from social justice. By contrast, social investment is a way of joining instrumental considerations with concerns about justice.

To be politically viable, social investment needs a problem-solving rationale. At a general level, that argument is about making the rising generation productive and making its members contributing members of society rather than a drag on productivity. At this level, however, the argument may be too general to have much political punch behind it. Perhaps for that reason proponents of greater investment in youths often turn to worries about crime as a factor. For instance, a recent Maryland election-year campaign for expanded youth opportunity offered the fact that Maryland's Department of Corrections had spent $901 million while its Office for Children had spent only $64 million. Moreover, costs are not confined to the allocation of tax revenue. Businesses and private institutions, as well as individuals, face security costs. Johns Hopkins University, for example, spends $15 million per year on security. Like public expenditures on security, private costs beg for alternative uses. Money spent on corrections and security measures is money spent inefficiently compared to money spent on prevention.

The question is how to make this case. The mere presentation of data is unconvincing. One challenge is to educate the public about the roots of behaviors particularly among youths and how life chances can vary by zip code. This is one of the tasks taken on by proponents of Maryland's Opportunity Agenda. This is no easy matter. Significantly, research indicates a class division over methods of crime prevention (Taylor 2001), with the middle class more inclined toward hard-line enforcement. The notion that behavior has social roots is a hard sell in highly individualistic America. Future savings from reduced crime, less costly criminal-justice processes, and fewer incarcerations are one way to bring home the advantages of a prevention strategy. But that line of argument runs counter to a deeply ingrained tendency to reduce complex problems to a matter of personal responsibility.

The political dynamics of social investment extend beyond the challenge of overcoming a cultural bias toward personal and individual explanations of behavior. The viability of social investment ultimately calls for reconciliation between political time and policy time. Policy problems rarely yield to quick fixes, but political time is short term—thinking long term is in many ways an unnatural act. Dealing with immediate demands is very much the typical order of the day at city hall and many other political offices (e.g., see the account by Rae 2006). As put by Bruce Vladeck, "Policymakers are always preoccupied with putting out today's fires ignited from kindling that has been piling up for some time" (1980, 256). He adds, "The political process has a rhythm all its own, one that differs substantially from the needs of sound policymaking or the patterns of the private activities that government seeks to encourage, regulate, or control. The perspective of public officials, both appointive and elective, rarely extends past the next election—never for more than four years and generally for less than two" (1980, 255). If there is disjuncture between policy time and political time, then one might wonder how this affects the development of physical infrastructure (e.g., convention centers, sports stadiums, and downtown hotels). After all, these are projects typically put forward as efforts that will yield long-term gain as economic stimulants. Do they, then, suffer from lack of political attention because proposed benefits are long term (and hard to measure)? There is little in the behavior of mayors and other local executives to suggest a weakness in political will behind such projects. But why not—what is there in such projects that prevents a policy–politics disjuncture or compensates for it? A plausible answer is that, although the posited economic gain is long term, the projects themselves are immediately tangible—they can be seen and are available for public use. By contrast, many programs for children and youths are not tangible, and their immediate users are mostly lower SES populations rather than the general public. Consider also a contrast with capital budgeting: capital expenditures can be paid for by bonds, thereby providing facilities in the near future while extending payment of their costs into a more distant time.

Finally, metropolitan fragmentation handicaps pursuit of social investment. Households are only one layer of inequality with the capacity to provide for future generations; local jurisdictions differ widely in their concentrations of well-off versus disadvantaged households (see Rae, this volume) and thus vary in need for social investment and in their capacity to respond to this need.

In summary, initiatives that represent investment in children and youths potentially face multiple political drawbacks. The altruistic motive of doing social and civic good may be too fragile to provide a firm political foundation for such programs. Further, their rationale as programs that advance community well-being run against the grain of an individualistic culture; hence they are programs that may not readily gain wide public support. Additionally, their purported benefits are long term and fit political time and space poorly. Moreover, they lack the kind of immediate tangibility that physical infrastructure yields. Given these multiple areas of vulnerability, one could question the political viability of social investment even in programs aimed at children and youths. Therefore, let us turn to some concrete cases and consider what can make social investment a politically feasible issue.

Cases

San Francisco's Children's Amendment

In his classic work on agenda setting, John Kingdon maintained that public policy is not to be understood solely in terms of power and influence—that the content of ideas is also important (1995, 125). Perhaps, but the reverse is also true (Moore 1988). San Francisco's Children's Amendment shows that superior argumentation is not enough; power is also important.[2]

San Francisco has the lowest percentage of children in its population of any major city in the United States. Yet in November 1991, through the referendum process, the city pioneered in allocating a percentage of its property-tax revenue for *expanded* children's services. Proposition J mandated for a ten-year period that 2.5 percent of the city's property taxes be devoted to this purpose. Moreover, San Francisco's action inspired its cross-bay neighbor, Oakland, to adopt a similar measure.

As an amendment to the city charter, Proposition J was more than a general statement of intention. It also called for an annual Children's Services Plan to be accompanied by public hearings and thus moved budgeting for children into an open political process. As this process developed over time, it came to involve varied forms of community engagement—including community summits, forums, focus groups, and neighborhood group meetings. With responsibility for its execution placed in the hands of city government and its agencies, the passage of the proposition was soon followed by the elevation of the Mayor's Office of Children, Youth and Their Families (with its one-person staff) into a full-fledged city department, coordinating multiple agencies.

The backers of the amendment also created a youth network of organizations and agencies dedicated to children's issues and standing at the ready to defend programs and monitor their implementation. With a further push from amendment backers, engagement also came to include the youths of the city in a variety of venues, including youth summits and a youth commission. Through the latter, youths became part of the planning process, the holders of youth budget hearings, operators of a philanthropic exercise, and participants in program evaluation.

Proposition J was a gravitational force that brought a diffuse base of support together and made it a visible factor in the city's civic and political life. Because J contained a sunset provision, a second Children's Amendment, Proposition D, was put forward in 2000. It raised the money set aside to 3 percent of the city's property tax revenue and provided for a fifteen-year period. Whereas J incurred significant opposition as well as support and passed by a relatively modest margin of 54.5 percent of the votes cast, D passed by 73 percent of the vote.

The origins of Proposition J contain important political lessons about the limitations of advocacy. The leadership force behind the proposition was Coleman Advocates for Children and Youth and its executive director, Margaret Brodkin. In 1987, Coleman brought together eighty-five children's organizations to put together a comprehensive children's agenda. At that point, few public officials in San Francisco thought about children as a constituency in the budget process. The Coleman-led coalition sought to change that. The city's mayor was the generally progressive Art Agnos, but his willingness to proclaim that children were a major priority had little or no budgetary substance to back that up. After three years of seemingly futile advocacy, the coalition opted for the referendum process. They were convinced that the people were ahead of the politicians. Brodkin put it this way:

> We began to get exasperated. It seemed we had out-advocated just about everyone in the City. We had more reports, more detailed proposals, more compelling cost-benefit arguments than anyone else. We never missed a budget meeting, and we were constantly coming up with more and more creative ways to make the point. It seemed like we were working harder and harder for fewer gains. But no matter how hard we tried, we couldn't convince local politicians that helping kids would help their political future. We just weren't seen as a large (or wealthy) constituency. No one thought that voting on children's services would yield voter support . . . No one saw children's advocates as a cohesive, or a well-established constituency. (Brodkin and Coleman Advocates 1994, 12)

To put the proposition on the ballot, backers of the Children's Amendment launched a petition drive that generated 68,000 signatures—well above the minimum number needed to go to referendum. Activists in the petition drive came from a variety of sources—from Teamsters who delivered newspapers to carriers to the Catholic Peace and Justice Commission, the Unitarian Church, and Greenpeace. The campaign was intense, but turnout was not large. Despite efforts to court business groups and reach across the ideological spectrum, endorsements broke along liberal–conservative lines. Supporters, however, included the Police Officers Association. Conservative state senator Quentin Kopp was the most vocal opponent. Opposition also came from the Chamber of Commerce, the Republican Central Committee, conservative neighborhood clubs, and the *San Francisco Chronicle*.

Margaret Brodkin gleaned several lessons from the campaign. One is that it turned conventional political wisdom on its head, "demonstrating that there is indeed political mileage to be gained in caring about children" (Brodkin and Coleman Advocates 1994, xi). The election results, along with some polling, painted a clear picture: "The older, richer, and whiter parts of town were more heavily opposed. The younger, less affluent, and more heavily minority parts of the city strongly supported" it (Brodkin and Coleman Advocates 1994, 49). Only the wealthier neighborhoods voted against the charter amendment, in some instances by as much as 80 percent; lower-income areas were the strongest supporters, also sometimes by as much as 80 percent. Note, however, that a survey in 2000 found that support for children's services was high in virtually all categories of the population, including the segment with no children (David Binder Research, commissioned by Coleman Advocates 2000). The mobilization lesson Margaret Brodkin drew is worth quoting at length:

> While it might be wise for child advocates to continue courting conservatives, it is naïve . . . to see the cause of children as ideologically neutral. Our cause is clearly about public responsibility for the welfare of our country's children. We believe that laissez faire, marketplace policies don't work when it comes to the well-being of children. We believe in aggressive government intervention to strengthen families and assure a minimum guarantee of health, education and welfare for children.
>
> Let's face it: conservatives generally don't like this sort of thing. They can take it in small pieces—a legislator here and there who will support this piece or that—but as a general policy direction they have rejected it. This is no secret to anyone working in the field of children's issues. However, the premise of much of our work is that we are going to "bring around" the conservative political establishment. Perhaps we should give that up, acknowledging the ideological premises of our commitments, and focus on motivating and organizing our potential allies to be a more powerful force. (Brodkin and Coleman Advocates 1994, 50)

The 2000 campaign for Proposition D turned out not to be an occasion to test Margaret Brodkin's alternative strategy of mobilization. In the context of a generally progressive city, the initial Children's Amendment proved to be enormously popular. The concentration of significant resources around a designated purpose carried out in a high-visibility manner with opportunity to enlist additional sources of active support (e.g., youths) gave children's issues a hard-to-resist place high on the city's agenda. The presence of a funding pool, the mandate for a city plan, and the continuing support of a network centered on an adept advocacy organization brought diffuse support into a stable coalition. Proposition D did not require a petition drive; the mayor and city council put it on the ballot. It carried overwhelmingly.

San Francisco's Children's Amendment demonstrates that social investment can be politically viable. However, in politics there are few, if any, permanent victories. After having named Margaret Brodkin head of the city's Department of Children, Youth and Their Families in 2004, Mayor Gavin Newsom fired her in 2009. He did so at a time when San Francisco, like many other local governments, faced a severe fiscal crunch. Apparently the mayor decided to divert some funding from direct children's services to keep park and recreation facilities open, and the mayor viewed Brodkin as an obstacle. Still the core coalition remained intact.

North Carolina's Smart Start

North Carolina's Smart Start brings intergovernmental relations into the spotlight and illustrates a much different form of politics from the San Francisco Children's Amendment. Whereas Coleman Advocates built its pitch around *social* responsibility for the next generation, Smart Start took shape as part of a strategy for preparing for North Carolina's *economic* future.

As the name suggests, Smart Start is a preschool program.[3] It is designed to increase school readiness by improving child care and providing preventive health care. It operates through a state-level nonprofit called the North Carolina Partnership for Children. It works in close collaboration with the state, and its core funding comes from the state government. The partnership also receives support from the business sector. Consider the remarks of an AT&T executive: "Smart Start is not just a children's issue—it is an economic development issue. Smart Start improves the quality of child care, ultimately making children better prepared for school. Improved child care eventually means a better qualified workforce and an improved quality of life—a major issue in recruiting industry to any area. With Smart Start, we are all winners" (Dombro n.d., 11). The state partnership's mode of operation is to provide money, technical assistance, oversight, and policy guidance to local nonprofit partnerships. The local partnerships are mandated to be inclusive—public agencies from health and schools to libraries; families; business people; providers across the gamut of government, nonprofit, and for-profit initiatives; faith-based entities; Head Start; and all parties with connections to child care and preschool programs.

Unlike San Francisco's Children's Amendment, Smart Start originated in the government sector with Governor James Hunt as its leadership force.

The governor, of course, did not operate in a vacuum. In 1991, the North Carolina Day Care Association, representing more than 1,500 early childhood professionals and advocates, asked the state legislature to appropriate $80 million for expanding and improving day care. They failed to get the appropriation but did get a study commission to examine the issue. That kept the issue alive, and when Governor Hunt, who had been out of office since 1985, began thinking about running for a third term, he embraced the issue and gave it political viability. As governor earlier, Hunt had initiated public kindergarten statewide. In 1991–1992, Hunt was hearing from some business leaders about the need for workforce development, starting with early childhood. North Carolina also had a high percentage of working mothers faced with significant child care needs.

Workforce development was no new policy theme for Hunt. Beginning when he first came into office as lieutenant governor and then governor in the 1970s and 1980s, he saw North Carolina as a low-wage state too long dependent on agriculture and textiles. As he put together his ideas into a program for the state, Hunt saw education, economic development, and higher-paying jobs as integrally related. Early on he recognized the global economy as the relevant context: "A world-class workforce requires world-class skills, which in turn require children to come to school ready to learn. Children who come to school healthy and prepared to succeed will develop into better workers, sustaining North Carolina's economy in years to come" (National Association of State Boards of Education 1998). During Hunt's campaign for governor, he convened experts to develop a white paper on early childhood needs. They called for a statewide initiative, and that became a major platform issue in his campaign. A week after the election, Hunt reconvened the experts to put together the specifics of what became Smart Start. The proposal encountered opposition, as some argued the state was taking over the raising of children. Conservative church leaders were among the most vocal opponents, charging in some cases that the program "will set children straight on the road to hell" (Kirp 2007, 245). Hunt countered by inviting a group of church leaders to the governor's mansion and reminded them that he came from a religious background and that he saw the responsibility to care for children. He said he knew "how important churches are to our communities," adding, "I want to help families who aren't coming to your church, who don't have support" (qtd. in Kirp 2007, 245). Several of the clergy were enlisted to talk up Smart Start to their congregations.

In the legislature, the division was largely along partisan lines, with the Democratic governor getting support mostly from Democratic legislators. The 1993 legislation provided for a pilot program covering twelve "pioneer" partnerships, representing eighteen counties. The county was the basic local unit, with smaller counties combining to form partnerships. By the year 2000, as Hunt's governorship was nearing a close, local partnerships covered all one hundred North Carolina counties. Though state money was the crucial resource, both the state partnership and the local ones raised private money and in-kind donations. In creating Smart Start, Governor Hunt's strategy was to tap local understanding of needs, encourage cooperation and coordination among local players, expand the resource base for the program, and include diverse stakeholders in such a way that they would develop ownership of the program.

As an instance of social investment, Smart Start involves much more than good feelings about a worthy goal. The state legislature began asking for evaluation one year into the program. This is unrealistically early but nevertheless indicative of a wariness about social spending. Business leaders and other donors also want assurance that the investment is being handled responsibly.

Predictably, as a decentralized and somewhat open-ended operation, Smart Start had some early administrative and fiscal problems, but these have been addressed and procedures tightened. External evaluation is another important ingredient, as it has also been with the children's programs in San Francisco. All of this has been handled in such a way as to maintain governmental and nongovernmental support at both the state and local levels. The program has garnered international recognition and won awards such as the Kennedy School's innovation prize. Governor Hunt passed the ballot-box test and was reelected in 1996 (for a fourth term) after the launching of Smart Start.

Like San Francisco's Children's Amendment, North Carolina's Smart Start shows that social investment can attract popular support. However, it does not manifest itself spontaneously. In both cases, leadership came through a significant institutional source, a long-established advocacy organization in San Francisco and the governor's office in North Carolina. In both cases, there was opposition and resistance that reflected a liberal–conservative divide, but in both cases, the salience of that divide faded as each program moved from initiation to implementation and actual service provision. The two cases differ in that business had no special role in San Francisco, but in North Carolina, with an emphasis on workforce and economic development, business played a large role. Most noteworthy, Smart Start give statewide coverage, thereby providing social investment in poorer jurisdictions that would have had great difficulty mounting such an effort on their own.

To underscore the range of strategies found in the politics of social investment, it is worth remembering that key leadership for San Francisco's Children's Amendment was centered in the nonprofit sector, but program responsibility was housed in the government sector, whereas key leadership for Smart Start came from the government sector, but program responsibility was housed in the nonprofit sector.

Crime Control: Lessons from Boston

For some, the answer to crime is straightforward—get tough and incarcerate lawbreakers. The United States has tried that and has a record-level prison population—a total of 2.3 million in 2008. That is just under 3 percent of the adult population. And despite this high rate of incarceration, crime is still a major problem in many low-income areas, and the financial cost of this system is huge. The social costs are even greater.

The police have never adhered to a one-track approach to crime prevention. Significantly, city departments have long sponsored athletic leagues for youths, and police officers regard working with youths as part of a needed strategy of prevention. It is not surprising, then, that San Francisco's Children's Amendment had the support of the Police Officers Association. Local support for prevention has now gone national as well with the creation of a nonprofit called Fight Crime: Invest in Kids. Launched in 1996, it has a membership that includes police chiefs, sheriffs, prosecutors, and other law-enforcement officers. The organization's policy focus is high-quality preschool education, prevention of child abuse, after-school and summer programs, and intervention to reach troubled youths. As a general principle, prevention thus has strong appeal within the law-enforcement sector.

Let us look at the problem on the ground. Here we encounter issues not raised by simple program advocacy. Action coalitions are less easily built and maintained. A Baltimore survey contains an interesting class contrast in responses to crime (Taylor 2001). Higher-income neighborhoods saw it as primarily a problem of averting victimization, and hence they favored patrols and direct application of the protective authority of the police. Lower-income neighborhoods were more inclined to see crime related to social problems, and hence, in line with the prevention approach, they favored improving social and physical conditions. However, despite a shared concern with prevention, law-enforcement agencies and lower-income residents, particularly residents of color, are hardly natural allies (Weitzer and Tuch 2006).

Moreover, criminal-justice units and agencies work largely independent of one another, sometimes at cross-purposes, with limited coordination, and often in an atmosphere of distrust of one another. Further, law enforcement often has little or no connection to social-service and opportunity-providing agencies. Additionally, in high-crime areas, police–community relations are laden with mutual antagonism, and police work typically is hampered by limited cooperation from community residents. Though the no-snitching norm is not embraced by all, it is held widely enough to hamper police investigations.

The overall question is how to remedy what is essentially a dysfunctional situation. What can we learn from recent law-enforcement work, specifically from what is called a problem-solving approach to policing (Weisburd and Braga 2006)? Boston's youth antiviolence campaign is instructive. It came, however, out of an extraordinary set of circumstances. As the 1990s opened, both the Boston police and the city's inner-city community faced a crisis. An urgent need to act created an uncommon but much needed "network of capacity." This capacity involved carrots, sticks, and what one participant called "a small but critically important piece of shared moral territory" (qtd. in Pruitt 2000, 27). In the face of a dramatic rise in youth homicide, there was a widely held aim of keeping kids alive and giving them a future—this was the shared moral responsibility that helped knit together a youth antiviolence effort.

Several elements went into the Boston campaign.[4] One was Operation Night Light—a police–probation office partnership to make sure that at-risk youths were abiding by the conditions of their release into the community. This came about as a small number of police and probation officers realized that they were seeing one another only on the occasion of attending the funerals of murdered youths. In talking, they found they could exchange useful information. They also learned they had complementary powers, and police and probation officers began to patrol together in postcurfew hours to keep a close eye on youths on probation.

Community enlistment into what criminal-justice specialist call a "network of capacity" took a more dramatic path. With youth violence on the rise, particularly within the African-American community, a dramatic event shook that community at its very foundation. An incident of gang warfare carried into an African-American church where a funeral was being held for a member of one of the gangs. An opposing gang pursued one of the murdered youth's friends into the church, guns drawn, and fired several shots. Urged forward by the shock of this event and building on previous work by individual ministers, black clergy came together to form the TenPoint Coalition for working with youths in troubled neighborhoods.

The police department faced its own crisis. In Boston in the early 1990s, complaints about police brutality and mismanagement were widespread, intensified by a mishandled murder investigation and a clumsy "stop and frisk" response to the rising level of gang violence. The Carol Stuart murder case particularly brought together several concerns about the Boston police. Stuart was a pregnant white woman murdered on her way home from Boston City Hospital. Initially, her husband, the actual murderer, told police investigators that the perpetrator was a black male. The police responded by saturating the neighborhood, a public-housing area, with stop-and-frisk practices targeted at black males. When it eventually turned out that the husband was in fact the one who committed the murder, multiple discontents with the police had gathered enough force to bring about an independent commission, which called for far-reaching reform, including more effective police–community relations at the street level.

Among other measures, the department created the Youth Violence Task Force to disrupt gangs and move toward a strategy of prevention. Without detailing all the steps, let me highlight the cooperation that developed between the task force and the TenPoint Coalition. The arrangement was that the coalition would employ its knowledge of the community to identify the central figures of violence, who would then be arrested or subjected to unremitting surveillance. Others would be cautioned that violence would not be tolerated and then be offered services to help them step away from a life of crime and violence. Members of the TenPoint Coalition were making the basic selection of who was to receive which form of intervention. They also worked with the police to get the message out about ending violence.

As this approach, known as Operation Ceasefire, took shape, it drew in multiple elements in a wide network of capacity. The stick of enforcement was linked with the carrot of opportunity provision. It meant offering the alternatives of job training, mentoring, jobs, after-school programs, special schools, and internships to those willing to forego gang life. The operation included an information and communication effort based on home visits to youths on probation or believed to be at risk, which worked through the clergy and others at the neighborhood level, programs at schools, and a wider information effort about imprisonment versus alternatives. Policing included attention to "hot spots," intensive patrolling, and sometimes smothering an area with enforcement efforts. At the same time, it involved varied forms of assistance, including a business-supported effort for expanded opportunities for disadvantaged youths. Although jail time for a few was part of the violence-prevention picture, it was mixed with expanded opportunity for others. Thus the acceptability of Operation Ceasefire within the inner city rested on something quite different from a purely punitive approach.

The TenPoint Coalition began to work more closely with a range of partners, such as the mayor's youth workers, schools, and probation officers, as well as the police. They also came to enjoy the active support of the key Roman Catholic figure in Boston at that time, Cardinal Bernard Law. A member of the coalition offered the view that Cardinal Law played a decisive role of extending an important spiritual and cultural influence to an overwhelmingly Irish Catholic police department.

The central lesson of Boston's experience with stemming youth violence is that effective law enforcement calls for community involvement. In turn, community involvement requires that hard-line enforcement be replaced by a more selective approach that includes the carrot of affording youths credible pathways to mainstream opportunities. In brief, law enforcement is well served by a social investment component.

Boston's network of capacity had several elements. One was cooperation among actors within the criminal-justice system—actors in agencies that spill over the boundaries of the central city itself and cover the intergovernmental system from top to bottom. In addition, the network encompassed cooperation between criminal-justice agencies and human-service agencies, with the contributions of the latter enhanced by the addition of support from the business and voluntary sectors. The faith community was also part of Boston's network. Last but not least, the network aligned the criminal-justice system with the inner-city community. As analysts Anthony Braga and Christopher Winship point out, the overall network was a very intensive body of relationships, created in Boston only by unusual conditions and not easily replicated elsewhere (2006; see also Tita et al. 2003). Even in Boston, the network has not been easy to maintain.[5] Still, from Boston's experience, we can see that in public safety, the equality–efficiency trade-off has little to offer. Instead of a crude trade-off between equality and efficiency, we need to consider how varied measures can be blended into an effective mix.

Conclusion

Conventional wisdom puts the primary burden to train the rising generation for its future place in society on the private household. Yet in today's world of advanced education and formal credentials, this mode of intergenerational responsibility is less and less able to do the job. The private household of modest or less means cannot by itself shoulder the responsibility of preparing children and youths for a productive adulthood alone. This assessment of postindustrial society sits poorly with those who see the private market as the universal answer to society's challenges. The problem of underinvestment in the future becomes salient only when we think about society or about the costs of inadequate social investment that come from crime and disorder in the long term.

All in all, Okun's equality–efficiency trade-off is an inadequate formula for today's world. Consider long-term consequences of neglecting social investment. A polarized society in which many are ill prepared to become productive members is unsustainable. By posing a trade-off of productivity with equality, Okun reduces the policy challenge to one of minimizing the safety net and holding in check demands that emanate from lower socioeconomic levels. If such a view of politics ever had a place, it is not in today's world. Contrary to Okun's assumption that justice (i.e., greater equality) and social well-being are at odds with one another, a future-minded perspective brings the two into close alignment.

The real political challenge is to enable citizens inclined to think mainly about the present to turn their attention to the future. From this perspective, politics is not about how to distribute the current supply of benefits; it is about investment—planning for and acting on behalf of the future. This is language that business executives can understand, as Governor Hunt demonstrated through Smart Start.

Ordinary citizens, of course, have a rational, calculating side that tends toward individual, near-term interests, but that is not the whole of human behavior. Feminist scholars remind us that that is only one side. If we bear in mind that the mother–child relationship is also a basic unit in society, then we can see that cross-generational ties have a place in political life. Cultivated so as to remind us of our social responsibility to the rising generation and fashioned into a mobilized electoral constituency, as with San Francisco's Children's Amendment, this social-minded side of human nature can yield political results. As a society, the United States has relied heavily on punishment and incarceration as an anti-crime strategy. This approach not only is socially destructive of family and community life but also has become costly in the sense of maintaining an oversized prison population while failing to give the nation a low crime rate. Circumstances beg for an alternative, and Boston's antiviolence campaign suggests one. It teaches us that crime control requires community cooperation, and this cooperation cannot be elicited by reliance on enforcement and punishment alone.

The Children's Amendment teaches about the importance of constituency building, Smart Start about workforce development as a window onto the future, and Boston's antiviolence campaign about the importance of the police–community connection. A deeper lesson underlying all three cases is that, yes, business can be a useful ally, but ultimately it is those in the lower ranks of the socioeconomic order who are the most dependable supporters of social investment. They are the ones closest to the reality of the unequal opportunity to prepare their children for the future. They were the core of electoral support in San Francisco. They are the labor component in North Carolina who are especially mindful of the need to move from a low-wage economy to a higher-wage future. They are the ones who suffer most from a punitive approach to law enforcement and the ones who see firsthand its inadequacies.

The political feasibility of social investment is profoundly affected by the fragmented structure of metropolitan regions. With their highly uneven distributions of well-off and disadvantaged households, metropolitan regions make stand-alone municipalities ill-suited for the pursuit of social investment. A large concentration of wealthy families provides a strong tax base but an electorate little disposed to support the policy aim. A concentration of poor people provides a supportive constituency but a weak tax base. A relatively prosperous central city like San Francisco provides a mix, but a small municipality with a big low-income population simply lacks the resources for much in the way of social investment. Thus ameliorating the consequences of the metropolitan arrangement, such as underinvestment in children and youths, cannot realistically be made the sole responsibility of most central cities, much less of low-income suburbs, though the metropolitan structure tends to do just that and to do so by concentrating social needs in jurisdictions that possess highly limited resources.

A social-investment agenda cannot, then, be pursued on something thought of simply as the regional stage; the actual metropolitan structure is too fragmented to constitute such a stage. Does its absence mean that no pursuit of a social-investment agenda is feasible, or are there alternative paths available? A theme running through my three minicases is that social investment as a form of social justice is feasible even in a formally fragmented setting. Thus we need to think of metropolitan areas as one layer (albeit underinstitutionalized) with multiple sectors in a process of multilevel governing. Consider the three minicases in that light:

1. *San Francisco's Children's Amendment.* The principal support for this initiative came from the nonprofit sector, with little initial support from city hall. The core of popular support came from the lower SES populations. Once the possibility was made concrete to them, it was they who, by their shared need, took a collective, long-term view. Within the Bay Area the pattern held, and the diffusion of innovation was not to more affluent suburbs (counties or municipalities) but to Oakland, a neighboring city with a high proportion of lower SES residents. San Francisco's action was multisector but not intergovernmental.

2. *North Carolina's Smart Start.* The key players in North Carolina's Smart Start were the governor and state officials. Working with the nonprofit sector and forging an intergovernmental (state–county) link, the government entities thus activated were not stand-alone municipalities but counties. The use of counties worked around the potential isolation of municipalities. Moreover, local coalitions were multisector, including business and civil society, as well as government. These multisector coalitions also got around the isolation of municipal governments.

3. *Boston's youth antiviolence campaign.* Like San Francisco's Children's Amendment, the Boston campaign was played out on a city stage. But as in North Carolina's Smart Start, the players were intergovernmental and multisector, as well as municipal. Mounting a full-fledged campaign required players from federal and state governments as well as business and, in a particularly prominent role, the faith community. Thus the absence of an explicit metropolitan stage did not mean that city activities occurred without significant external resources.

Overall, then, the metropolitan context is something more complicated than an explicitly metropolitan stage. The subnational framework for pursuing social investment can be expansive, as in North Carolina's Smart Start. Though the formal governmental context is structured so as to isolate cities with "their" problems, the actual reality is more complex. Thus those who would advance social justice in a metropolitan context are well advised to keep a wider, less formal framework in mind and seek sundry ways to counter the isolation of municipalities. Ad hoc arrangements can be constructed to cope with the fact that there is no formal metropolitan stage. Smart Start in particular reveals the vital part that intergovernmental connections can play, especially when reinforced by cross-sector supports. The three experiences examined here show that under the right circumstances, social investment is politically viable. In its pursuit, the first step is to discard formulaic thinking.

In its early days the equality-efficiency trade-off served as a maxim intended to throw light on an aspect of national welfare policy. As with many maxims, applying it indiscriminately to a wide variety of situations seems unwise. The social-investment experience points to a complex reality and shows that social policy, especially in a postindustrial world, does not reduce to a simple trade-off. Viewed narrowly from the perspective of an isolated municipality, Okun's trade-off could be a factor. But viewed more expansively, fragmentation and isolation need not be the final words.

Notes

1 Some might argue that, for a particular state or locality, investing in youths offers limited return because those who are educated are likely to move to some other jurisdiction. This is certainly a plausible pattern, but another way of looking at this issue is that youths who experience underinvestment are especially likely to remain in the state and locality, adding to a future population that is apt to be unproductive, and contributing to the costs incurred by the state and locality. Hence mobility among those invested-in youths may reduce future benefit, but the lack of mobility for those that are underinvested in is almost certain to add to future costs and make the locality a less attractive site for a mobile population.

2 Important sources include Brodkin and Coleman Advocates (1994), David Binder Research (2000), Harder + Company Community Research, and McLaughlin et al. (2009).

3 Sources on Smart Start include Bryant et al. (2003), Dombro (1999), Dombro (n.d.), Fleming and Doig (2000), and Kirp (2007).

4 Several published accounts are available, among them Berrien and Winship (2002, 2003), Braga and Winship (2006), Kennedy (2002, 2006), and Pruitt (2000).

5 Michael Owens reports that the TenPoint Coalition has itself been beset by internal conflict (2007, 217).

References

Berrien, Jenny, and Christopher Winship. 2002. "An Umbrella of Legitimacy: Boston's Police Department–Ten Point Coalition Collaboration." In *Securing Our Children's Future: New Approaches to Juvenile Justice and Youth Violence*, ed. Gary S. Katzmann, 200–228. Washington, D.C.: The Brookings Institution.

———. 2003. "Should We Have Faith in the Churches? The Ten-Point Coalition's Effect on Boston's Youth Violence." In *Guns, Crime, and Punishment in America*, ed. Bernard E. Harcourt, 222–48. New York: New York University Press.

Braga, Anthony, and Christopher Winship. 2006. "Partnership, Accountability, and Innovation: Clarifying Boston's Experience with Pulling Levers." In *Police Innovation*, ed. David Weisburd and Anthony Braga, 171–87. New York: Cambridge University Press.

Brodkin, Margaret, and Coleman Advocates. 1994. *From Sand Boxes to Ballot Boxes*. San Francisco: Coleman Advocates for Children and Youth.

David Binder Research. 2000. *San Francisco*. San Francisco: San Francisco Voter Survey on Children.

Dombro, Amy L. 1999. "Getting Started." Raleigh: Partnership for Children and Families and Work Institute.

Fleming, Jana, and Sean Doig. 2000. *Building Trust, Developing Community: Lessons from North Carolina's Smart Start Initiative*. Chapel Hill: Frank Porter Graham Child Development Center at the University of North Carolina.

Harder + Company Community Research. 2000. *Making a Difference for San Francisco's Children*. San Francisco: Coleman Advocates for Children and Youth.

Kennedy, David M. 2002. "A Tale of One City: Reflections on the Boston Gun Project." In *Securing Our Children's Future: New Approaches to Juvenile Justice and Youth Violence*, ed. Gary S. Katzmann, 229–61. Washington, D.C.: The Brookings Institution.

———. 2006. "Old Wine in New Bottles: Policing and the Lessons of Pulling Levers." In *Police Innovation*, ed. David Weisburd and Anthony Braga, 155–70. New York: Cambridge University Press.

Kingdon, John W. 1995. *Agendas, Alternatives, and Public Policies*. New York: HarperCollins.

Kirp, David L. 2007. *The Sandbox Investment*. Cambridge, Mass.: Harvard University Press.

McLaughlin, Milbrey W., Richard Scott, Sarah Deschenes, Kathryn Hopkins, and Anne Newman. 2009. *Between Movement and Establishment*. Palo Alto, Calif.: Stanford University Press.

Moore, Mark H. 1988. "What Sort of Ideas Become Public Ideas?" In *The Power of Public Ideas*, ed. Robert Reich, 55–83. Cambridge, Mass.: Harvard University Press.

National Association of State Boards of Education. 1998. "State Improvement Initiatives." 4, no. 9.

Okun, Arthur M. 1975. *Equality and Efficiency: The Big Tradeoff*. Washington, D.C.: The Brookings Institution.

Owens, Michael L. 2007. *God and Government in the Ghetto*. Chicago: University of Chicago Press.

Peterson, Paul E. 1981. *City Limits*. Chicago: University of Chicago Press.

Pruitt, Bettye H. 2000. "The Boston Strategy: A Story of Unlikely Alliances." Robert Wood Johnson Foundation, http://www.bostonstrategy.com.

Rae, Douglas W. 2006. "Making Life Work in Crowded Places." *Urban Affairs Review* 41:271–91.

Schneider, Anne, and Helen Ingram. 1993. "Social Construction of Target Populations." *American Political Science Review* 87, no. 2: 334–47.

Taylor, Ralph B. 2001. *Breaking Away from Broken Windows*. Boulder, Colo.: Westview Press.

Tita, George, K. Jack Riley, Gregory Ridgeway, Clifford Grammich, and Allan Abrahamse. 2003. *Reducing Gun Violence: Results from an Intervention in East Los Angeles*. Santa Monica, Calif.: Rand.

Vladeck, Bruce C. 1980. *Unloving Care*. New York: Basic Books.

Weisburd, David, and Anthony A. Braga. 2006. "*Advocate*: Hot Spots Policing as a Model for Police Innovation." In *Police Innovation*, ed. David Weisburd and Anthony A. Braga, 225–44. New York: Cambridge University Press.

Weitzer, Ronald, and Steven A. Tuch. 2006. *Race and Policing in America*. New York: Cambridge University Press.

III

PLANNING FOR JUSTICE

6 REDEVELOPMENT PLANNING AND DISTRIBUTIVE JUSTICE IN THE AMERICAN METROPOLIS

SUSAN S. FAINSTEIN

REDEVELOPMENT POLICY, INTENDED TO TRANSFORM the built environment on land already containing structures, constitutes the principal place-targeted approach to bettering urban areas within the United States. Major programs for redevelopment have occurred under both national and local guidance and have involved a variety of strategies. The purpose of redevelopment policy has been to improve the quality and efficiency of existing cities and, increasingly, of suburbs. Because of the interests already vested in occupied space, it has been a particularly contentious political arena. As originally framed after World War II, urban programs were envisioned as providing public investment so as to make cities competitive with suburbs and to replace dilapidated housing with high-quality residences. Later the primary emphasis switched to enhancing metropolitan competitiveness.

My critique of these programs is that they perpetrated injustice even while their supporters claimed that they were intending to benefit the poor and people of color who increasingly were the occupants of inner-city neighborhoods. Facile equations of neighborhood improvement with amelioration of the situation of residents allowed for replacement of the existing population by business enterprises or groups with higher incomes. Arguments that economic development programs would generate tax revenues allowing expenditures on social welfare pointed to a potential that was rarely realized. In the words of Bent Flyvbjerg (1998, 228), "Rationalization presented as rationality is a principal strategy in the exercise of power." In the instance of redevelopment programs, the unjust treatment of disadvantaged populations was consistently rationalized as being in their own long-term interest.

This chapter examines the forces shaping American redevelopment policy and its outcomes. My central argument is that nearly sixty years of programs have involved significant changes in administrative form, funding, scale, justifications, content, public participation, and the composition of redevelopment coalitions. At the same time, however, the separation of physical and social components of redevelopment efforts has changed little, and the distribution of benefits has largely favored developers and business interests regardless of the alleged aims of the program. Consequently, while redevelopment programs have contributed to revival of previously declining cities, they have acted as agencies for producing greater justice within metropolitan areas only at those rare times when grassroots mobilizations have pressed for a more equitable distribution of benefits. As will be discussed later in the chapter, justice is defined as reflecting the criteria of equity, democracy, and diversity.[1]

To support my argument I briefly trace the history of government-sponsored redevelopment programs in the United States since the Housing Act of 1949, which set forth the federal Urban Renewal program, and portray their distribution of benefits. That history is periodized according to each phase's general thrust, and although there was always local variation, there has never been more than at the present. The causal factors underlying the shifts delimiting each period are analyzed. These factors, which are numerous and interactive, include political pressures and changes in national and urban regimes; economic restructuring; changing demographics; and ideological currents.

In an earlier work my coauthor and I (Fainstein and Fainstein 1986) identified three periods subsequent to the 1949 act, which we labeled directive (1950–64), concessionary (1965–74), and conserving (1975–81). From the vantage point of 2008, I would name a fourth period (1982–2008) as privatized. It is striking that the break points between the periods are quite marked, with the exception of the fourth, which is continuous with its predecessor but can be differentiated by the deepening of preexisting currents. The remainder of this chapter presents the characteristics of each period, describes the planning doctrines associated with it,[2] summarizes the relationship between the spatial and social outcomes of the policies, and explicates an approach to evaluating programs based on a concept of just outcomes.

The Directive Period (1950–64)

Title I ("Slum Clearance and Urban Development") of the Housing Act of 1949 inaugurated a vigorous response by city governments to the threat of suburbanization, the growth of slums, and the perceived obsolescence of the urban built environment (von Hoffman 2000). The act made federal funding available to local urban renewal authorities for clearance of large sites, with the expectation that they would be developed primarily by private and institutional investors according to a predetermined plan (Fainstein 1988, 1998). It was thought that the existing pattern of small, irregular land holdings deterred investment in modern structures and that rationalization of ownership under relatively few developers was a prerequisite to improvement. Title I required that the land seized be predominantly residential, but it did not mandate the replacement of housing units destroyed. Thus it called for slum clearance but not for building affordable housing (Weiss 1980).

Based on the concept that experts knew best how cities should be redeveloped, city governments embarked on programs aimed at extirpating those areas of their territory deemed blighted, regardless of the sentiments of present occupants. Planners saw renewal programs as providing them the opportunity to realize their dreams of imposing order on the unruly city, eliminating blight, and achieving these objectives within the strictures of a comprehensive plan. Thus Alfred Bettman, the first president of the American Society of Planning Officials (ASPO), is credited with developing the strategies underlying Title I of the 1949 act (Gerckens 1995). In his testimony before the U.S. Senate's subcommittee on postwar planning, Bettman argued, "The existing lot and street layout of the [blighted] areas is obsolescent in the sense that it does not fit modern technology, and the rebuilding cannot, as a practical or economic matter, occur without the cure of this deeper obsolescence by a redesigning of the areas . . . in the light of the general master planning of the whole urban territory in which they are located" (1945, 5–6).[3] That the poverty of residents led to the neglect of the building stock was rarely articulated; rather the focus was on the physical characteristics of neighborhoods and the means of upgrading them with little recognition of the need to assist the residents.

Ultimately, whether or not urban renewal's rearrangement of the urban fabric offered a basis for urban revival depended less on physical form than on broader economic trends. If by dint of local entrepreneurship or strategic location the city occupied a niche in the national system of cities whereby it was attractive to investors, then the new office buildings and modern apartments constructed on the former sites of tenements and factories drew occupants and businesses into the central city. Regardless, however, of whether or not the city achieved aggregate economic improvement, lower-income neighborhoods and especially residents of color received few benefits from urban renewal programs during the directive period. Even though public housing was erected on some of the cleared land, units built never fully replaced units destroyed, and the segregation of uses prescribed by the planning doctrine of the times meant that the new housing projects were isolated from retail and social services (Listokin 1991; Schwartz 2010). Furthermore, small, locally owned businesses lost their clienteles, and deindustrialization was often exacerbated by demolition of still-operating manufacturers. Within the terminology used by Hayward and Swanstrom in the introduction to this book, the policies of the directive period, by their blindness to the distributive outcomes of renewal programs and the resulting social impacts, constituted thick injustice. They were unjust in that they rewarded developers and downtown businesses at the expense of low-income residents and workers, pushed residents of areas identified as slums into other, less well-located blighted areas, and took no account of existing social networks. The rhetoric of the sponsors of these programs, however, never communicated their less savory intent but rather spoke to restoring the vitality of yesteryear while simultaneously, as Bettman claimed, overcoming obsolescence.

The Concessionary Period (1965–74)

Before the 1960s Herbert Gans (1959), a sociologist–planner who throughout his long and illustrious career consistently attacked programs for urban betterment developed at the expense of the poor, was a lonely voice arguing that the principal beneficiaries of urban redevelopment programs should be the affected community and not developer interests. He commented that "clearance destroys not only housing, but also a functioning social system, the existence of which is not even recognized by current relocation procedures" (1959, 19). The early 1960s, however, witnessed a drumbeat of disapprobation of urban renewal and highway programs from intellectual critics. Jane Jacobs's *Death and Life of Great American Cities* (1961, 4) challenged the tenets of reduced densities and comprehensiveness so dear to the hearts of planners, crying that "this is not the rebuilding of cities. This is the sacking of cities." Her polemic echoed Gans's (1962) critique of the destruction of Boston's West End neighborhood and was picked up by Peter Marris (1962, 183), who contended, "On the whole then, it seems fair to say that relocation has provided only marginally better housing, in very similar neighborhoods, at higher rents, and has done as much to worsen as to solve the social problems of the families displaced. The dispossessed enjoy as their reward a distant view of luxury apartments rising over their old homes."[4] The intellectual attacks on urban renewal, however, had little impact on planning practice until the rise of urban social movements in the mid-1960s. Spurred by the success of the civil rights movement in the South and President Lyndon Johnson's declaration of a war on poverty, protests against redevelopment programs began to receive a response from local public officials and the federal government (Fainstein and Fainstein 1974; Keyes 1969). The Economic Opportunity Act (EOA) of 1964 established community action programs within poor neighborhoods, which received federal funds directly and spent their resources on social and educational programs. The mandate for maximum feasible participation of the poor contained in the EOA (Boone 1972) presaged citizen participation requirements in the urban renewal law, and in 1968, local urban renewal authorities were mandated to set up project area committees to represent affected community residents. The Demonstration Cities and Metropolitan Development Act of 1966 (Model Cities) focused on poor neighborhoods (Frieden and Kaplan 1975). Requiring that neighborhood residents have substantial representation on planning bodies affecting their areas, the act emphasized community preservation, coordination of physical and social planning, and rehabilitation. In 1970, the Uniform Relocation Assistance Act finally ensured that displaced residents would receive adequate relocation payments. Despite the concessions to mobilized communities evidenced by these new programs, large-scale urban renewal projects aimed at downtown regeneration continued, provoking fierce reactions where they impinged on residential areas.

Reflecting the political and social divisions between supporters of continued urban restructuring and opponents of large-scale, public interventions, the planning profession divided between those working for central-city redevelopment agencies, who still adhered to the model of comprehensive planning, and neighborhood-based planners, who focused on their particular piece of the city and often took adversarial positions toward the center (Needleman and Needleman 1974). The latter worked for poverty and Model Cities agencies as well as community-based organizations. In the planning literature the split was reflected in the articles published in the *Journal of the American*

Institute of Planners. Paul Davidoff's influential call for advocacy planning appeared in 1965, but most pieces concerned with redevelopment during this period focused on analytic techniques. Whether implicitly or explicitly, comprehensiveness remained the goal; Lindblom's (1959) critique of comprehensiveness for its impracticality and Altshuler's (1965) skepticism regarding the generalist planner's claim to knowledge of the public interest are never acknowledged in these articles. Mostly, as in the comment of Flyvbjerg quoted previously, they rationalized the exercise of power, not so much by making broad arguments for redevelopment programs, but rather by transforming political decisions into technical ones.

Still, during the concessionary period, planning to some degree shifted away from its commitment to a unitary public interest, and many recognized that the problems of low-income neighborhoods would not be vanquished purely through trickle-down policies. This recognition led to a division of labor among policy makers. A minority perceived the existence of slums as a consequence of social inequality rather than obsolete physical structures and spent their work lives addressing that issue. The majority continued to emphasize comprehensiveness and focus on land use, transportation, and environmental systems that would provide the template for urban improvement. Overall the balance between justice and injustice changed, with more equitable outcomes occurring even while demolition of communities and subsidies to developers continued.

The concessionary period, along with the entire postwar era of major federal involvement in urban redevelopment, ended with the passage of the Housing and Community Development Act (HCDA) of 1974. This act terminated the federal urban renewal, Model Cities, and public-housing programs, replacing them with Community Development Block Grants (CDBG) and Section 8 housing programs.[5] The Nixon–Ford presidencies, the decreasing influence of central city electorates, the Republican Party's "Southern Strategy," and the gradual dismantling of the poverty program all marked the end of an epoch that had begun with the New Deal and, for better and worse, involved active intervention in urban transformation. The move to block grants meant that the central cities that had received substantial federal subventions to support their urban renewal programs could no longer afford large-scale public land-acquisition and capital-expenditure programs for redevelopment purposes. Even though local business interests had promoted urban renewal programs, the business-friendly Republican administrations shied away from policies that benefited northern cities, preferring the formula-based block grants that distributed money to their suburban and southern constituencies.[6]

The Conserving Period (1975–81)

The mid-1970s constituted a crisis moment for older American cities. The country was undergoing a rise in unemployment that particularly hit manufacturing centers as jobs disappeared by the millions. Inflation tripped off taxpayers' revolts and further undermined the situation of city governments that faced increased expenses with declining revenues and withdrawal of federal support. Welfare rolls and crime rates were rising, white flight and business departures to suburban office parks and shopping malls accelerated, while housing abandonment turned central areas into vacant lots. Tracts that had been bulldozed by urban renewal still awaited private investment. Cleveland declared bankruptcy, while New York's fiscal crisis ended with financial control vested in two unelected, business-dominated governing boards.

During this period, development trajectories became increasingly uneven within and between cities (see Beauregard 1989). In contrast to the cities that could entice private investment due to their converting economies, many of the old manufacturing centers of the Midwest, as well as eastern industrial locations like Lowell and Philadelphia, simply foundered. Their economic plight arose as major industrial firms lost out to global competition, were acquired by other firms, introduced labor-saving technology, or moved to lower-cost areas. Between 1968 and 1977 Detroit lost 208,000 jobs, or one-third of its employment base (Hill 1986, 99). Abandonment, rather than gentrification, was the principal issue in many midwestern and northeastern cities.

Cities responded to their plight by developing new methods for enticing private investment. No longer able to rely on federal support, they devised a variety of tax incentive and below-market-rate interest loan measures aimed at reducing development costs. Typically a developer or a municipal government would envision a project, and then public money or tax forgiveness would be used to supplement the private investment. The approach meant the end of comprehensive planning, as investment proceeded on an opportunistic, project-by-project basis.

Within urban neighborhoods community development corporations (CDCs)—nonprofit, neighborhood-based, nongovernmental organizations (NGOs)—became the principal vehicle for affordable housing and, to a lesser extent, commercial development (Rubin 2000). Growing out of the advocacy organizations spawned during the preceding period, CDCs put together multiple sources of financing to develop housing. As direct federal funding of housing under Section 8, new construction and substantial rehabilitation programs for housing dwindled, CDCs rehabbed abandoned buildings and constructed new structures on vacant lots. Provisions within the national tax code gave breaks to private investors in low-income housing, and CDCs could tap into syndicates of investors looking for tax benefits, as well as various philanthropic and state funds to finance their activities. Unlike public housing, which had always been opposed by real-estate interests and by this time had become highly stigmatized, construction by NGOs fit the privatization ideology of the time.

Redevelopment thus proceeded piecemeal, with almost total reliance on private investment funds as the source of capital, and tax and regulatory relief providing the stimulus. Ambitious megaprojects gave way to smaller, interstitial efforts (Altshuler and Luberoff 2003). Efforts at transforming central business districts continued, but they were more limited in scope than in the previous period and more dependent on individual entrepreneurs. City economic development offices became ingenious packagers of funds, using tax-free industrial revenue bonds, tax increment financing districts (TIFs), special development districts, and enterprise zones to entice investors (Fainstein and Fainstein 1986).[7]

After the termination of the federal urban renewal program, the planning literature related to urban revitalization reflected modest ambitions in its focus on policies linking housing and neighborhood upgrading to office development. Public–private partnerships, under which government and private entities formally agreed to work together on projects, were vaunted as the appropriate form of organization for development. Much attention was paid to gentrification, a term coined by the British sociologist Ruth Glass that had only recently become part of the planner's vocabulary. The debate over gentrification centered on whether it represented a desirable "back to the city" movement (Auger 1979) or whether it was the successor to urban renewal's displacement of low-income citizens (Hartman 1979), and whether it was sparked by consumer demand or developers' greed (Smith 1979). Reflecting the continuing split among planners that had begun during the 1960s, dissidents were highly critical of such neighborhood upgrading, while supporters celebrated the urban "renaissance."

The Carter administration (1976–80) provided some federal support for neighborhood redevelopment and required that CDBG funds be directed to impoverished areas. By 1981 and the onset of the Reagan administration, however, the federal emphasis on community revitalization had almost vanished, and the orientation of city governments had moved decisively from the removal of slums and blight to promoting economic development (Clarke 1984; Fainstein and Fainstein 1989). Economic restructuring had produced numerous disused waterfronts and railroad yards, allowing construction to take place on the periphery of CBDs without displacement of residents. The festive retail marketplace came into its own, and planners began to regard lively streetscapes as more desirable than sober office buildings (Frieden and Sagalyn 1989).

Reliance on tax subsidies, public–private partnerships, and an office-led strategy could not cope with private industry's lack of interest in the declined cities of the Midwest and Northeast, particularly in those cities with large black populations. Only Chicago (Squires et al. 1987) and Minneapolis (Nickel 1995), of the northern cities between the Alleghenies and the Rockies, were able to achieve redevelopment success. They employed TIF financing to enlarge their CBDs and nurture the new service economy, enabling them to boast of new, lively downtowns. Within these, as in other converting cities, however, success in the aggregate was accompanied by widening disparities between the well-to-do and the poor (Squires 1989). Despite the efforts of community-based organizations, injustice, as measured by inequitable outcomes, once again thickened.

Privatized Redevelopment (1982–)

Trends toward privatization that began in the 1970s intensified under the Reagan, Clinton, and first and second Bush administrations. The greater efficiency of market processes became the conventional wisdom, while city governments continued to confront lean budgets and tax resistance that inhibited them from using their own capital budgets to finance development projects. The centerpiece of urban policy under the Clinton administration—empowerment zones—represented a rare infusion of federal funds to foster area-based urban economic development in poverty locations during this period. The program, which provided federal tax forgiveness and deregulation to entice private investment and also injected federal funds into social services, was limited to a handful of cities; evaluation indicated that "zone initiatives had little impact" (Oakley and Tsao 2006).[8] Even parks, long assumed to be a public responsibility, were expected to be self-financing as a consequence of revenues produced by adjacent real-estate development.[9] The predictable result was that most redevelopment depended on its potential profitability and was highly susceptible to the real-estate cycle (Fainstein 2001).[10] As in the conserving era, planning was largely project based, and its capacity to achieve results increasingly varied from city to city, depending on local leadership and the general economic fortunes of the metropolitan area.

The coalition supporting redevelopment endeavors has narrowed since 1981. As large firms became increasingly globalized, the local elites who had participated in organizations that framed the city's planning strategies began to break up. Strom (2008) has identified a narrower group of property developers, tourism executives, and leaders of nonprofit institutions as the major nongovernmental figures within contemporary urban growth regimes.[11] Gone are the department store proprietors, utility executives, local newspaper owners, bankers, and corporate magnates with deep roots in their localities and a nostalgic vision of a revived downtown. Strom asserts that the new coalitions have less of a focus on remaking downtown and greater interest in amenities, festivals, and safety. She sees business improvement districts, which exist in outlying as well as central areas, as important in shaping the urban agenda and argues that the old split between neighborhoods and downtown has consequently become attenuated.

Strom's hypothesis probably is correct if divisions over redevelopment strategies are categorized geographically. The politics of redevelopment ceased to revolve around whether capital will be invested downtown or in residential neighborhoods, suburbs or central cities, but rather around the type of investments made. Governments continue to pour money into convention centers and sports venues as entertainment has become identified as a more reliable catalyst to economic development than office construction (Fainstein and Judd, 1999). Although residential neighborhoods receive assistance from CDBG and other, locally raised funds, the amount expended is dwarfed by the sums flowing into these larger enterprises. Deteriorating older residential suburbs and satellite cities with low-income populations are generally losers by any measure: they lack the professional staffs and CDCs of central cities, they have low revenue-generating capacity, and they have little political influence.

Within central cities developers have proved willing to build in formerly shunned neighborhoods in response to incentives. Efforts to attract capital into poorer areas have depended primarily on the low-income housing tax credit (LIHTC). A product of the 1986 Tax Reform Act, this program eliminated the depreciation benefits formerly offered to limited partners in syndicated investments for affordable housing and substituted a credit restricted to corporations (Schwartz 2010, ch. 5). By 2003, over 1.2 million housing units had been constructed under the program. Both private and nonprofit developers could tap into the credit, the available amount of which depended on annual congressional allocations.[12]

Investment by individual homeowners, who benefited from the requirements of the 1977 Community Reinvestment Act (CRA), also helped to infuse capital into formerly deprived neighborhoods (Schwartz 2010, 242–46). The act gave community groups standing to challenge proposed bank mergers. To avoid such blockages of their ambitions, banks entered into agreements to increase their lending in once redlined neighborhoods. The effectiveness of the act's stipulations lessened, however, as more lending was being conducted by nonbank financial institutions; moreover, restrictions were removed from interstate banking, thus freeing banks from ties (and therefore obligations) to particular places.

After the subsidence of megaprojects post-1974, they gradually began to make a comeback. Establishing a new model for inner-city development, they embodied a design orthodoxy that jettisoned earlier aims of lowering densities and separating uses. Now mixed uses and the twenty-four-hour city became the desiderata of planners (Love 2006–7). In fact, land emptied of structures forty to fifty years earlier under the urban renewal program began to attract investor interest in response to advanced services firms' desire for central locations and increased consumer demand for downtown residences (Birch 2006).

Public–private partnerships, including New York's Battery Park City, Columbus Center, and Times Square schemes, burgeoned during the last two decades of the twentieth century and attracted investments of billions of dollars (Fainstein 2001, 2005). Similar large projects in Los Angeles, San Francisco, and Chicago likewise indicated the willingness of private capital to utilize tax incentives, as well as publicly provided loans and infrastructure investments to build major projects, on a scale that often exceeded the developments built during the heyday of urban renewal. In the new millennium, New York has two huge mixed-use schemes (Atlantic Yards in Brooklyn and Hudson Yards in Manhattan) proposed, and two new stadiums (for the Yankees and Mets baseball teams) constructed.[13] All four of these projects involve public–private partnerships that absorb very large public expenditures through tax subsidies and infrastructure provision; they epitomize top-down planning justified in the name of economic development; and in the cases of Atlantic Yards and Yankee Stadium, they are occurring in impoverished areas away from the Manhattan central business district.[14]

The commitment to sports venues—two stadiums plus an arena in Atlantic Yards—represents a widely observed pattern throughout the country, where despite virtually unanimous analytic findings that investment in sports produces neither economic development nor neighborhood improvement, sports-related development continues apace (Long 2005). The principal means by which advocates for low-income groups achieve benefits from major developments is through the use of community benefits agreements (CBAs), which developers negotiate either directly with community representatives or with the intercession of city officials. Usually the deal is made when the developer wishes a concession from the public sector, such as regulatory relief, a tax subsidy, or infrastructure provision. The extent to which such deals actually create favorable outcomes for the public depends on structuring the deal so that developers give up benefits equivalent to the concessions they receive, the criteria for developer contributions are clearly specified, and effective monitoring and penalties for noncompliance exist (Kayden 2000; Weber 2007, 2008; Wolf-Powers 2010). Unfortunately, these criteria are often not met.

Another component of early urban renewal programs that has reappeared is clearance and reconstruction. Rather, however, than the target being tenement houses and marginal businesses, it is the public housing constructed under the 1949 act. Justified as breaking up concentrated poverty and the vicious circle allegedly associated with it, the HOPE VI program replaces distressed public housing with mixed-income developments (Goetz 2003). Often the projects targeted for removal are located in waterfront areas or adjacent to an expanded downtown. Thus like urban renewal of the 1950s and 1960s, the program is being used to clear areas of populations perceived as threatening to middle-class users (Bennett, Smith, and Wright 2006).

Cities throughout the country have seized on HOPE VI as a vehicle for removing public housing from desirable locations and using the sites for large development schemes. Nowhere has this process gone farther than in Chicago, where the city has replaced its enormous projects, including the Cabrini-Green and Robert Taylor Homes, with new, mixed-income construction.[15] Critics of the process contend that the city administration was motivated by a desire to improve the city's public image and to upgrade areas for middle-class habitation. They point to inadequate relocation procedures, the scarcity of good housing elsewhere to accommodate the dislocated, and the longtime lapse between eviction and the availability of new units for those allowed to return to the site. While new HOPE VI developments typically conform to Jane Jacobs's precepts of mixed use and mixed income, they lack the layered appearance of old city neighborhoods that grew by accretion. More important, as in the urban renewal projects she criticized, communities are broken up and people are moved involuntarily.[16]

The confidence expressed in earlier days that physical programs alone produced economic regeneration has dissipated. There is a growing focus on events like Olympic games and activities such as festivals and farmers markets as generators of redevelopment. The consensus is that such "soft" measures, along with the development of entertainment and cultural milieus, are the best approach to attracting interest in central locations by consumers, investors, and the much-desired "creative class." Considerably more attention is being paid to the region as the locus of economic activity and the beneficial effects of constraining peripheral growth on central city improvement (Swanstrom 2006; Nelson et al. 2004).

A series of overlapping approaches has come along to stimulate central city economic development. These include promoting high-tech industry (Markusen, Hall, and Glasmeier 1986); developing festive retailing (Frieden and Sagalyn 1989); stimulating clustering of related economic activities (Porter 2000); fostering Disney-influenced entertainment milieus (Hannigan 1998); bringing in tourism through sports-related development, iconic architecture, and cultural events (Judd 2003; Judd and Fainstein 1999; Hoffman, Fainstein, and Judd 2003); attracting creative people through cultural distinctiveness (Florida 2002; Markusen and Schrock 2006; Currid 2007), and deconcentrating the poor (Imbroscio 2008). These strategies do not require redistributive measures but rely instead, as was the case under urban renewal, on trickle-down. Unlike urban renewal, however, they are explicitly market oriented in their orientation. Their unabashed goal is economic development, not residential improvement or urban beautification, although innovative design has increasingly been incorporated within them.

The effects on equity and diversity of these recent initiatives are controversial. They are less likely to have a direct negative impact on the poor than did urban renewal programs, and to the extent that they add amenities available to everyone, they may enhance public life. Sharon Zukin (2010), however, asserts that commercial upgrading and sanitizing of public spaces is erasing authenticity and depriving the urban working class of their cultural inheritance—that paradoxically what is rationalized as planning for diversity is in fact destroying genuine diversity. Evaluation of the cultural effects of city marketing, niche retailing, and festivalization is so subjective that coming to any firm conclusion presents considerable difficulty. Zukin has nostalgia for a manufacturing city that has faded from existence and regards the more glamorous terrain associated with boutiques and coffee shops as exclusionary. It is questionable, however, whether the white-collar proletariat now resident in American metropolises would share her negative feelings toward cappuccino. At any rate, current improvements in the urban milieu, even if they represent a culture somewhat at odds with a traditional working-class way of life, cannot be seen as constituting a level of injustice comparable to evicting families from their homes or demolishing their place of work.

The Interaction between Spatial and Social Injustice

Until the 1980s, redevelopment efforts had largely targeted central cities. Suburbia, however, has increasingly become the site of poverty, deteriorated housing, and abandoned commercial buildings. Uneven development has transformed the earlier condition of impoverished inner cities and wealthy outlying areas into a metropolitan checkerboard, wherein some suburbs have become ghettoized, older shopping malls vacated, low-income people of all races are living in suburbs, and metropolitan centers are witnessing gentrification. During the 1990s, concentrations of extreme poverty lessened, but the number of people experiencing poverty grew (Jargowsky 2003). Although Hayward and Swanstrom in their introduction rightly consider isolation of the poor as an underlying initial contributor to thick injustice, present trends indicate that disrupting past patterns of segregation through either gentrification or outmigration of poor and minorities does not diminish the structural forces producing income inequality. One of the aims of urban redevelopment programs has always been to retain or attract middle-class families into central cities. Recently environmental concerns have heightened the perception that everyone would benefit from more compact development. But given that schools and infrastructure had already deteriorated as a consequence of middle- and upper-class flight from the city, returnees are unlikely to bring about changes that would benefit existing impoverished populations. Rather dense environments disproportionately attract nonfamily households—singles, young couples, retirees—who, even if they do not directly displace poor communities, diminish their political power, undermine their social connections, and have little interest in improving schools. The newcomers do not interact with their impoverished neighbors; therefore, they do not provide the role models and social connections that are the alleged positive outcomes of proximity. In fact, Robert Putnam (2007) has found that neighborhood diversity, even when it does not generate hostility, reduces neighborliness and social trust. Moreover, to the extent that well-to-do families with children come to or remain in central cities, they typically either opt out of the public school system or disproportionately send their children to schools with competitive admissions.

Efforts at suburban integration have largely proved unstable, as vacancies in integrating areas tend to be taken up by minorities until a tipping point is reached. Furthermore, arguments that poor minorities in central cities who lacked access to outlaying jobs would benefit from a suburban location were largely fallacious. The studies did not really consider that suburbanites almost always drove to work even if their employment was also in the suburbs. Many of the participants in the federal Moving to Opportunity program who originally did move to outlying locations found that, even though their housing and security conditions improved, their employment situations did not, they suffered from social isolation, and they lost access to the social services concentrated within the city (Briggs, Popkin, and Goering 2010).

The relationship between spatial and social inequality is highly complex and path dependent. If postwar suburban development had occurred without discrimination against African-Americans and if exclusionary zoning had never been permitted, then the malign effects of spatial segregation would have been averted. That area homogeneity now exists, however, and that municipal control of public services has produced extremely uneven access means that a move toward heterogeneity and metropolitan government will not erase the distributional effects of the past. Space has been used by the privileged to protect their positions, and changes in those spatial arrangements cannot readily undo their previous effects and may even reinforce them.

If with the aims of achieving social integration and reducing sprawl with its negative environmental effects, we move toward denser, more compact cities, then we may, in fact, exacerbate past inequities. Land prices at the center would rise, and without compensatory programs to make housing affordable, poor people would be forced into more crowded conditions. Many of the households that moved to peripheral locations did so because these were the only areas they could afford. Elimination of the choice to trade greater space for proximity to the center might well result in the increased domination of central locations by the wealthy. As long as inequalities of power and income arise out of the economic system, rearranging space will not lessen them without accompanying resource redistributional programs.

Redevelopment and Distributive Outcomes

We are now in a position to look back at nearly sixty years of programs aimed at restoring America's cities to their former glory. In that time, the definition of the urban problem has switched from slums and blight to joblessness and concentrated poverty (what Europeans term social exclusion), while the concern with the migration of business out of downtown has merged with a broader consideration of metropolitan competitive advantage. Numerous programs have come and gone. To some extent they have succeeded in reviving downtowns, improving neighborhoods, and staunching outward migration of people and industry, although the amount of success varies according to local leadership and the strength of the metropolitan economy. As many names as the programs have had, with the exception of public housing, the war on poverty, and Model Cities, their major purpose has been to attract private money through using public subsidies for corporate retention or relocation and real-estate development. The three aforementioned programs targeted at poor neighborhoods have now vanished, and the current approach is unabashedly directed at economic development and the dispersal of poor people—with the latter used to encourage property development initiatives in their former locales.

We can thus make the following generalizations:

- In terms of urban policy (i.e., policy that is geographically targeted to cities), physical property improvement has been equated with social improvement. Property-led economic development assumes that providing structures for business firms will create new jobs. Social programs are not connected with physical ones and are rather administered on an individual basis.

- The need to attract private investment skews projects to favor developer interests. Emphasis on physical development of retail and office space as the key to job creation ignores the types of jobs created, which frequently do not fit the skill set of local residents or, for low-skilled jobs, do not promise a living wage. Dependence on cross-subsidies for affordable housing provision requires a sufficient number of market-rate units to insure profitability.[17] The LIHTC essentially bribes private investors to provide capital for low-income housing construction; direct federal subsidy would be much more efficient.

- The reliance on public–private partnerships insulates large-scale development from democratic input. Community development agreements have become an important vehicle for circumventing the barriers to public input by offering an avenue for demanding benefits to local communities, but nevertheless the profit-making participants in the partnership generally shape the overall character of the project. In smaller projects where the private partner is a nonprofit entity like a CDC, community interests have more control and take the initiative in shaping the project, but dependence on a variety of funding sources constrains their planning. Moreover, the capacity of CDCs is limited, and in most places, the scale of their operations is small relative to need.

- Redevelopment planners must operate within the limits set by market factors, by federal and local legislation, and by the agendas of their political masters, who in turn are heavily influenced by local and extralocal growth coalitions. Planning consultants who promote particular kinds of investments, especially convention centers and sports venues, bolster the predilections of local officials seeking the glory of bringing in a team or cutting the ribbon before the new convention facility.

Inflated claims are made regarding the job and revenue streams created by new development (Flyvbjerg 2003) and the benefits that poor people will gain by "moving to opportunity" (Briggs, Popkin, and Goering 2010). Community advocates within urban bureaucracies are not sufficiently powerful on their own to move redevelopment into different channels. They do, however, have the capacity to challenge fabricated numbers with careful analysis. When they have the backing of mobilized constituencies, either when acting as spokespersons for community groups or as "guerrillas within the bureaucracy" (Needleman and Needleman 1974), they can be in the position to develop alternative plans. Ironically it is when real estate markets fail during the inevitable downturns that the greatest openings for more innovative developments occur, as land prices fall and properties become vacant.[18] Even within the confines of developer-initiated megaprojects, planners can persevere to make the projects serve broader publics through hard bargaining. Courses in planning schools on negotiation tend to view the planner as a mediator, but what planners need to learn is how to be effective in pressing a deal on the better-paid, private-sector negotiator sitting across the table. It is now generally accepted that planning is about power, politics, and implementation and not simply the application of technical knowledge—this is nowhere more true than in the arena of redevelopment planning.

Popular mobilization for greater justice in redevelopment planning is a prerequisite for the creation of projects that tilt more in favor of lower-income residents. The Los Angeles Alliance for a New Economy (LAANE) represents one locally based model that demands significant concessions in return for any public subsidy to developers. Its program calls for commitments to a living wage by firms that receive public subsidies and the provision of health and job training benefits. What is especially notable about this model is that it brings together community groups and labor unions in a common cause. Similar groups have formed in other cities, many of them linked up in a national Right to the City Alliance. In New York, the Working Families Party has pressed for wage commitments in subsidized projects, while the Right to the City group has staged protests and taken over residential buildings. For these local movements to become truly effective, however, they must, as the urban movements of the 1960s did, affect the national political scene. So far this has not happened. Despite the Obama administration's sympathy for the urban working class, it has been preoccupied by other matters, and the president has barely mentioned urban programs beyond the need to staunch foreclosures.

European countries have much more prominent national urban policies than does the United States. Virtually all invest more heavily in housing programs for both construction and rental assistance. In the Netherlands, for example, although commitment to social housing provision has shrunk, affordable housing still usually constitutes half of the units in new construction in the major cities. The United Kingdom under the last Labour government encouraged local governments to negotiate agreements with developers wherein the developer would make legally binding commitments to provide public benefits in return for the right to develop ("planning permission").[19] These agreements were increasingly used to support the provision of services and infrastructure, such as transportation facilities, recreational venues, education, health, and affordable housing. Within most European countries, it is largely assumed that neighborhood revitalization efforts will combine physical and social strategies—ironically the American Model Cities program set the template for these approaches even as it was eliminated in the United States.

The European examples indicate that, even in the context of global competitiveness, more just planning is possible. It requires, however, a political force that presses for it. In Europe left-wing parties are the principal agents for a more equitable urban agenda, but even conservative parties, carrying out a tradition of paternalism and operating within a different ideological framework, support a larger government role in providing social assistance.

An Outcomes-Oriented Approach to Redevelopment

If American policy makers are to promote alternatives, they need to have a set of criteria by which to evaluate proposals for redevelopment. Progressive urban planners and policy makers have overemphasized process to the detriment of outcomes, as democracy and mediation rather than program outcomes have become the lodestars of their practice. To be sure, democracy in itself is a desirable practice, not simply a means to an end, and therefore should be included among principles of justice. At the same time, however, public participation can be contrary to other elements of justice, as will be discussed later. Determining the justice of urban policy requires scrutinizing its consequences by examining the resulting distribution of benefits, not just evaluating the circumstances under which it was made (Campbell 2006).

There can be considerable debate concerning the content of urban justice. Nevertheless, I would posit three general principles that characterize a just urban policy: equity, diversity, and democracy. The criterion of equity follows on the work of John Rawls, which has become the dominant philosophical argument within liberal democratic societies. As Hayward and Swanstrom, referring to Rawls and subsequent philosophers assert in their introduction to this book, "People with a very wide range of beliefs about justice . . . should repudiate the inequalities of resources, opportunities, and powers that characterize the contemporary metropolis." From this it follows that just policies do not reinforce inequality but rather result in more equitable outcomes.

The principal criticism of Rawls by those who wish to broaden his definition of justice is that he overemphasizes material outcomes and does not sufficiently concern himself with discrepancies of power and self-esteem resulting from differences based in gender, ethnicity, or other group characteristics (see especially Young 1990; Honneth 2003). Although group differences often correlate with material disadvantage, they still have an autonomous element that is not simply overcome by income equalization. Based on these arguments and their obvious relevance to issues of metropolitan segregation and inferior access to housing and services, I name diversity as one of the three principles of urban justice. Philosophers use the term "recognition" to refer to just treatment of the "other"; however, within the context of the metropolis and in accordance with common usage, "diversity" or "social inclusion" seems the more appropriate term.

Democracy is, as indicated previously, a principle in accordance with the traditions of liberal societies and, by its advocates, usually considered to contribute to just outcomes. The logic is that inclusion of subordinate groups in decision-making processes is a good in itself not only by making people feel empowered and acting as a vehicle for education but also by forcing elites to take nonelite interests into consideration. Proponents of deliberative or thick democracy regard participation that extends beyond periodic elections into the policy-making process as essential to justice (Gutmann and Thompson 1996). As a practical problem, however, inclusion in situations where power is unequally distributed initially does not usually lead to redress of inequality. When, as is frequently the case, participation is dominated by propertied interests—whether homeowners or developers—the result is frequently exclusion and unequal distribution. Moreover, lower-income people often lack the personal resources to participate effectively even if they are nominally included and, due to the dominance of certain ideas promulgated by ruling regimes (e.g., that everyone benefits from policies promoting economic development), they may opt for policies not in their best interests. Thus while democracy needs to be included in the list of guiding principles of justice, it is not sufficient, and an evaluation of its impact in relation to equity is always necessary.

Sustainability, interpreted as producing environmental equity between present and future generations, is a corollary to the principle of equity. For the purposes of this chapter, it is collapsed into that principle, but it does produce an additional constraint in relation to redevelopment policy.

The three principles of equity, diversity, and democracy lead to the following more specific guidance for policy makers (Fainstein 2010):

1. All new housing development should provide units for households with incomes below the median, either on-site or elsewhere, with the goal of providing a decent home and suitable living environment for everyone. This follows a precedent established in the United Kingdom, where all major developments must have a percentage of their units allocated for below-market-rate housing. As happens in Amsterdam, nonprofit developers could be allocated space in new projects. Housing units developed to be affordable should remain in perpetuity in the affordable housing pool or be subject to one-for-one replacement. (Until recently demolition of public housing in the United States required one-to-one replacement, but this rule was eliminated. Moreover, most subsidized housing built by private developers needs to remain affordable only for a limited period.)

2. Households or businesses should not be involuntarily relocated for the purpose of obtaining economic development or community balance except in exceptional circumstances. When relocation is needed for the construction of public facilities, to improve housing quality, or to increase densities so as to accommodate additional population, adequate compensation requires that the dislocated be given sufficient means to occupy an equivalent dwelling or business site, regardless of whether they are renters or owners and independent of the market value of the lost location. Reconstruction of neighborhoods should be conducted incrementally so that interim space is available in the vicinity for displaced households who wish to remain in the same location.

3. Economic development programs should give priority to the interests of employees and small-business owners. All new commercial development should provide space for public use and to the extent feasible should facilitate the livelihood of independent and cooperatively owned businesses.

4. Megaprojects should be subject to heightened scrutiny; be required to provide direct benefits to low-income people in the form of employment provisions, public amenities, and a living wage; and, if public subsidy is

involved, should include public participation in the profits. If at all possible, they should be developed incrementally and with multiple developers.

5. Planners should take an active role in deliberative settings in pressing for egalitarian solutions and blocking ones that disproportionately benefit the already well off.

Context affects the extent to which these ideas can be applied—it is easier to make demands on developers when the real estate market is hot, but on the other hand, there is more opportunity for nonprofit development when it is slack. Most important is that justice, not growth, should be the operative rhetoric surrounding development activities. Physical development aimed at improving the quality of a place without assisting the people who originally occupied it constitutes a form of thick injustice. Redevelopment policy is only just when it is carried out in tandem with programs for improved wages, housing, and social services. The first step toward achieving a more just form of redevelopment is to change the discourse surrounding programs so that justice becomes a touchstone for policy initiatives. Accomplishment of real change, however, requires more than rhetorical backing but must be based in activist social movements of the sort that briefly had impact during the 1960s and 1970s and are nascent today.

Notes

1 In Fainstein (2010), building on the works of philosophers John Rawls, Iris Marion Young, Nancy Fraser, and Martha Nussbaum, I develop a concept of the just city as embodying these principles. They are elaborated briefly later in this chapter.

2 See Faludi and van der Valk (1994) for a discussion of the term "planning doctrine," referring to the broad type of planning that is adopted by a particular society.

3 Bettman successfully defended zoning before the Supreme Court in *Euclid v. Ambler* (1926).

4 Much of planning scholarship ignored the critique of urban renewal and instead focused on establishing a scientific, apolitical basis for planning. See, inter alia, Robinson, Wolfe, and Barringer (1965); Steger (1965); Mao (1966); Wingo (1966); and Schaaf (1969). Bennett Harrison (1973) was exceptional in using economic analysis as a tool for investigating the redistributional effects of the Model Cities program.

5 The principal program within Section 8 provided subsidies to renters, allowing them to rent units within the private market by limiting their contribution to the payment to 25 percent (later raised to 30 percent) of their income.

6 Many southern cities had never mounted urban renewal programs out of fear of federal oversight.

7 TIFs are districts wherein increases in property tax revenues accountable to new development are plowed back into the area or used to pay off loans initially used for the area's revitalization; special development districts target subsidies and tax and regulatory relief to particular areas; enterprise zones (EZs) are state-designated development districts.

8 The idea of the zones had been around since the Reagan administration under the rubric enterprise zones (EZs); while the federal government took many years to adopt the program after it was first proposed, many state governments had established EZs providing exemptions from state taxes and other incentives (Peters and Fisher 2003).

9 The halting progress of New York's Hudson River Park and Boston's Rose Kennedy Greenway is a product of expectations of financing coming as an externality of development. Many of New York's established parks now depend for their maintenance money on private conservancies, restaurants, and use of the parks for corporate events.

10 At the time of this writing, the credit crisis in real-estate finance is blocking progress in a number of developments that seemed well on track just a short time ago.

11 In cities like New York, where large development firms like the Related Companies are headquartered, their heads participate in the local growth coalition. In other cities, however, such major players are not actors but rather are brought in by city economic development authorities.

12 In contrast, under the original urban renewal program, the principal incentives available to for-profit developers were cheap land and publicly provided infrastructure.

13 In addition, Columbia University is developing a new campus in a mainly vacant area of West Harlem, although some eminent domain and business displacement is required.

14 When the affected Bronx community board rejected the Yankee Stadium plan because it destroyed a much-used park, the response of the Bronx borough president was to remove the members voting no from the board. He now heads President Obama's Office of Urban Policy.

15 White House senior advisor Valerie Jarrett spearheaded Chicago's HOPE VI project.

16 There is considerable debate over whether or not poor people dispersed from public housing benefit. See Boston (2005a, 2005b) and Goetz (2003, 2005).

17 Cross-subsidies exist when developers use part of their profits from market-rate housing to lower the prices of other units. Most such programs provide some form of assistance to developers in return, although in locations with inclusionary zoning all significant developments are required to offer affordable housing.

18 In New York during the 1970s and 1980s, property abandonment resulted in the city's acquiring a large stock of "in rem" housing, taken through accelerated tax delinquency proceedings. These structures were rehabilitated or razed for new construction on a large scale by CDCs; the reconstruction of the South Bronx, once a national symbol of urban decay, is largely attributable to this activity. After the real-estate booms of the 1990s and 2000s, very little property remained available

for affordable housing developers. Foreclosures now make possible an aggressive program to buy up vacated property for affordable housing, but whether this will happen remains to be seen.

19 The Labour Party suffered defeat in 2010. It is too soon to know what the policy of the new, Conservative–Liberal Democrat coalition government will be with regard to cities.

References

Altshuler, Alan A. 1965. *The City Planning Process*. Ithaca, N.Y.: Cornell University Press.

Altshuler, Alan A., and David Luberoff. 2003. *Megaprojects*. Washington, D.C.: The Brookings Institution.

Auger, Deborah A. 1979. "The Politics of Revitalization in Gentrifying Neighborhoods: The Case of Boston's South End." *Journal of the American Planning Association* 45, no. 4: 515–22.

Beauregard, Robert A. 1989. "Postwar Spatial Transformations." In *Atop the Urban Hierarchy*, ed. Robert A. Beauregard, 1–44. Totowa, N.J.: Rowman and Littlefield.

Bennett, Larry, Janet. L. Smith, and Patricia A. Wright, eds. 2006. *Where Are Poor People to Live?* Armonk, N.Y.: M. E. Sharpe.

Bettman, Alfred. 1945. "To the Honorable Chairman and Members, Sub-committee on Housing and Urban Redevelopment, Committee on Postwar Planning, U.S. Senate." *Journal of the American Institute of Planners* 11, no. 2: 5–10.

Birch, Eugenie L. 2006. "Who Lives Downtown?" In *Redefining Urban and Suburban America*, ed. Alan Berube, Bruce Katz, and Robert E. Lang, 29–60. Washington, D.C.: The Brookings Institution.

Boone, R. W. 1972. "Reflections on Citizen Participation and the Economic Opportunity Act." *Public Administration Review* 32:444–56.

Boston, Thomas D. 2005a. "The Effects of Revitalization on Public Housing Residents." *Journal of the American Planning Association* 71, no. 4: 393–407.

———. 2005b. "Response." *Journal of the American Planning Association* 71, no. 4:410.

Briggs, Xavier deS., Susan J. Popkin, and John Goering. 2010. *Moving to Opportunity*. Oxford: Oxford University Press.

Campbell, Heather. 2006. "Just Planning: The Art of Situated Ethical Judgment." *Journal of Planning Education and Research* 26: 92–106.

Clarke, Susan E. 1984. "Neighborhood Policy Options: The Reagan Agenda." *Journal of the American Planning Association* 50, no. 4: 493–501.

Currid, Elizabeth. 2007. *The Warhol Economy: How Fashion, Art, and Music Drive New York City*. Princeton, N.J.: Princeton University Press.

Davidoff, Paul. 1965. "Advocacy and Pluralism in Planning." *Journal of the American Institute of Planners* 31, no. 4: 544–55.

Fainstein, Norman I., Susan S. Fainstein, Richard Child Hill, Dennis Judd, and Michael Peter Smith. 1986. "Regime Strategies, Communal Resistance, and Economic Forces." In *Restructuring the City*, rev. ed., 245–82. New York: Longman.

Fainstein, Susan S. 1988. "Urban Renewal." In *Handbook on Housing and the Built Environment*, ed. Elizabeth Huttman and Willem van Vliet, 403–16. Westport, Conn.: Greenwood Press.

———. 1998. "Urban Redevelopment." In *The Encyclopedia of Housing*, ed. Willem van Vliet, 614–17. Thousand Oaks, Calif.: Sage.

———. 2001. *The City Builders*. Rev. ed. Lawrence: University Press of Kansas.

———. 2010. *The Just City*. Ithaca, N.Y.: Cornell University Press.

Fainstein, Susan S., and Dennis R. Judd. 1999. "Global Forces, Local Strategies, and Urban Tourism." In *The Tourist City*, ed. Dennis R. Judd and Susan S. Fainstein, 1–20. New Haven, Conn.: Yale University Press.

Fainstein, Susan S., and Norman Fainstein. 1974. *Urban Political Movements*. Englewood Cliffs, N.J.: Prentice-Hall.

———. 1989. "The Ambivalent State: Economic Development Policy in the U.S. Federal System under the Reagan Administration." *Urban Affairs Quarterly* 25, no. 1: 41–62.

Faludi, Andreas, and Arnold van der Valk. 1994. *Rule and Order: Dutch Planning Doctrine in the Twentieth Century*. Dordrecht: Kluwer.

Florida, Richard L. 2002. *The Rise of the Creative Class*. New York: Basic Books.

Flyvbjerg, Bent. 1998. *Rationality and Power*. Chicago: University of Chicago Press.

———. 2003. *Megaprojects and Risk*. Cambridge: Cambridge University Press.

Frieden, Bernard J., and Lynne B. Sagalyn. 1989. *Downtown, Inc.: How America Rebuilds Cities*. Cambridge, Mass.: MIT Press.

Frieden, Bernard J., and Marshall Kaplan. 1975. *The Politics of Neglect*. Cambridge, Mass.: MIT Press.

Gans, Herbert. 1959. "The Human Implications of Current Redevelopment and Relocation Planning." *Journal of the American Institute of Planners* 25, no. 1: 15–26.

———. 1962. *The Urban Villagers*. New York: Free Press.

Gerckens, Lawrence. 1995. "Alfred Bettman." http://www-personal.umich.edu/~sdbest/up594/people/Abettman.htm.

Goetz, Edward G. 2003. *Clearing the Way*. Washington, D.C.: Urban Institute Press.

———. 2005. "Comment: Public Housing Demolition and the Benefits to Low-Income Families." *Journal of the American Planning Association* 71, no. 4: 407–10.

Gutmann, Amy, and Dennis Thompson. 1996. *Democracy and Disagreement*. Cambridge, Mass.: Harvard University Press.

Hannigan, John. 1998. *Fantasy City*. New York: Routledge.

Harrison, Bennett. 1973. "The Participation of Ghetto Residents in the Model Cities Program." *Journal of the American Institute of Planners* 39, no. 1: 43–55.

Hartman, Chester. 1979. "Comment on 'Neighborhood Revitalization and Displacement': A Review of the Evidence." *Journal of the American Planning Association*, 45, no. 4: 488–91.

Hill, Richard Child, Susan S. Fainstein, Norman I. Fainstein, Dennis Judd, and Michael Peter Smith. 1986. "Crisis in the Motor City." In *Restructuring the City*, rev. ed., 80–125. New York: Longman.

Hoffman, Lily M., Susan S. Fainstein, and Dennis R. Judd, ed. 2003. *Cities and Visitors*. Oxford: Blackwell.

Hoffman, Alexander von. 2000. "A Study in Contradictions: The Origins and Legacy of the Housing Act of 1949." *Housing Policy Debate* 11, no. 2: 299–326.

Honneth, Axel. 2003. "Redistribution as Recognition: A Response to Nancy Fraser." In *Redistribution or Recognition?* ed. Nancy Fraser and Axel Honneth, trans. Joel Golb, James Ingram, and Christiane Wilke, 110–97. London: Verso.

Imbroscio, David. 2008. "United and Actuated by Some Common Impulse of Passion: Challenging the Dispersal Consensus in American Housing Policy Research." *Journal of Urban Affairs* 20, no. 2: 111–30.

Jacobs, Jane. 1961. *The Death and Life of Great American Cities.* New York: Vintage.

Jargowsky, Paul A. 2003. "Stunning Progress, Hidden Problems: The Dramatic Decline of Concentrated Poverty in the 1990s." *The Living Cities Census Series.* Washington, D.C.: Brookings Institution.

Judd, Dennis R., ed. 2003. *The Infrastructure of Play.* Armonk, N.Y.: M. E. Sharpe.

Judd, Dennis R., and Susan S. Fainstein, ed. 1999. *The Tourist City.* New Haven, Conn.: Yale University Press.

Kayden, Jerold. 2000. *Privately Owned Public Space.* New York: Wiley.

Keyes, Langley C. 1969. *The Rehabilitation Planning Game.* Cambridge, Mass.: MIT Press.

Lindblom, Charles E. 1959. "The Science of 'Muddling Through.'" *Public Administration Review* 19, no. 1: 79–88.

Listokin, David. 1991. "Federal Housing Policy and Preservation: Historical Evolution, Patterns, and Implications." *Housing Policy Debate* 2, no. 2: 157–85.

Long, Judith Grant. 2005. "Full Count: The Real Cost of Public Funding for Major League Sports Facilities." *Journal of Sports Economics* 6: 119–43.

Love, Tim. 2006–2007. "Urban Design after Battery Park City." *Harvard Design Magazine,* no. 25: 60–69.

Mao, James C. T. 1966. "Efficiency in Public Urban Renewal Expenditures through Benefit–Cost Analysis." *Journal of the American Institute of Planners* 32, no. 2: 95–107.

Markusen, Ann R., and Greg Schrock. 2006. "The 'Artistic Dividend': Urban Artistic Specialisation and Economic Development Implications." *Urban Studies* 43, no. 10: 1661–86.

Markusen, Ann R., Peter Hall, and Amy Glasmeier. 1986. *High Tech America.* Boston: Allen & Unwin.

Marris, Peter. 1962. "The Social Implications of Urban Redevelopment." *Journal of the American Planning Association* 28, no. 3: 180–86.

Needleman, Martin L., and Caroline E. Needleman. 1974. *Guerrillas in the Bureaucracy.* New York: Wiley.

Nelson, Arthur C., Raymond J. Burby, Edward Feser, Casey J. Dawkins, Emil E. Malizia, and Roberto Quercia. 2004. "Urban Containment and Central-City Revitalization." *Journal of the American Planning Association* 70, no. 4: 411–25

Nickel, Denise R. 1995. "The Progressive City? Urban Redevelopment in Minneapolis." *Urban Affairs Review* 30, no. 3: 355–77.

Oakley, Deirdre, and Hui-Shien Tsao. 2006. "A New Way of Revitalizing Distressed Urban

Communities? Assessing the Impact of the Federal Empowerment Zone Program." *Journal of Urban Affairs* 28, no. 5: 443–71.

Peters, Alan, and Peter Fisher. 2003. "Enterprise Zone Incentives: How Effective Are They?" In *Financing Economic Development in the 21st Century*, ed. Sammis B. White, Richard D. Bingham, and Edward W. Hill. Armonk, N.Y.: M. E. Sharpe.

Porter, Michael E. 2000. "Location, Competition, and Economic Development: Local Clusters in a Global Economy." *Economic Development Quarterly* 14, no. 1: 15–34.

Putnam, Robert D. 2007. "E Pluribus Unum: Diversity and Community in the Twenty-First Century." *Scandinavian Political Studies* 30, no. 2: 137–74.

Rubin, Herbert J. 2000. *Renewing Hope within Neighborhoods of Despair*. Albany: State University of New York Press.

Schaaf, A. H. 1969. "Economic Feasibility Analysis for Urban Renewal Housing Rehabilitation." *Journal of the American Institute of Planners* 35, no. 6: 399–404.

Schwartz, Alex F. 2010. *Housing Policy in the United States*. Rev. ed. New York: Routledge.

Smith, Neil. 1979. "Toward a Theory of Gentrification: A Back to the City Movement by Capital, Not People." *Journal of the American Planning Association* 45, no. 4: 538–48.

Squires, Gregory D., ed. 1989. *Unequal Partnerships*. New Brunswick, N.J.: Rutgers University Press.

Squires, Gregory D., Larry Bennett, Katherine McCourt, and Philip Nyden. 1987. *Chicago: Race, Class, and the Response to Urban Decline*. Philadelphia: Temple University Press.

Steger, Wilbur A. 1965. "The Pittsburgh Urban Renewal Simulation Model." *Journal of the American Institute of Planners* 31, no. 2: 144–50.

Strom, Elizabeth. 2008. "Rethinking the Politics of Downtown Development." *Journal of Urban Affairs* 30, no. 1: 37–61.

Swanstrom, Todd. 2006. "Regionalism, Equality, and Democracy." *Urban Affairs Review* 42, no. 2: 249–57.

Weber, Rachel. 2007. "Negotiating the 'Ideal Deal': Which Local Governments Have the Most Bargaining Leverage?" In *Reining in the Competition for Capital*, ed. Ann R. Markusen, 141–60. Kalamazoo, Mich. W. E. Upjohn Institute.

———. 2008. What Makes a Good Economic Development Deal?" In *Retooling for Growth*, ed. Richard M. McGahey and Jennifer S. Vey, 277–98. Washington, D.C.: The Brookings Institution.

Weiss, Marc. 1980. "The Origins and Legacy of Urban Renewal." In *Urban and Regional Planning in an Age of Austerity*, ed. Pierre Clavel, John Forester, and William W. Goldsmith, 53–80. New York: Pergamon.

Wingo, Lowdon, Jr. 1966. "Urban Renewal: A Strategy for Information and Analysis." *Journal of the American Institute of Planners* 32, no. 3: 143–54.

Wolf-Powers, Laura. 2010. "Community Benefits Agreements and Local Government." *Journal of the American Planning Association* 76, no. 2: 141–59.

Young, Iris M. 1990. *Justice and the Politics of Difference*. Princeton, N.J.: Princeton University Press.

Zukin, Sharon. 2010. *Naked City: The Death and Life of Authentic Urban Places*. New York: Oxford University Press.

7 JUSTICE, THE PUBLIC SECTOR, AND CITIES

Relegitimating the Activist State

THAD WILLIAMSON

THE ASSAULT ON EGALITARIAN SOCIAL JUSTICE in the United States over the past forty years has also been an assault on the legitimacy of vigorous public action to forward substantive goals. This is no coincidence: egalitarian conceptions of social justice invariably assume that the state will be the principal mechanism for establishing just social arrangements and rectifying inequalities (Rawls 1971; Dworkin 2000). In contrast, neoliberal conceptions of governance aim to both straitjacket the public sector and stymie efforts toward meaningful egalitarian redistribution. Given this strong internal connection between attractive conceptions of social justice and the idea of an active, competent public sector, advocates of urban social justice need to develop an account of how public-sector leadership on behalf of normatively desirable ends can be relegitimated. In this chapter, I focus on how we might begin to rehabilitate the idea of a vigorous public sector at the local level, given the existing political climate. As theorists since Tocqueville have recognized, local-level democratic practice is the building block (for better or worse) of larger-scale democracy, and (to use Rawlsian terminology) a society cannot be well ordered, stable, and just if local political and economic life is characterized by large inequalities and the predominance of private interests over public concerns.[1]

This chapter proceeds in two parts. In the first section, I argue that rehabilitating a vigorous public sector will require establishing a practical conception of the "public interest" that is capable of guiding policymakers and citizens. After discussing the relationship between ideas of social justice and the public interest, I go on to introduce conceptions of effective public-sector leadership—the "New Public Service"—developed by contemporary theorists of public administration in response to the neoliberal assault on the state. This engagement with theory is driven by a practical question: how can we begin at the local level to relegitimate the idea of a vibrant public sector that has the ability to curb private interests and advance social justice?

In the second section, I introduce a case study of creative public leadership in Richmond, Virginia, that corresponds to the "New Public Service" in important respects. Specifically, I examine how a city planner (Rachel Flynn) used a participatory process to galvanize public support for a new downtown master plan that vigorously challenges the traditional prerogative of developers in the city by calling for public control of riverfront property. The relative success of that effort, the resistance it has encountered, and its inherent limitations all shed light on the challenges involved in rehabilitating an activist public sector in inhospitable settings.

Social justice advocates who presume that the state will be a principal mechanism for rectifying injustice must develop an account of how the public sector can play this constructive role. In particular, those concerned with advancing social justice at the metropolitan level must wrestle with four critical issues: First, predominant theories of public management and urban public leadership generally are not predicated on the idea of an activist public sector acting to rectify inequalities and injustices. Second, government policy and actions have often taken a direct role in constituting or reinforcing social injustices, and in many cases, small- and large-scale public action at the local level has been biased toward the interests of business elites (Holland et al. 2007). Third, as presently constituted, local public sectors often lack the capacity to undertake the agendas frequently proposed by social justice advocates and green urbanists. In particular, we have relatively few examples of effective large-scale public action that also exhibits the virtues of transparency, openness to civic participation, and sensitivity toward all affected groups. Fourth, the public sector too often displays incompetence in the tasks that it already takes on, and corruption of various kinds is a recurrent problem in municipal government.

Social justice advocates need to explain why we should believe, despite these challenges, that the state is capable of acting in a vigorous way to correct social injustices and advance the public interest (especially our massive ecological challenges). This account should have two major components. The first is a *constitutional* theory of how to organize local and metropolitan government, including specification of the powers government should have vis-à-vis private actors, specification of the division of labor between more local and metropolitan-wide governments, and specification of the mechanisms by which government will be rendered inclusive, democratic, and accountable. The second needed component, and the focus of this chapter, is an account of how the public sector, once constituted, can or should go about acting on behalf of social justice and the public interest. What is needed is a positive theory of public administration on behalf of normatively desirable ends. Central to such an account must be a workable conception of what "the public interest" is and how it is to be pursued in practice.

Social Justice and the Public Interest

In its simplest sense, the public interest is to be distinguished from factional rule or domination by one segment of the community. To appeal to the "public interest" as a normative standard for evaluating public policy is to insist that the advocates of a given proposal explain why such an action is to the benefit of the larger community and not just the interests (material or otherwise) of its advocates. This does not mean that a proposal needs to directly benefit every member of the community, or even most of them, to be in accord with the public interest. For example, when disadvantaged groups press for more resources, they need not be forced to show that their demands would maximize the community's aggregate utility. Instead, they can reasonably appeal to the public interest that the community as a whole has in all citizens having adequate resources to develop themselves and pursue their aims. In other words, disadvantaged groups should be able to appeal to substantive conceptions of social justice in making arguments about why they should get more resources. This is the primary impetus motivating John Rawls's conception of social justice: to move away from utilitarian methods for measuring what the public interest is and to insist upon the normative priority of improving—maximizing—the position of the least well off (Rawls 1971).

This example already illustrates the complex relationship between social justice and the public interest. For thinkers like Rawls, the "public interest" should be seen as a subset of a larger-order conception of social justice—a conception intended to guide the organization of our institutions and to serve as a normative benchmark for policy making. This does not mean, however, that the notion of a public interest is unimportant.

In a well-ordered Rawlsian society, the concerns of government are not limited simply to implementing social policies or political–economic arrangements that achieve distributive justice. As Rawls stipulates, the government must also, for instance, attend to and provide public goods more generally (e.g., defense and security, public infrastructure, education, ecological protection; Rawls 1971). In urban contexts, there is strong reason to believe that it is in the broad interest of the community as a whole to provide not only public safety and workable infrastructure but also ample recreational opportunities, green and open spaces, and usable public space in general.[2] Providing such goods through public channels, rather than leaving them to the market, will lead to a more egalitarian distribution of these much-needed amenities. The public provision of such goods also reinforces the fundamental Rawlsian idea that society is to be seen as a scheme of social cooperation among free equals, not a Hobbesian world in which each takes what he can get and relates to others on purely instrumental grounds.

Note also that the relevant distributional question in urban contexts is not simply how to maximize the position of the least well off. It is also how to keep the very wealthy and most powerful actors from monopolizing the most attractive places and opportunities within the city. Often advocates of distributive justice fall into the habit of only thinking about how to improve the lot of the poor vis-à-vis the middle class. From the standpoint of larger-order social justice, however, an equally important question in contemporary capitalist societies is how the poor and middle class together can keep the very rich and powerful from running away with the overwhelming bulk of accumulated wealth, which can then be converted into excess political power and the capacity to redevelop the city as a playground for the affluent rather than as a shared landscape equally accessible to all. Needless to say, such a city also cannot realize the difference principle or anything like it. When local residents challenge the predominance of corporate developers and their efforts to shape land use so as to maximize profit opportunities in order to promote what Logan and Molotch term "use values" (Logan and Molotch 1987), they can reasonably claim that they are acting on behalf of the "public interest" and that their opponents' proposal benefits only a small faction rather than the community as a whole. Obviously, these claims to be acting in the name of the "public interest" must be subject to critical scrutiny. The previous example presents what might be viewed as a relatively easy (though not uncommon) case in which the "public interest" is invoked to protect the well-being of the overwhelming majority of the community against the interests of a powerful and affluent elite or of a particular private actor. But consider the opposite scenario, in which the overwhelming majority of the community invokes the "public interest" not as a defense against rapacious elites but in order to marginalize already oppressed groups belonging to the "least well off," as in proposals to forbid panhandling by the urban homeless (Mitchell 2003). Rawlsian principles of social justice aim to preclude attempts to punish the least well off in the name of promoting the good of "the community as a whole" (or more likely, the interests of relatively affluent people and business owners annoyed by the presence of homeless people). In a just society, we would expect a stable social ethos favorable to the least well off to be in place, making adoption of such policies unlikely; in the highly unjust, "nonideal" cities that we actually inhabit, preventing such outcomes in practice will likely require (at the least) structuring policy deliberations such that persons most affected by a given policy receive adequate voice and representation.[3]

This counterexample demonstrates the importance of linking one's account of the "public interest" to an account of social justice. From a Rawlsian point of view, this means clarifying that by "public interest," one is not referring to a simple aggregation of preferences or interests satisfied, to the views or interests of the median resident, or to the views or interests of any particular political majority. But what is the "public interest" if not one of these things? Three principal strategies are available to answer that question. The first is to define the public interest in procedural terms (in a broadly Habermasian framework). Posit an ideal decision-making process in which all points of view have equal access of expression, in which citizens are committed to listening to one another and open to the possibility of revising their preferences and positions, and in which the "unforced force" of the better reason trumps the demands of self-interested actors (Habermas 1984). The result of such a deliberative process might be regarded as the "public interest." A second strategy is to attempt to specify some set of public goods or "values" that cannot be realized by market processes but require public action to establish, defend, and extend. There is a shared public concern with maintaining a sustainable environment but good reason to doubt that market processes will secure that value—and hence the justification for the state taking an active role on behalf of realizing such public values (Bozeman 2007).

A third strategy defines the public interest not in terms of the product of an ideal decision procedure or as a list of specific public goods and values but in terms of our shared interest in living in a political regime of a certain kind. Specifically, we have a shared interest in living in a regime characterized by adherence to democratic norms, limited social inequality, a broad distribution of economic opportunity, and politics that are not dominated by the demands of the most economically powerful groups (Elkin 2006). It is this third, more substantive conception of the public interest that I wish to endorse here, although properly understood it incorporates important aspects of the first two approaches as well. An advantage of this way of thinking about the public interest is that it allows social justice considerations to be built into its very framework: we have a shared interest in creating, sustaining, and improving a regime of a particular kind—that is, one that is socially just.

But this formulation taken alone is too simple. First, as it is stated so far, it presumes the possibility of universal consensus about concrete principles of justice and the nature of the just regime. But in the real world, there is no consensus about the content of social justice, let alone Rawls's version of it (Cohen 2003), and it is obvious that many actors are motivated primarily by self-interest rather than social justice concerns and that the already powerful have greater capacity to advance and protect their interests than other groups.

Second, to be a useful concept, the "public interest" needs to be able to play a concrete role in specific policy debates. Specifically, actors should be asked to justify and make arguments on behalf of their policy preferences with reference to the public interest. While "public interest" in the ultimate sense is to be understood as the good of living and sharing a just, democratic, and prosperous regime, actual policy debates typically focus on concrete, intermediate goods (e.g., how to use this piece of land, whether to fund a proposed program, how to promote economic development), in which the relationship of the regime as a whole to the good in question may not be obvious. Just as claims about the meaning of justice, the requirements of democracy, and the best route to prosperity are controversial, so, too, will be all claims about the "public interest." Even if there were a rough consensus about the kinds of cities we wished to build, there would be significant disagreements about the best policy means to those ends.

In practice, acting to promote the public interest requires making a set of provisional judgments concerning, as Stephen Elkin puts it, "what is the public interest here in this case" (Elkin 1999, 43). Such judgments are best made in the context of a deliberative process in which as many viewpoints and perspectives as possible are canvassed. This conception of the public interest should be sharply distinguished from strong communitarian claims that local political life can or should be modeled on establishing a unitary identity that covers over or represses fundamental differences of identity and perspective. As Iris Marion Young argues, in a diverse society "the perception of anything like a common good can only be an outcome of public interaction that expresses rather than submerges particularities" (Young 1990, 119). Note, however, that Young is neither arguing against public deliberation nor rejecting the possibility of identifying shared interests; rather she is insisting that the public sphere be structured so as to be accessible and welcoming of difference. Indeed, Young deploys a critique of the domination of urban politics and development by private interests that is closely related to (in fact draws on) the conception presented by Elkin and other writers. Moreover, Young goes on to provide a "normative account of city life" that might be interpreted as a substantive account of the sorts of public goods cities should provide or exhibit: nonexclusionary social differentiation, variety, eroticism, publicity (Young 1990). To criticize simplistic conceptions of a public interest based on the model of a homogenous community does not imply that we can do without a conception of the public interest altogether or preclude the possibility and necessity of coming to workable judgments about how to advance the public interest in an inclusive, democratic process (Schwartz 2008). There is every reason to be suspicious of attempts by policy makers and elites to declare they know what the "public interest" is—or what "justice" is—and impose it. But when political discussion goes well, and distinctive points of view have the opportunity to be expressed and taken seriously, then resulting judgments about the content of the public interest in specific cases carry a strong, albeit always provisional, legitimacy.

This conception of the public interest draws on Elkin's efforts to provide a revised constitutional theory of a "commercial republic." While Elkin's interest is in stipulating the kinds of institutional arrangements that can sustain a democratic polity writ large, he places particular importance on the structure of local political arrangements as the essential building blocks of a meaningfully democratic regime. Local politics, Elkin argues, must be the site where citizens in a large-scale polity attain skill in discerning "what the public interest is" in particular cases, gain an appreciation of the value of deliberation, and learn to distinguish good leadership from bad. Active, public-minded citizenship must be encouraged; this in turn implies the presence of active, public-minded public officials who see themselves as seeking to attain the public interest rather than simply managing bargains among interest groups. It also implies that local politics must not be dominated by business interests. Equally important, local politics must have a strong deliberative element and must not be structured so as to lock into place or reinforce existing inequalities.

Relegitimating the Public Sector

Elkin's account stipulates that local politics should have the following features: a culture of civic participation and deliberation; an active public sector with the competence, resources, and legitimacy to act on behalf of the community as a whole; and competent public officials who attempt to discern the public interest and act upon it. Each of these requirements contradicts neoliberal accounts of public sector management that have become predominant in recent decades. Persistent fiscal strains, the privatization wave, and ideological attacks on bureaucrats have combined both to constrain government action and undermine its legitimacy.

In this context, two new ideologies of public management have emerged, offering a critique of traditional "command-and-control" government. Drawing on the observation that bureaucracies often must perform ambiguous tasks in ways that are shaped more by politics than by efficiency, these approaches assume that government is least inefficient and most effective when organized so as to mimic the market. "New Public Management" theories call for turning government control of resources and provision of services to private firms when possible and adopting a government-by-contract model. The strong assumption is that government is inherently inefficient because it lacks market accountability; consequently, privatization of government functions whenever feasible is normatively desirable (Morgan, England, and Pelissero 2006). The second approach, "Reinventing Government," calls on public officials to act as entrepreneurs and find new ways to generate revenue and hold down costs (Gaebler and Osborne 1992). For both approaches, the default assumption is that government ought to be "run like a business"; New Public Management holds the further assumption that government action is legitimate only in cases of "market failure." While the

Reinventing Government framework sanctions innovative public-sector entrepreneurial activity in potentially interesting ways, neither approach envisages an active public sector capable of taking aggressive action to forward the public interest and rectify social injustice. Yet each of these frameworks has had a substantial impact on the practice of public management in American cities (Doherty and Stone 1999; Morgan, England, and Pelissero 2007; Holland et al. 2007).

Janet and Robert Denhardt's work provides the most systematic attempt to date to provide a positive theory of public administration as an alternative to both command-and-control and market-based paradigms. Denhardt and Denhardt's notion of the "New Public Service" aims to recover and rearticulate the notion that public officials can and should be publicly minded and concerned with advancing the public interest and that this is best done by inculcating among officials an ethic of serving the public, as opposed to imposing one's will on others. This conception of public service stands in direct contrast to public choice theory's assumption that all actors, including public officials, are ultimately motivated by self-interest (whether narrowly or expansively defined). Denhardt and Denhardt's highly plausible claim is that the reductive public choice account of public-official behavior can become a self-fulfilling prophecy (witness the federal response to Hurricane Katrina) and that, conversely, sustaining a culture and ethos of public-minded behavior within public institutions requires being very explicit about the value of public service and developing a theoretical account of how public-minded officials can and should act (Denhardt and Denhardt 2003).

Denhardt and Denhardt thus approvingly cite Jeffrey Luke's conception of "catalytic leadership" as an appropriate model for the public sector. In this model, the tasks of "leaders" (public officials) are fourfold. First, public leaders must call attention to a specific issue and problem in order to "[create] a sense of urgency about its solution, and [trigger] broad public interest." Second, leaders need to get all stakeholders engaged in the issue, with a particular focus on ensuring diverse interests and perspectives are at the table. Third, working in concert with assembled citizens, alternative strategies for action need to be explored. Fourth, once action in a particular direction is under way, leaders must "build support" for it "among 'champions,' power holders, advocacy groups, and those holding important resources. The leader must then turn to institutionalizing cooperative behavior and becoming a network facilitator" (Denhardt and Denhardt 2003, 151; adapted from Luke 1998, 37–148).

This approach is an admirable attempt to specify a positive account of democratically minded, justice-inclined public administration. Especially important is the internal connection drawn between the legitimacy and long-term effectiveness of public actions and the willingness and ability to engage affected and interested citizens in the process. Nonetheless, we might doubt whether public officials learning how to incorporate citizen participation and involvement in the policy process is sufficient to redress background structural inequalities in a meaningful way. The work of Richard Box offers an important corrective on this point. Box calls on public administrators to understand from the outset the nature of the political–economic system in which they operate and to see themselves as subversives—that is, as agents fighting against the dominant logic of the existing political–economic system. The ideal public-sector worker, in his view, is not only the civic-minded public servant but also the official who uses her position and the resources available to her to struggle against both the tendency of state power to reinforce background inequalities and background inequalities themselves (Box 2004).

Case Study: Downtown Planning in Richmond, Virginia

Taken together, Denhardt and Denhardt's and Box's respective conceptions of public leadership call for catalytic leadership from public officials who are capable of mobilizing and collaborating with civic groups and who understand the political environment in which they operate. Leadership in this vein has at least a chance of harnessing public power toward normatively desirable and democratically legitimate ends. How might these conceptions work in practice? The following section considers the work of Richmond's community planning director Rachel Flynn, who devised and attempted to implement a new downtown master plan for the city. Flynn's efforts approximate most closely the idea of "catalytic leadership" but also incorporate aspects of Box's approach.

Richmond, Virginia, is hardly promising terrain for innovative public-sector leadership. The metropolitan area is a classic case of a central city with a majority African-American population and high levels of poverty (nearly 25 percent) surrounded by more affluent suburbs. Due to the geographic and political separation of cities and counties in Virginia, meaningful regional cooperation among the metropolitan area's governments is limited in scope, and there are no cooperative arrangements with a significant redistributive content. Politics in the city proper have generally been dominated by powerful local business interests such as local corporations and the real estate industry. Civic participation in the city is generally weak and usually racially divided and continues to be hampered by a long history of mutual racial distrust (Corcoran 2010); participation in public meetings and other efforts to lobby public officials is often disproportionately white. There are no powerful cross-racial organizations operating in the city and Industrial Areas Foundation–style community-organizing efforts to date have had very limited impact. Land use and redevelopment issues in the city have traditionally been the prerogative of developers and real estate interests (Silver 1984).

The case study that follows concerns both the public interest and distributive justice, though not in the more common sense of policies and practices affecting the least well off. Rather, this is a case of mobilizing the public at large to prevent powerful economic interests from imposing their will on the political process and claiming the most valuable real estate in the city. It is also about an attempt to reassert the legitimacy of direct public action for public ends and of city planning in a relatively conservative political context that has often been hostile to both ideas.

Starting in 2007, Flynn spearheaded a process leading to the adoption and implementation of a new master plan for downtown Richmond. Flynn is an experienced urban planner with progressive sensibilities who previously worked in Lynchburg, Virginia (doing political battle, on occasion, with Jerry Falwell and Liberty University). Flynn was hired by then-mayor L. Douglas Wilder in March 2006 and charged with revitalizing Richmond's downtown, which has been decaying as a commercial center and residential location for decades. Despite the presence of the state capital, a branch of the Federal Reserve, numerous law and financial firms, a major state university, and a historically significant river, large swaths of the city's downtown remain underused or vacant, with few recognized and widely used spaces or pedestrian attractions.

The substance of Flynn's work has consisted of initiating a process to transform downtown into a more pedestrian-friendly, urbanist environment with expanded public space, dramatically improved public access to the James River, and more green amenities, such as trees. At the heart of Flynn's strategy for downtown is a renewed focus on capitalizing on its urbanist strengths, such as its small blocks and tight grid. This means focusing on storefront commerce, moving parking lots underground, lowering the parking space requirement for new buildings, putting an end to high-speed one-way streets, and in general encouraging pedestrian activity and alternative forms of transportation such as biking and (potentially) streetcars. The boldest part of the plan, however, is a proposal to construct a continuous riverfront park alongside the James River running through the heart of the city, anchored by a large public park to be located on currently vacant (but privately owned) land. Currently public access to the river is limited and uneven, and much of the riverfront area is unattractive; transforming the James River into Richmond's "great, wet Central Park" became one of the plan's catchphrases. Taken as a whole, the downtown plan is a thinly veiled criticism of decades of haphazard development and the city's failure to capitalize on its most outstanding asset, the James River, and an explicit claim that the public can do better by moving aggressively to purchase key properties and build an attractive new waterfront park accessible to all by foot.

Flynn built public support for this approach by providing extensive opportunities for civic participation in the formation of the plan. In summer of 2007, a series of planning charrettes were held, in which citizens were asked about their ideas for downtown and the general outcomes they would like to see the master plan realize. At least eight hundred residents (of roughly 195,000) participated in at least one of these meetings (exceeding Flynn's expectations). These discussions did not begin on a blank slate—Flynn's urbanist principles were used as a takeoff point—but in theory at least, "everything" with respect to land use, development, and streetscapes was on the table. As the plan was drafted, further meetings were held to solicit citizen feedback, and citizens were given the chance to interact directly with planning staff. Over a one-week period, an ongoing open house was held, allowing citizens to see the plans in formation, ask questions of city planning staff and design firm Dover, Kohl and Partners, and provide input. This process was intended both to generate input for the plan and to create a constituency of engaged citizens willing and able to advocate publically on behalf of the plan. This participatory approach, along with Flynn's perceived competence, played a major role in bolstering her credibility and political security and in winning support for the plan from much of the mainstream business and real estate leadership in the city (outside of affected development interests).

But Flynn has not just enlisted citizens in a planning exercise; she has acted self-consciously as a *political* agent in mobilizing support for the plan. Flynn has worked in concert with local smart growth and preservationist organizations to promote the plan and to solicit citizens willing to speak on behalf of the plan before city council and in public forums and also has spent extensive time consulting with experienced political observers and civic leaders in the city, strategizing about how to navigate the plan through the political process and an often developer-friendly city council. Indeed, the danger with the master plan all along has been that its teeth would be cut out at the implementation stage under pressure from developers negatively affected by the proposals. Flynn took steps throughout this process to prepare for a fight, and in 2009, a fight arrived.

The conflict derives from the contradiction between the aspirations of the master plan and a private developer's proposals to build high-rise luxury condos along the James River (the "Echo Harbour" project), permanently impacting the view of the river from atop historic Church Hill, on exactly the parcel of land designated by the city for a riverfront park. The project would simultaneously squash the possibility of an attractive, continuous public riverfront park and impede the view of the James River for which the city is named.[4] Lawyer James Theobald, representing development firm USP Rocketts, sharply criticized the master plan and the process as disrespectful of property rights in a series of public hearings in 2008 and 2009. Immediately after the passage of the plan by the city council in October 2008, council member Bruce Tyler, an architect for one of the firms involved in the Echo Harbour proposal, announced he would seek amendments to the plan in coming months.

Spring and summer 2009 saw a protracted struggle over Tyler's attempts to amend the plan so as to weaken its commitment to a continuous public riverfront park and weaken the standards by which future special use-permit requests will be judged. For instance, in the original plan, the public option for establishing a park is listed first; in the revised plan, a private development option for the property in question is listed first. More important, Tyler favored striking out a provision mandating that all special-use permits be evaluated in terms of the specific character and zoning designation of the land under question. This is significant because the proposed height of the condominium proposal violates existing zoning for riverfront property, and the developers would need a special-use permit (under both current zoning and the new plan) to go forward. Planning commission and city council meetings throughout 2009 featured citizens overwhelmingly speaking out against the condominium proposal, but Theobald and USP Rocketts continued to lobby on behalf of the proposal. Behind the scenes, the firm made extensive efforts to sway planning commission and city council members (almost all council members receive significant campaign funding from development interests). After months of hearings and delays, the revised plan was approved on July 27, 2009; the amendment backed by Tyler to weaken special-use permit language failed by one vote.

What is the public interest in this case? Proponents of the Echo Harbour development have made two kinds of arguments: a property rights–based argument that, in effect, developers and property owners should be allowed to do what they want, and an argument that the development will create jobs and tax revenues and not disrupt public access to the river. Theobald and USP Rocketts have made almost no effort to argue that the condominium plan in fact fits the aspirations of the downtown plan strongly endorsed by citizens and approved by the city council. Those aspirations are for the city to use the James River to reestablish the city's identity and to make public space and public access to the river the heart of that identity. The force of the argument for the public park proposal and against riverfront condominiums is not simply about providing more or better recreational or aesthetic amenities to citizens or about providing a better way to stimulate downtown economic activity (though the downtown plan embraces both those goals as well) but about creating a signature location that people can identify with the city. This in turn is seen to be in the public interest because it would bolster the city's unique identity, give residents a new shared space to be proud of, and reinvigorate pride and interest in Richmond's unique qualities. Further, the long process by which the new master plan was adopted and the civic participation it engendered lends the specifics of the plan credibility as an expression of what the community (more precisely, the civically active part of the community) would like to see happen.

The alternative proposal for the land in question has none of these qualities; it is a proposal, largely unwanted by city residents, to build a fairly generic, high-rise condo and create a space that will be the terrain of high-end residents and consumers, taking much of the best riverfront view and access in the process. Approval of the Echo Harbour proposal would further send a strong signal that no matter what the public says it wants, developers have sufficient influence and political muscle to impose their will on land-use planning. That in turn has very negative implications for the future of democratic politics in Richmond. Advocates for the downtown master plan can thus contend that there is both a smaller-order public interest in this case in seeing the public's aspirations for a large riverside park realized because of the specific public goods that that project is expected to provide and a larger-order public interest in seeing the expressed will of the community and overwhelming views of local residents honored because of the implications that carries for where political power really lies in the city.

In the process of this debate, Flynn has emerged as a lightning-rod figure: a hero to almost all the citizens involved in the process, who view her as a champion for the public good, but an arrogant annoyance to several members of city council. After an April 2009 planning commission meeting in which Flynn flatly refused a commissioner's request to seek an accommodation with Echo Harbour developers about the project, saying it was not her job to compromise what the public wanted and the principles of the plan, at least three council members wrote to the mayor requesting Flynn's termination. Flynn withstood this pressure and continued in her job for the next two years as an advocate for the plan's goals. The future of the proposal to create a true riverfront park remains uncertain, however. City council removed money set aside by the mayor to buy up riverfront properties from both the fiscal 2009–10 and fiscal 2010–11 budgets, meaning Flynn and the city could not act to acquire the properties needed to establish the proposed park. In the meantime, despite losing on the downtown plan amendment language, Theobald and USP Rocketts have not withdrawn the project or abandoned hope of obtaining a special-use permit for it. As of April 2011, the fate of the contested riverfront possibility is still undecided.[5] Flynn herself announced her resignation from city government in March 2011 to take a consulting position in Abu Dhabi.

While this example of public-sector leadership contains significant flaws and a still-uncertain outcome, the downtown plan process represents a breakthrough in contemporary Richmond politics. Flynn's work changed the discourse about downtown development in Richmond and shown that there is fairly wide citizen support for strong public action on behalf of urbanism. The idea that the city should be shaped by the public, not the developers, has been widely embraced. Because of the way citizens have been mobilized and the legitimacy the planning process has commanded, Flynn has been able to take strong stands and directly criticize powerful interests and figures in the city.

Nonetheless, Flynn's efforts were hampered by the relatively weak level of civic organization in Richmond. White, well-educated persons represent the overwhelming majority of persons involved both in the charrette-based public-planning process and in advocacy groups like Partnership for Smarter Growth and the Alliance to Conserve Old Richmond Neighborhoods. This is highly problematic in a city that is majority African-American and has allowed critics like Tyler to claim that the downtown plan process reflected the views of a small group of self-selected people. Although the city government and some activists did reach out to African-American organizations and the plan was endorsed by some important African-American leaders (including new mayor Dwight Jones, who succeeded Wilder in 2009), success in generating extensive African-American participation was limited.[6]

In this regard, the debate over the downtown plan has reenacted a recurrent dilemma for social justice advocates in Richmond: the political mismatch between the task of promoting justice within the metropolitan region as a whole and the task of promoting justice within the city itself. There is good reason to think the downtown plan, if enacted, would draw more people back into living downtown, in turn stimulating commercial development in the currently dilapidated Broad Street corridor. Such resettlement of downtown would strengthen the city's tax base and allow it to capture a greater proportion of regional economic growth. Yet while the plan may benefit the city as a whole, its promised benefits for the least well off in Richmond are either indirect (e.g., possible access to jobs created by increases in commercial activity downtown) or intangible (e.g., the benefit of living in a more pedestrian-friendly city). From the perspective of the least well off, the downtown plan looks like just another effort to make life more comfortable for middle-class urban dwellers.

Likewise, the relative success of the downtown planning process has depended precisely on the fact that it has been perceived simultaneously as progressive and nonthreatening. As noted, most mainstream business groups in the city have been broadly supportive, as have those developers who stand to benefit from opportunities to build higher-density, mixed-use developments within the downtown study area. But it is much more difficult to imagine an initiative in the Richmond metropolitan area aimed at directly benefitting "the least well off"—that is, directly attacking poverty in the city via a substantial outlay of public resources—gaining such widespread support. Indeed, Richmond's metropolitan structure makes such an initiative extremely difficult, since it would involve making a claim on resources controlled by politically distinct suburban counties.

This case thus illustrates both the possibilities and limitations of "New Public Service"–type public leadership in helping to reinvigorate the public sector. Succinctly put, leadership that seeks to engage citizens and calls attention to positive possibilities for significantly improving the city can, in fact, call into being civic forces that were previously dormant and draw new people into the policy-making process. When combined with shrewd and, at times, forceful political judgment, activist public leaders can also shepherd proposals to change the way the city is developed through the political process, compromising on some details but not the essentials. But public leadership alone cannot overcome inherent structural flaws in the metropolis. In the Richmond case specifically, despite efforts to engage the African-American population (which led to the inclusion of affordable housing language in the final plan) and support from several key African-America leaders, grassroots participation in the debate about the downtown plan remained disproportionately white and middle class. While the process Flynn initiated was not inherently exclusionary, it did not do nearly enough to overcome or alter long-standing inequalities of political participation and voice in the city.

The second limitation refers to the fact that Richmond's metropolitan governance structure—or lack thereof—means that, at present, challenging fundamental structural inequalities is simply off the political table. There is no plausible way by which another Rachel Flynn could initiate a process intended to fundamentally rectify inequalities of public education in the metropolis, since each school district is separate and suburban residents have no interest in such reform (Ryan 2010). What city officials can and cannot do is thus shaped by the structure of metropolitan governance already in place—hence, the importance for metropolitan social justice to establish both (a) an account of what a just metropolitan constitution for American's urban areas would look like and (b) a more-than-wishful-thinking account of how sharply divided metropolises might meaningfully move in that direction in the future.

Importantly, this does not mean that city officials in Richmond or elsewhere have no capacity to attempt to improve the city's position and promote the shared interests of its citizens. Flynn found an opportunity to do so in the fact that a major, unique natural resource of the city (the James River) has yet to be fully tapped as a signature attraction and central community location for the city, and there is reason to believe that if the vision of the plan were fully realized, then the city would reap multiple benefits and be in a stronger position relative to its suburban neighbors. Moreover, and central to our concern here, it would help rehabilitate the idea that the public sector can act successfully on behalf of public aims. But while the public aims involved in the downtown master plan are significant and worth fighting to achieve, they simply do not address the fundamental structural inequalities characterizing the Richmond metropolitan area.

Conclusion

This assessment naturally raises a question: what would the politics capable of addressing such fundamental inequalities and injustices look like in a place like Richmond, especially given the area's very unfavorable metropolitan political structure? One prerequisite of such a politics, and the focus of this chapter, is public support for using public power to constrain private actors and regulate market processes in order to achieve substantive public goals. This idea is fundamental to almost all attractive conceptions of social justice, and it is an idea that has been under attack in the United States at all levels of government in recent decades. Despite its inherent limitations, the effort to create a new downtown master plan in Richmond has had significant success in beginning to rehabilitate that basic idea. Indeed, perhaps the most promising aspect of the downtown master-plan debate in Richmond is that Flynn's core assertion—that the public should have the first claim on the best and most valuable undeveloped land in the city—found significant resonance in a city that has traditionally been deferential to private developers.

But reestablishing the legitimacy of meaningful public sector action is not enough if larger-order social justice issues are to be tackled. The next step in Richmond must involve the forging of the kind of coalition that was almost completely absent in the struggle over the downtown plan: a genuinely multiracial coalition committed to establishing not just public space and other public goods but also more direct steps to address poverty and improve the position of the "least well off." It is possible that one or more local public officials might play a catalytic role in helping mobilize low-income residents in the city in a more direct fashion and help forge a coalition between middle-class and low-income residents on behalf of a concrete goal. The most promising candidate issue in this respect is dramatically improving public transportation in the city, an issue that directly affects low-income residents in the city and is a goal supported by almost all the advocates who mobilized on behalf of the downtown master plan. Improving public transportation is also a regional issue (transit to Richmond's suburbs is generally limited, meaning many jobs are out of reach of carless Richmond residents). A strong, cross-class, multiracial coalition of Richmonders and supportive suburban residents could potentially challenge the regional status quo and begin correcting one very significant social injustice (unequal access to employment).

Regardless of whether creative public-sector leadership in support of that goal is forthcoming, the burden of building a truly multiracial coalition on behalf of social justice must rest with civic and grassroots activists committed to creating and sustaining long-term solidarity across difference. At particular historical moments, public-sector leaders can play a critical role in framing issues and mobilizing constituents to address key problems, but they cannot create powerful, cross-cutting social movements out of whole cloth. That job falls to citizens.

Notes

Discussions with Planning Commission member Amy Howard, John Moeser (Virginia Commonwealth University professor of urban planning emeritus), and numerous citizen participants in the process have helped inform this chapter. Informal conversations with Rachel Flynn in 2008 and 2009 and an extensive formal interview with Flynn in June 2010 have provided additional insight into the process. The author has also attended or participated in several public hearings related to the downtown plan.

1 With the advent of the Obama administration, some Progressives such as Peter Dreier believe that attention should shift to national-level policy (Dreier 2009). While better national policies would have many positive ramifications for cities, to date there is little evidence that the large-scale stimulus programs or any of the other initiatives of the Obama administration has or will materially change public attitudes toward the state and the legitimacy of public action. While it remains possible that a large-scale, federal domestic project, successfully implemented, might have that effect, continued attention to local and metropolitan structures of democratic practice remains essential—independent of the future direction of federal policy.

2 Rawls's views on the extent to which a just society should provide public goods that do not provide direct benefits to all citizens evolved over time; whereas in *A Theory of Justice* he takes a strong position that it is not just to tax some to provide cultural goods (e.g., museums) they may not themselves enjoy, in subsequent writing he backs off that position and accepts the legitimacy of governments providing a range of goods intended to bolster local quality of life and distinctive character. See Freeman (2007, 392–98) for an instructive account on this point.

3 This example—quite deliberately—points to a much larger difficulty beyond the scope of this chapter that needs to be fully resolved: the unhappy fact that the further society is marked by invidious degrees of inequality and unjust social relations, the more likely it is that political processes in their normal operations will tend to reinforce such inequalities. There is no easy remedy for this problem, and it is not one that thinkers like Rawls, who devoted most of his attention to ideal theory as opposed to examining possibilities for advancing justice in the politics of actually existing capitalist societies, provide much guidance for. The hope of deliberative theorists is that well-structured deliberative processes can at least minimize

political inequalities between citizens and permit the possibility of the political process being used to narrow inequalities. This idea remains more hope than reality (but see Fung [2004] for some instructive exceptions), and greater attention to this question by democratic theorists and others is an urgent imperative.

4 William Byrd II named the city "Richmond" in 1737 because the view of the James River from atop Church Hill closely resembled the view of the River Thames from Richmond Hill outside London; the location today is considered a historical site and is a prime attraction for visitors to the city.

5 In August 2010, Mayor Dwight Jones announced plans to commission a new $500,000 study of how to "improve and expand access along the downtown riverfront," inclusive of the land involved in the Echo Harbour controversy (Jones 2010).

6 Notably, in June 2010, the charrette technique was again used in Richmond to launch a significant planning effort, this time regarding the revitalization of the area around the Bon Secours Richmond Community Hospital in the city's overwhelmingly poor and African-American East End. These charrettes, cosponsored by Bon Secours, the city, and the Richmond Redevelopment and Housing Authority, were well attended by African-Americans and heavily publicized in the local African-American media.

References

Biegelesen, Amy. 2007a. "Master Plan Sessions Confront Race, Push Details." *Style Weekly*, August 12.

———. 2007b. "Master Planners Return to Dispel "Sea of Whiteness."'" *Style Weekly*, September 19.

———. 2008. "In Like Flynn." *Style Weekly*, January 16.

———. 2008. "Master Panned." *Style Weekly*, October 28.

———. 2009. "Flynn's Last Stand?" *Style Weekly*, May 7.

Box, Richard C. 2004. *Critical Social Theory in Public Administration*. Armonk, N.Y.: M. E. Sharpe.

Bozeman, Barry. 2007. *Public Values and Public Interest: Counterbalancing Economic Individualism*. Washington, D.C.: Georgetown University Press.

Church Hill People's News. n.d. http://www.chpn.net.

Cohen, Joshua. 2002. "For a Democratic Society." In *The Cambridge Companion to Rawls*, ed. Samuel Freeman. Cambridge: Cambridge University Press.

Corcoran, Rob. 2010. *Trustbuilding: An Honest Conversation on Race, Reconciliation, and Responsibility*. Charlottesville: University of Virginia Press.

Denhardt, Janet V., and Robert B. Denhardt. 2003. *The New Public Service: Serving, Not Steering*. Armonk, N.Y.: M. E. Sharpe.

Doherty, Kathryn M., and Clarence N. Stone. 1999. "Local Practice in Transition: From Government to Governance." In *Dilemmas of Scale in America's Federal Democracy*, ed. Martha Derthick. Cambridge: Cambridge University Press.

Dreier, Peter. 2009. "There Is No Urban Crisis: Progressive Politics and Urban Policy in the Obama Era." Paper presented at "Justice and the American Metropolis" conference, St. Louis, Mo., May 9. 2009.

Dworkin, Ronald. 2000. *Sovereign Virtue: The Theory and Practice of Equality.* Cambridge: Cambridge University Press.

Elkin, Stephen L. 1999. "Citizen and City: Locality, Public-Spiritedness, and the American Regime." In *Dilemmas of Scale in America's Federal Democracy,* ed. Martha Derthick. Cambridge: Cambridge University Press.

———. 2006. *Reconstructing the Commercial Republic: Constitutional Theory after Madison.* Chicago: University of Chicago Press.

Freeman, Samuel. 2007. *Rawls.* New York: Routledge.

Fung, Archon. 2004. *Empowered Participation: Reinventing Urban Democracy.* Princeton, N.J.: Princeton University Press.

Gaebler, Ted, and David Osborne. 1992. *Reinventing Government: How the Entrepreneurial Spirit Is Transforming the Public Sector.* Reading, Mass.: Addison-Wesley.

Habermas, Jürgen. 1984. *The Theory of Communicative Action.* Vols. 1 and 2. Trans. Thomas McCarthy. Boston: Beacon Press.

Holland, Dorothy, Catherine Lutz, Donald Nonini, Lesley Bartlett, Marla Frederick-McGlathery, Thaddeus Gulbrandsen, and Enrique Murillo Jr. 2007. *Local Democracy under Siege: Activism, Public Interests, and Private Politics.* New York: New York University Press.

Jones, Will. 2010. "Study to Explore Expanding Access to Richmond's Riverfront." *Richmond Times-Dispatch,* August 15.

Logan, John, and Harvey Molotch. 1987. *Urban Fortunes: The Political Economy of Place.* Berkeley: University of California Press.

Luke, Jeffrey. 1998. *Catalytic Leadership.* San Francisco: Josey-Bass.

Mitchell, Donald. 2003. *The Right to the City: Social Justice and the Fight for Public Space.* New York: Guilford Press.

Morgan, David R., Robert E. England, and John P. Pelissero. 2006. *Managing Urban America.* 6th ed. Washington, D.C.: CQ Press.

Rawls, John. 1971. *A Theory of Justice.* Cambridge, Mass.: Harvard University Press.

Richmond, Virginia. 2008. Richmond Downtown Plan. *Official Richmond Web site,* October. http://www.ci.richmond.va.us/forms/DowntownPlan.aspx.

Ryan, James. 2010. *Five Miles Away, A World Apart: One City, Two Schools, and the Story of Educational Opportunity in Modern America.* New York: Oxford University Press.

Sarvay, John. n.d. *Buttermilk & Molasses.* http://floricane.typepad.com/buttermilk/richmonds_downtown_plan/index.html.

Schwartz, Joseph. 2008. *The Future of Democratic Equality: Rebuilding Social Solidarity in a Fragmented America.* New York: Routledge.

Silver, Christopher. 1984. *Twentieth Century Richmond: Politics, Planning, and Race.* Knoxville: University of Tennessee Press.

Williamson, Thad. 2009. "Echo Chamber." *Style Weekly,* April 28.

Young, Iris Marion. 1990. *Justice and the Politics of Difference.* Princeton, N.J.: Princeton University Press.

IV

JUSTICE AND INSTITUTIONS

VOTING

AND JUSTICE

ELECTED CITY OFFICIALS MAKE DECISIONS that affect the lives of both city residents and outsiders. Local public schools have an impact on the communities in which graduates live wherever they are. City zoning policies influence not only the nature of city life but also that of neighboring communities. City police do not simply arrest local residents; sometimes, they patrol looking for outsiders. On these and many other policy issues, however, when local elected officials look to the general population for guidance, they tend to care principally about the views held by the people eligible to vote for them. It is not surprising that city officials answerable only to local voters do not pay much attention to the views of those who live in a neighboring jurisdiction. It is equally unsurprising that city officials care more about the voting population than they do about the views of city residents who are ineligible to vote. The reason for this focus on local voters' opinions need not be attributed to the reductionist idea that all city officials care about is their own reelection. It is, after all, a principle of democracy that elected officials are supposed to care about the interests of the people who elect them even if they are not running for reelection.

Determining who is eligible to vote for local elected officials is, therefore, a key component of the organization of local decision making. It is also a key example of what Hayward and Swanstrom call, in their introduction to this volume, "thick injustice." Exclusions from the franchise operate far below the surface of American politics, and they tend to be hidden or obscure. Chances are most people in the United States think that America long ago embraced universal suffrage. With African-Americans, women, and young adults over eighteen now added to the electorate, it seems reasonable to treat the decisions made by popularly elected local officials as representative of what local residents want. And it seems equally reasonable to treat the decisions made by neighboring localities as legitimate, notwithstanding their impact on outsiders. After all, voters in other cities should have the right to control their officials, too. Besides, popularly elected state governments are empowered to correct interlocal abuses if there are any.

In this chapter, I argue that this rosy picture of electoral legitimacy is inaccurate. I do so by focusing on the thick injustice that remains part of the legal structure that defines the local electorate. Not every adult resident is eligible to vote in the United States. Moreover, the definition of residency is itself problematic. Indeed, as we shall see, sometimes nonresidents are allowed to vote—but sometimes they are not. The justification for my focus on voter eligibility is straightforward. If the rules that determine the local electorate were changed, then a very different group of people would be able to influence the decisions that local officials make about matters such as education, zoning, and police behavior. Changing these rules thus has the potential to alter the relationship between city policy and social justice.

Before we turn to the legal definition of the local electorate, two preliminary points are worth noting. The first is that many local decisions are not made by locally elected officials. Most importantly, city policy is significantly determined by state law. As David Barron and I have described at length, the state government directly controls major local issues. State law also specifies the kinds of issues that cities are empowered to deal with on their own. Even on those matters delegated to the local government, the state routinely overrules contrary local decision making (Frug and Barron 2008). And the role of elected state officials is only the beginning of the list of those entitled to make important local decisions. State-created public authorities are another significant local decision maker. Decisions about mass transit, roads, water distribution, and energy policy, like dozens of other issues, are often in the hands not of elected city or state governments but of officials appointed by the governor, frequently with little or no city input. Once empowered, these public authorities—such as the Massachusetts Turnpike Authority or the Port Authority of New York and New Jersey—can have a decisive influence on the development policy of a city, such as the "Big Dig" in Boston and the rebuilding of the World Trade Center site in New York. Finally, the private sector plays a critical role in local policy making. I refer here not simply to the fact that private investment decisions are a key influence on city development policy. Substantial portions of city territory are controlled by private organizations—by homeowners associations, office parks, and malls. The rules that govern these parts of town are primarily (although not entirely) established by these private organizations. Moreover, in many cities public streets are patrolled by employees of business improvement districts—organizations created to deal with issues such as safety, sanitation, and street life. Under state law, the leadership of these organizations is normally elected by local property owners, not by local residents generally. (There are more than one hundred business-improvement districts in New York City alone.) My focus on voting rules for elected city officials thus deals with only a fraction of the decisions that affect a city's future. The size of this fraction varies from city to city. But everywhere it is important enough to be a subject of interest simply by itself.

The second introductory point concerns the relationship between this chapter and the important literature on what is called, following Robert Dahl, the *principle of affected interests* (Goodin 2007; Dahl 1989; Dahl 1970). The literature grapples with a central puzzle of democratic theory: how does one determine who should be entitled to participate in a democratic decision-making process? The principle of affected interests addresses this question by exploring the virtues of, and difficulties with establishing, a particular test for the franchise: those who are affected by a government's decisions are entitled to vote for its officials. One problem with implementing such a standard is that countless outsiders—sometimes the whole world—are affected by decisions that they have no role in influencing. (Much of the world, for example, is affected by American foreign policy.) Another problem is the standard's apparent circularity: who decides who is affected by a government policy? A democratic electorate composed of people who are affected cannot decide this question: determining who is affected is a preliminary issue that constitutes the group, and that question needs to be decided by another democratic process.

In this chapter, I advocate adding to the franchise categories of people—noncitizens, felons, part-time residents, and residents of neighboring jurisdictions within the same metropolitan area—who are affected by city decision making. To this extent, I embrace the goals associated with the principle of affected interests. At the same time, however, my focus on city decision making is not simply an application of it. For cities, there is no circularity problem. In the United States, local self-government is not a matter of community self-definition. Although there are exceptions, decisions about voting eligibility are made not by the localities themselves but by state law. (As we shall see, the occasional claims that the kind of voting restrictions discussed in this chapter violate federal constitutional law are usually rejected.) The definition of the local political community is thus in the hands of outsiders, not just insiders. Moreover, when a state defines the local electorate, it is not simply deciding who is affected by city policies. Defining the local franchise is a way of making urban policy. By including some of the people affected by a city's decisions while (inevitably) excluding others, state law determines what a city is and whose interests it represents. In judging the present qualifications for—and any proposed changes in—the local franchise, the critical issue, then, is not whether everyone affected will be included (they will not be) but whether the role of the city, as distinguished from the other locations for democratic decision making at the state and national level, is properly being defined.

Voting by Residents

Noncitizens

Voting in city elections in the United States is almost everywhere limited to city residents. But not all adult city residents qualify. One important group that is excluded from the electorate are those who are not citizens of the United States. This population in major American cities is significant. According to the 2000 census, the four most populous cities in the United States all have a large population of adult noncitizens. New York's adult noncitizen population is 22.9 percent, Chicago's 16.4 percent, Los Angeles' 32.2 percent, and Houston's 22.9 percent. Other major cities are similar: Phoenix (17.5 percent), San Diego (16.6 percent), Dallas (22.3 percent), San Francisco (16.7 percent), and San Jose (24.9 percent) are illustrative. In California, 85 cities have a population consisting of at least 25 percent noncitizens, and in 12 (small) California cities, the noncitizen adult population constitutes the majority of local residents (Hayduk 2006; Avila 2003).

The idea of enfranchising adult noncitizens is not new. In the United States, many cities permitted noncitizen voting in the nineteenth century (Hayduk 2006; Raskin 1993; Neuman 1991–92). Even now, there are a few isolated places where noncitizens can vote (most importantly, perhaps, for Chicago's local school councils; Hayduk 2006; Harper-Ho 2000). Other cities—including New York City and Cambridge, Massachusetts—have considered proposals to permit adult noncitizens to vote in local elections. Nevertheless, most of current examples of adult noncitizen voting are found outside the United States. Almost forty countries allow noncitizens to vote in some elections, most of them on a local basis.[1] The most important example is the European Union. Article 19 of the Treaty of the European Union (Treaty of the European Union 1997) provides that "every citizen of the Union residing in a Member State of which he is not a national shall have the right to vote and to stand as a candidate at the municipal elections in the Member State in which he resides, under the same conditions as the nationals of that State." To be sure, there are qualifications. The member states can restrict membership in municipal executive bodies to their nationals; they can have special rules for referenda; and they can apply duration-of-residency requirements when the nonnational population exceeds 20 percent of eligible voters.[2]

Even more important, this provision only applies to nonnationals from other European Union countries. It excludes, in other words, the large number of local residents from the rest of Europe, Asia, and Africa. This exclusion has been the subject of intense debate in Europe for decades. Gerald Neuman has examined the debate in Germany where, unlike the United States, rules governing the naturalization process traditionally rendered generations of children of foreign guest workers permanent aliens even if they were born in Germany (Neuman 1991–92). (In 2000, the law was changed to allow naturalization for those who have resided in Germany for eight years and met other qualifications.) That these resident aliens are ineligible to vote is not just a political decision. In 1990, the German Federal Constitutional Court held unconstitutional the efforts of the German states of Schleswig-Holstein and Hamburg to include noncitizens in the vote for local elections. Other countries have been more receptive. Sweden, for example, has permitted all foreign nationals to vote and run for office in local elections since 1975 (Neuman 1991–92).

Notwithstanding these complexities, suffice it to say that many European countries have at least accepted some aspects of the idea of alien suffrage. It could be extended even there. More important for our purposes, it could be adopted in the United States in a way that's appropriate for American cities. No doubt, efforts to do so would be controversial. Those who favor the idea emphasize notions of social justice—arguing that those subject to the laws of the locality should have a voice in selecting the people who make them. Often, the slogan "no taxation without representation" is used in this regard. (We shall return to this slogan shortly.) Opponents worry about devaluing the naturalization process and about the lack of knowledge that noncitizens might have about the United States and its history. There is also a dispute about whether noncitizens would actually vote if given the chance. Even if the idea were adopted in the United States, lots of details would have to be worked out. Since the United States is not a member of an organization analogous to the European Union, opening the franchise to noncitizens would potentially include a much larger range of people. Decisions would need to be made about duration-of-residence requirements and the appropriate entitlements of undocumented aliens. At the moment, the important point is simple: the debate over noncitizen voting is one ingredient in determining the relationship between voting and justice.

Felons

More than five million people in the United States are disenfranchised because they are felons. What this means varies from state to state. In twelve states, depending on the crime and when it was committed, those who have been convicted of a felony are disenfranchised for life. In eighteen states, the franchise is restored when the period of parole or probation ends; in five states, it is restored after parole ends (even if the felon is still on probation); in thirteen states, it is restored upon release from prison. In two states (Maine and Vermont), felons may vote from prison. And felons are not the only people disenfranchised after committing crimes. Five states—Colorado, Illinois, Michigan, South Carolina, and Maryland—disenfranchise people convicted of some misdemeanors.[3]

The Supreme Court has made clear that the United States Constitution does not prohibit barring felons from the vote.[4] Litigation therefore has focused on a narrower issue: whether the Voting Rights Act, which prohibits voting practices that result in the denial of the vote on account of race, restricts the disenfranchisement of felons. This approach has resulted in a number of split decisions in the lower federal courts, but felon disenfranchisement has been upheld against this attack as well. Even though the legal challenges in the United States against felon disenfranchisement have so far failed, the controversy over the wisdom of the policy has continued. In 2001, the National Commission on Federal Election

Reform, cochaired by Jimmy Carter and Gerald Ford, recommended the enfranchisement of felons who have completed their sentence (including parole and probation; Keeney 2008).

Again, international experience is different. Permanent felon disenfranchisement is rare around the world, and some countries—Denmark, Israel, Spain, and Switzerland, for example—allow felons to vote from prison.[5] The legal challenge against felon disenfranchisement has also produced different results elsewhere. Courts in Canada, South Africa, and Australia have held aspects of felon disenfranchisement unconstitutional (Keeney 2008).[6] Perhaps the most significant opinion was rendered by the European Court of Human Rights. In 2005, the court ruled that the United Kingdom's disenfranchisement of all incarcerated prisoners violated the provision of the European Convention on Human Rights that ensured people's free choice of their legislature (Keeney 2008).[7]

Unlike noncitizen voting, most of the debate on felon disenfranchisement has focused on the state and even the national level rather than the local level. In the United States, the size of the problem is significant in many states—particularly in Florida, which houses the largest prison population in the nation. (This is usually mentioned in the context of the 2000 Presidential election.)[8] Denying felons the vote also has significant national implications. As Paul Street puts it, "21st century America's very disproportionately black and urban prisoners count toward the political apportionment (representation) accorded to predominantly white and rural communities that tend to host prisons in, say, 'downstate' Illinois or 'upstate' New York" (2003, 4). Disenfranchised, imprisoned minorities, in other words, count in giving white, rural voters more power over state and national issues (and, therefore, over the criminal laws that imprison them in the first place).

As Street argues, felon disenfranchisement is a local issue as well. Local prisoners are valuable commodities—they contribute to the economic development of the places where they are incarcerated not only in terms of calculating population for development grants but also in terms of organizing the local economy. "Visitors to such a very visibly white downstate town as Ina, Illinois (home of the Big Muddy Correctional Center)," Street writes, "would be surprised to learn from the Census Bureau that that community is 42 percent African-American and 90 percent male" (Street 2003, 5). If one focuses on those on parole and probation, then the local impact is even clearer. Like noncitizens, felons released from prison spend their lives in a city but can be disregarded by the elected officials whose decisions affect them as much as their neighbors.

As with noncitizen voting, the extension of the franchise to felons is controversial. Advocates emphasize the fundamental nature of the vote, the disproportionate impact of felon disenfranchisement on racial minorities, particularly African-Americans, and the fact that, on release, felons are generally (and should be) treated as having paid their debt to society. Opponents emphasize the disqualifying nature of having committed a crime and the importance of maintaining minimum standards for the franchise. (Some commentators note, more skeptically, that felons are unlikely to vote Republican; Robbers 2008; Street 2003.)

Defining Residents

Although voting is generally limited to residents (other than those just mentioned), there remains the issue of defining residence. One group of people that have trouble qualifying are the homeless. There are somewhere between two and three million homeless people in the United States today, two-thirds of them adults.[9] Not long ago, it was not uncommon to have a requirement that residents live in a "traditional dwelling" to be eligible to vote, a requirement that on its face barred the homeless from voting. A number of courts, however, have held that such a requirement imposes an unconstitutional infringement on the right to vote.[10] The National Voter Registration Act of 1993 also makes clear that the lack of a traditional dwelling cannot be the basis for denying the right to vote.

Still, despite the extent of their formal legal protection, the homeless face considerable difficulties in exercising their right to vote. Mailing address requirements are common; the mobility of the homeless make it difficult for them to meet registration deadlines; and identification documents (birth certificates, drivers licenses) are particularly hard for the homeless to get (Ozdeger and Baltimore 2006). Activists have sought to enhance homeless voting not just with registration drives and education programs but also with specific suggestions about how to help the homeless overcome these obstacles. Proposals include allowing the homeless to establish a nonresidential mailing address, enabling them to register as living in a park or on a street, and facilitating their ability to satisfy identification requirements. The National Coalition for the Homeless has proposed a Model State Homeless Voter Registration Act, which has been adopted in some states, designed to further goals like these. Notwithstanding these efforts—and despite the formal legal protection—the homeless voting level is low in most jurisdictions (Ozdeger and Baltimore 2006; Miller and Gonzales 2002).[11] And it is not just the homeless whose lack of a permanent home presents obstacles for some people to exercise their right to vote. A recent case denied the claim of illegal disenfranchisement brought by people who lived in recreational vehicles. The court upheld the local decision that the commercial mailboxes used for the required mailing address were inadequate.[12]

Others face even greater obstacles. A number of people, for example, live in town a portion of the year and yet are denied the ability to vote in local elections. One might think that this exclusion is reasonable on the grounds that actual presence in the jurisdiction for an extended period of time is a proper qualification for voting. But actual presence is not part of the legal requirement for voter qualification. Someone serving in the military or engaged in business or missionary activity outside of the country is a resident of the American municipality where they once lived even if he or she has not been in the city for years. The legal standard for voting is not residence if by that term one means physical presence in the city. The legal standard is based on the term "domicile." An individual's domicile is the place where he has a "fixed, permanent, and principal home to which, even with extended periods of living elsewhere . . . he intends to return."[13] One can be a domiciliary of only one place—the one that he claims as his permanent home. Moreover, although an individual can have residences in multiple locations, he can vote only in the local election where he is domiciled. Once domicile is established, the individual can leave town virtually forever and still vote in local elections.

The fact that voting rights are based on domicile enables people with no recent knowledge of the city to vote in local elections and prevents part-time residents who are domiciled elsewhere from voting. A leading New York case, *Wit v. Berman*, illustrates the problem.[14] Harold Wit and Donald Ebel both had a home in New York City for over forty years, and they each spent much of the year there. But they also lived in East Hampton and South Hampton, respectively, and that was where they were registered to vote. Denied the ability to vote in New York City elections as well, they sued, arguing that the denial was an unconstitutional infringement of their right to vote. The Second Circuit Court of Appeals rejected their claim. Domicile, the court reasoned, provides a workable standard for deciding whom to allow to register, whereas an effort to allow everyone who claims an interest in a local election to vote would be administratively unmanageable (how much of an interest would be enough?). Under New York law, the court said, the plaintiffs are entitled to choose which city to vote in. They can decide to be domiciled in either place. Requiring them to make this choice did not "in any sensible use of the word 'discriminate'"[15] against them.

It is important to recognize that the *Wit* decision did not decide whether people like Harold Wit and Donald Ebel should be allowed to vote in both local elections. All it decided was that it was not unconstitutional for the state to limit them to one local election. There is nothing to suggest that, if a state decided to allow them to vote in both elections, there would be any legal problem with its doing so. Indeed, people like Harold Wit and Donald Ebel have been enfranchised in just this way. A leading case is *May v. Town of Mountain Village*.[16] Mountain Village is a resort community. In a referendum, local residents voted to allow owners of summer homes, resident only part of the year, to vote in local elections. The Tenth Circuit Court of Appeals upheld that decision, rejecting the claim that, by doing so, the vote of full-time residents would be unconstitutionally diluted.

Thus both excluding part-time residents and including them are constitutionally permitted. The court in *Wit* recognized that the current domicile-focused rule is hard to defend:

> Particularly in modern times, domicile is very often a poor proxy for a voter's stake in electoral outcomes because many of an individual voter's varied interests are affected in elections in which they do not vote. Some, or even many, voters may reasonably perceive that their primary concerns are affected more by outcomes in elections in which they do not vote than by outcomes in elections in which they do vote. There are endless examples of the bad fit between domicile and a voter's interest in electoral outcomes. For example, a person who works in a factory, or owns one, located in a municipality other than where the person lives, has interests in that municipality's tax, traffic, law enforcement and other policies.[17]

The court held, however, that it would be administratively impossible to determine which of these kinds of interests should qualify people for the vote. (We shall return to this question later.)

If it *were* administratively feasible to include part-time residents in the vote, would it be the right thing to do? One might be tempted to say that it would not be if one focused solely on Harold Wit, Donald Ebel, or the owners of vacation homes in Mountain Village. After all, one of their principal claims is that they owned houses in both localities, and it was this connection that they emphasized as entitling them to vote. This kind of emphasis is often phrased in terms of the slogan "no taxation without representation." Such a focus tends to lead to the idea that property owners should be entitled to vote in more than one local election, but that nonproperty owners should not be. Yet even the "taxation without representation" slogan does not necessitate this distinction. After all, people who work in the factory that the *Wit* court imagined might pay local income or sales taxes whether or not they own property in the locality.

Still, the idea of linking voting and taxes might seem troubling. But part-time resident voting need not be so limited. After all, farm workers who work during harvest season often live part of the year in a locality. They do not own property, but they might be included in the concept of a nonresident voting population. (There was a brief filed in the *Wit* case by farm workers supporting the demand for a local vote.) The same can be said about domestic workers who "live in" part of the week and go "home" on the weekends. As the *Wit* court suggests, however, once one begins to include these examples, those who work in town but live elsewhere easily spring to mind. The argument for part-time residents' eligibility to vote thus fades into the issue of nonresident voting, the topic I discuss next.

Before I do, it is worth noting the extent of current support for voting based on property ownership rather than on residency. One might have thought the idea of limiting the franchise to property owners was decisively rejected in the United States in the nineteenth century. Not so. To see why, one might begin with the familiar notion that so-called shareholder democracy is organized on a one dollar–one vote, not a one person–one vote, basis. From there, it may not seem such a stretch to apply the same voting rule to homeowners' associations, another private property form. And so it is: owners, not residents, vote in homeowners' associations, with voting power usually allocated according to assessed value. Add to this the organization of elected public authorities—some of them, too, are organized in the same way: property owners, not residents, vote. This allocation of the franchise for public authorities has been upheld by the United States Supreme Court. The same property-based franchise has been upheld as well by a lower federal court for business improvement districts.[18]

But that is not all. One commentator wants to extend the business-improvement-district model to residential areas in major cities—again, allowing a supermajority of owners rather than residents to control decision making, with the votes allocated according to assessed value (Ellickson 1998).[19] Others want it to go further, arguing that development decisions should be made not by a city in an eminent domain process but by "land assembly districts"—neighborhood organizations organized in terms of property ownership, not on a one person–one vote basis (Heller and Hills 2008). To be sure, these extensions of a property-based franchise are just proposals. Yet even the current forms of property-owner voting raise troubling questions of the relationship between voting and justice. The basic idea of a property-owner franchise—that those who pay taxes should control public policy—is derived from the familiar idea of the market: those who pay should call the tune. The organization of politics, by contrast, is based on notions of equality, not on the ability to pay. Democracy is allocated on a basis of one person–one vote, regardless of wealth. This point is so obvious that it would not be worth making were it not for the examples of existing property-based voting (and proposals for more) just outlined.

Nonresident Voting

The most radical way to expand the franchise is to embrace nonresident voting in local elections without restricting the entitlement to part-time residents. Allowing people who work in a city to vote would be an easy place to start. After all, employees can spend more of the day in a city than those who sleep there at night and work elsewhere. Much of what the city does—police, sanitation, infrastructure maintenance, transportation policy, and the like—affects these employees, as well as residents. Defining the category of those who are employed in a city seems no more daunting than defining residence.

I know of no place that has added local workers to the franchise. But an interesting variant of the idea—one with instructive differences from a proposal to enfranchise workers—informs the current organization of London's most famous local government, the one square mile of the city's financial center known as the "City of London." The franchise of the City of London is based on the fact that "the City is the only area of the country in which the number of workers significantly outnumbers the residents and therefore, to be truly representative of its population, offers a vote to City organizations so they can have their say on the way the City is run."[20] It is not the workers themselves but the organizations for which they work that the City of London enfranchises. To be sure, a sole proprietor or individual partner in an equity firm is entitled to cast his or her own vote. But most of the votes are allocated to organizations, both incorporated and unincorporated. The organizations are given a number of votes that correspond to the size of their workforce: for example, 1 vote for an organization with 9 employees or fewer, 5 votes for one with 25 employees, 19 votes for one with 500 employees, and 79 votes for one with 3,500 employees. While the actual ballots are cast by those who work in the city, the scheme makes clear that it is the organization's decision, not the individual's, that determines how to vote. The City of London's enfranchisement of local businesses is thus a variant of the property-owner vote, as well as a variant of a worker franchise. Although those with businesses in the city might be tenants, not owners of property, it is their presence as businesses that give them the right to vote.

One way to extend the idea of nonresident voting beyond workers would be to come up with additional categories of people who would be entitled to the franchise. The problem with expanding the list in this way is that it is hard to distinguish among the wide variety of groups interested in city decision making. As Justice Rehnquist observed in an important voting-rights case, many others, in addition to workers and part-time residents, have an interest in the outcome of city elections: "A city's decisions inescapably affect individuals living immediately outside its borders. The granting of building permits for high-rise apartments, industrial plants, and the like on the city's fringe unavoidably contributes to problems of traffic congestion, school districting, and law enforcement immediately outside the city. A rate change in the city's sales or ad valorem taxes could well have a significant impact on retailers and property values in areas bordering the city. The condemnation of real property on the city's edge for construction of a municipal garbage dump or waste treatment plant would have obvious implications for neighboring nonresidents."[21] "Yet," Justice Rehnquist went on, "no one would suggest that nonresidents likely to be affected by this sort of municipal action have a constitutional right to participate in the political processes bringing it about." His opinion for the Court thus upheld the constitutionality of limiting the franchise to residents even in a case that involved the rights of people who lived on the outskirts of the city and were subject to extensive city regulation through the city's state-authorized extraterritorial jurisdiction.

In 1993, I proposed a version of nonresident voting that abandoned the attempt to determine the legitimate and illegitimate types of nonresident interest in local elections (Frug 1993). Instead, I proposed allowing the voters themselves to decide whether their interest in the result was sufficient to lead them to vote in a local election. Under the proposal, everyone would get five votes that they could cast in any local election, with the localities being defined by traditional city boundaries. My proposal limited the eligible local elections, however, to those in the metropolitan area in which the voter lived. The justification for this limit was based on my view of urban policy: the lack of metropolitan governance structure is a major problem for virtually every major city in the United States. Enabling voters to influence policy in neighboring cities—and limiting their additional votes solely to neighboring city elections—is a way of changing the parochial definition of self-interest that now undermines regional decision making. People would be unlikely to vote in an election they did not care about. But there would be a wide variety of reasons for their vote (increasing the amount of affordable housing available, a demand for gentrification, improving crime control near a workplace, the creation of open space, etc.). It is hard to say precisely what would happen in such a voting system. But it seems likely that the property taxes generated by shopping malls and office parks would be allocated more broadly than simply to those who live in the city where they are located. Indeed, the allocation of all tax revenue—and city policies more generally—are likely to focus more on the needs of the metropolitan area than on a single locality. Above all, such an electoral scheme would radically change the idea of what a city is—and of who is included in a reference to such a locality. The "self" in the phrase local self-interest would become a gesture toward an unknown and unspecifiable multiplicity.

This proposal generated an extensive critique by Professor Richard Briffault in a subsequent article (Briffault 1996). One of his objections was practical. The proposal would have limited impact, he argued, because few nonresidents would be tempted to vote in a neighboring jurisdiction's election. Indeed, he suggested, the most likely impact would be suburban targeting of central city elections rather than the other way around because the central city is the dominant focus of popular and media attention. Briffault's more fundamental objection to opening the franchise to nonresidents, however, was not practical but conceptual. "Cross-border voting," he said, "could undermine political self-determination at the local level." It would do so by transforming the local political debate and discussion into a regional, media-focused election, by undermining local control of the results of local decision making, by reducing the opportunity to build local politics on neighborhood face-to-face politics, and by making it difficult to tailor local decisions to the preferences of local residents.

Rich Ford has offered what, at least to me, is a decisive answer to these objections (1996). The proposal for nonresident voting that Ford was defending was not the same as mine: he did not limit the votes to five and he might be willing to open the franchise to interested nonresidents across the state, not just within the metropolitan region. Still, his response works as well for my proposal as it does for his. On the practical level, Ford pointed out that even Briffault concedes that *some* people are interested enough in policies implemented by cities other than where they live that they would likely vote in their elections. And this includes city voters interested in suburban polices (or seeking alliances with suburban residents to change central city policies) as well as the reverse. Turning the more important, conceptual objection, Ford responds, "Briffault's second critique is that if the proposal did have an effect, it would be to deny local residents self-government. In one sense, this critique is simply a restatement of the proposal. Since the proposal is designed to eliminate residence as a requirement of the franchise, it is definitionally true that the proposal will 'deny' residents the exclusive rights to vote in local elections. However, it does not follow that the proposal destroys local self-government. Instead, the proposal redefines the self that governs" (1191).

Nonresident voting is designed to reorient the current resident-focused definition of the term "self-interest." A city with nonresident voters might still be parochial, but it would not be parochial in the same sense of the term. The answer to the common question "where do you live?" would no longer be a reference simply to one's street address. It would recognize that one "lives" not just at one's place of residence but when one is at work or out for the evening. One "lives" as well in one's imagination—when, for example, making plans to move to or work in a jurisdiction now closed because land-use laws favor residents over newcomers. As Justice Rehnquist noted in an earlier quotation, one "lives" even when staying put while being subjected to a neighboring city's zoning, taxation, and environmental policies.

Justice

Although it is clear that many people now legally or practically excluded from the franchise could be included in it, the question remains:

would their inclusion promote or inhibit social justice? Underpinning Briffault's objection to nonresident voting and others' objections to the other extensions of the franchise canvassed in this chapter is the notion that the extensions of the franchise inhibits social justice. The more people one includes, the argument runs, the less of a voice current voters have. Law-abiding citizens are entitled to be the voting population; those excluded are not omitted because of some indefensible discrimination against others (as with race or gender qualifications). They can become members of the voting population themselves by obeying the law, becoming a citizen, and moving to town. There is nothing unjust about these requirements for the franchise. On the contrary, diluting the vote of law-abiding citizens threatens to take from them the right of self-government, an essential ingredient in the notion of social justice.

Those who seek to extend the franchise appeal to social justice as well. They focus not on current voters but on those that they would add to the voting rolls. The denial of the right to vote to those now excluded, they argue, is itself a denial of the right of self-government. It is not just "taxation without representation" that has this effect—although that it one of its consequences. Being subjected to the exercise of governmental power without a voice in its design is denial of an essential element of freedom. Ron Hayduk, arguing for noncitizen voting rights, quotes Benjamin Franklin: "They who have no voice nor vote in the electing of representatives do not enjoy liberty, but are absolutely enslaved to those who have votes" (Hayduk 2006).

Like supporters of extending the franchise to noncitizens or felons, I do not seek to enfranchise everyone affected by local decision making. I include only residents of the metropolitan area in the franchise (and Ford does not propose going beyond state boundaries). Here is a fundamental reason why extending the franchise in local elections has to have limits. As Robert Dahl has argued, an effort to include everyone affected by local decision making has no defensible stopping place. It can readily be extended to everyone in the nation, maybe even the world (Dahl 1982; Dahl 1970). Yet the idea of a universally inclusive "locality" is incoherent. When the local and the global become identical, the idea of the "local" loses its meaning. (Similar problems arise for those who focus on national, rather than local elections; there, too, people outside territorial boundaries are regularly affected by government decision making; Goodin 2007.)

Any effort to expand the current franchise must therefore decide not only whom to include in the franchise but whom to exclude. Some people will count as part of the community, while others will remain invisible. The invisibility of the nonvoter is striking not only today but also in Tocqueville's great book *Democracy in America* (Tocqueville 1969). Tocqueville observes at one point, "In the United States, except slaves, servants, and paupers supported by the towns, there is no class of persons who do not exercise the elective franchise, and who do not indirectly contribute to making the laws" (240). What is remarkable about this sentence is not just the casual dismissal of "slaves, servants, and paupers," although that is notable enough. Contemporaries, too, think that we have attained universal suffrage yet casually dismiss those, canvassed in this chapter, who are not included in the phrase. Even more remarkable, I think, is the fact that there was a class of persons who did not exercise the franchise when Tocqueville wrote that he does not even feel the need to put into his "except" clause: women. For many contemporaries, noncitizens and felons remain equally invisible.

The rules that define the franchise define membership in the political community. As Michael Walzer puts it, "The theory of distributive justice begins . . . with an account of membership rights. It must vindicate at one and the same time the (limited) right of closure, without which there could be no communities at all, and the political inclusiveness of existing communities" (1983, 63). Walzer's discussion of community membership does not focus on voting rights. But his point—and his ambivalence—is equally relevant here. Voting is a critical form of defining insiders and outsiders, of distinguishing "us" and "them." Each of the groups discussed in this chapter have a claim for inclusiveness. But every political community has its limits—its outsiders.

I embrace the social justice arguments for extending the franchise to all those discussed in this chapter: noncitizens, felons, the homeless, part-time residents, and nonresidents who live in the metropolitan area. That is why I have focused on these potential voters in this chapter. I recognize that their inclusion is controversial. Including aliens in the franchise is one form of a community-building exercise, while excluding them is another form of the same endeavor. Those who want to enfranchise people on parole or probation envision that such a change would improve both the felons' self-perception and others' attitudes toward them. Opponents seek to establish the primacy of law-abiding citizens. When I propose extending the franchise to metropolitan residents, but not others, I seek to reinforce a regional consciousness in American elections and in American policy making. Others want to reinforce a more circumscribed, local consciousness.

As I stated at the outset, state government defines what it means to be local and thus what it means to belong (Ford 1999). Indeed, these decisions are made by officials elected by state residents narrowly defined—without the inclusion of those whose vote is under debate. This kind of state role in formulating city policy is familiar to students of local government law, and it is often a matter of concern. But when dealing with the question of the definition of the local franchise, it has its advantages. This double structure—an enlarged local franchise that remains subject to state-imposed rules formulated by a more limited electorate—might help make the change more palatable. It also provides a mechanism for correcting mistakes if the proposed expansion has undesirable consequences not adequately foreseen at the time the change was made. Besides, such a structure is not unusual. The issue whether to enlarge the voting population is normally posed to a narrow group of people whose influence would be limited by such an expansion. Every expansion of the franchise—to nonproperty owners, former slaves, and women—has been made in this way.

There are also good reasons to begin the task of enlarging the franchise with local elections. The kinds of issues that cities are responsible for—providing local services, regulating land use, patrolling the streets, stimulating economic development—have immediate, direct effects on the everyday life of those now excluded from the franchise that it is easy for everyone to recognize. It is not surprising that noncitizen voting has largely been adopted in local rather than national elections. At the same time, the metropolitan nature of city life describes the daily experience of countless city residents; it is not unusual for them to cross local boundaries to work, go out, or shop on a daily basis. Focusing on these connections seems a good way to begin thinking about how far to expand the franchise. A focus on the city seems justified not only because it is more immediate but also because it is more limited. It allows differing conceptions of the relationship between voting and justice to coexist even within the same state; some cities can even be permitted to experiment with specific changes while others opt not to do so. This variety would allow experience with these changes to be part of the mix when an expanded franchise on a wider territorial basis is considered. This notion of trying out different conceptions of the relationship between voting and justice will not please those who consider justice a single idea, applicable throughout not just the state but the world. But it is consistent with notions proposed by advocates of local experimentation (subject ultimately, to be sure, to centralized standards) with the meaning of similar concepts, such as the equal protection of the laws (Barron 1999).

Limiting voting reform to localities means that the state can decide the meaning of a political community on the local level differently than on the state level. Isn't it unjust, one might object, to have a differential citizenship on a local or state basis? After all, state and national policies matter, too. Wouldn't a local emphasis make those in the expanded local franchise second-class citizens because they cannot vote for higher officials? Perhaps. But the countervailing arguments seem more persuasive to me. On issues such as nonresident voting, it is important to recognize that only some nonresidents are allowed to vote—in my proposal, only those who reside in the metropolitan region. How can the omission of those just outside the regional boundary be defended? One way to defend it is to point out that, although the definition of region is controversial, it is determined by state law. State officials selected by both regional insiders and outsiders not only draw the relevant boundaries but also exercise substantial power over the region and its cities. This countervailing balance, it seems to me, helps justify the impact on both insiders and outsiders of the regional boundaries being drawn. Of course, this kind of argument does not help those (whether felons or noncitizens) who cannot convince the state to expand the local franchise to them. This problem of persuasion would exist as well if the franchise at the state level were under consideration. Even for these potential voters, starting at the local level makes sense. If the expansion of the electorate generates support at the local level, then it can help create a political constituency for change at the state level. It was not an issue of voting that led Justice Brandeis famously to defend decentralization as creating a kind of laboratory.[22] But this is an issue where the argument fits very well.

Notes

1 http://www.immigrantvoting.org/material/TIMELINE.html.
2 http://www.europarl.europa.eu/factsheets/2_4_0_en.htm.
3 http://felonvoting.procon.org/viewtopic.asp (2004 figures).
4 *Richardson v. Ramirez*, 418 U.S. 24 (1974).
5 http://felonvoting.procon.org/viewresource.asp?resourceID=000289.
6 *Suave v. Canada*, 3 S.C.R. 519 (2002); *National Institute for Crime Prevention and*

the Reintegration of Offenders v. Minister of Home Affairs, CCT 3/04 (S. Afr. 2004); Roach v. Electoral Commissioner, 81 ALJR 1830 (Australia 2007).

7 Hirst v. United Kingdom, 38 Eur. H.R. Rep. 40.

8 http://felonvoting.procon.org.

9 http://www.nationalhomeless.org/publications/facts/How_Many.pdf (2007 figures).

10 Pitts v. Black, 608 F. Supp. 696 (S.D.N.Y. 1984); Fischer v. Stout, 741 P.2d 217 (Alaska 1997).

11 You Don't Need a Home to Vote! http://www.nationalhomeless.org/getinvolved/ projects/vote/index.html.

12 Teel v. Darnell, 2008 WL 474185, 2008 WL 1751532 (E.D. Tenn. 2008).

13 Wit v. Berman, 306 F.3d 1256, 1260 (2d Cir. 2002).

14 Wit v. Berman, 306 F.3d 1256, 1260 (2d Cir. 2002).

15 Wit v. Berman, 306 F.3d 1256, 1264 (2d Cir. 2002).

16 132 F.3d 576 (10th Cir. 1997).

17 Wit v. Berman, 306 F.3d 1256, 1261 (2d Cir. 2002).

18 Ball v. James, 451 U.S. 355 (1981); Kessler v. Grand Cent. Dist. Management Ass'n, Inc., 158 F.3d 92 (2d Cir. 1998).

19 "Hyper-egalitarian commentators tend to be hostile to . . . institutions that are governed by property owners . . . History, theory, and constitutional precedents, however, all cast doubt on the soundness of hyper-egalitarians' normative position" (Ellickson 1998, 90).

20 http://www.cityoflondon.gov.uk/Corporation/LGNL_Services/Council_and _democracy/Councillors_democracy_and_elections/appointment_proccess.htm.

21 Holt Civic Club v. City of Tuscaloosa, 439 U.S. 60 (1978).

22 New State Ice Co. v. Liebmann, 285 U.S. 262 (1932).

References

Avila, Joacquin. 2003. Political Apartheid in California: The Debate over Non-Citizen Voting. Los Angeles: UCLA Chicano Studies Research Center.

Barron, David. 1999. "The Promise of Cooley's City: Traces of Local Constitutionalism." University of Pennsylvania Law Review 147:487–612.

Briffault, Richard. 1996. "The Local Government Boundary Problem in Metropolitan Areas." Stanford Law Review 48:1115–71.

Dahl, Robert. 1970. After the Revolution? New Haven, Conn.: Yale University Press.

———. 1982. Dilemmas of Pluralist Democracy. New Haven, Conn.: Yale University Press.

———. 1989. Democracy and Its Critics. New Haven, Conn.: Yale University Press.

Ellickson, Robert. 1998. "New Institutions for Old Neighborhoods." Duke Law Journal 48:75–110.

Ford, Richard Thompson. 1996. "Beyond Borders: A Partial Response to Richard Briffault." Stanford Law Review 48:1173–95.

———. 1999. "Law's Territory (A History of Jurisdiction)." Michigan Law Review 97:843–929.

Frug, Gerald. 1993. "Decentering Decentralization." *University of Chicago Law Review* 60:253–338.

Frug, Gerald, and David Barron. 2008. *City Bound: How States Stifle Urban Innovation.* Ithaca, N.Y.: Cornell University Press.

Goodin, Robert E. 2007. "Enfranchising All Affected Interests and Its Alternatives." *Philosophy and Public Affairs* 35:40–68.

Harper-Ho, Virginia. 2000. "Noncitizen Voting Rights." *Law and Inequality* 18:271–94.

Hayduk, Ron. 2006. *Democracy for All: Restoring Immigrant Voting Rights in the United States.* New York: Routledge.

Heller, Michael, and Rick Hills. 2008. "Land Assembly Districts." *Harvard Law Review* 121:1465–1527.

Keeney, John. 2008. "Felon Disenfranchisement." In *America Votes,* ed. Benjamin Griffith, 91–104. Chicago: Section of State and Local Government Law, American Bar Association.

Miller, Jennine, and Peter Gonzales. 2002. "'I Matter! I Vote!': Overcoming the Disenfranchisement of the Homeless and Formerly Homeless Voter." *Temple Policy & Civil Rights Law Review* 11:343–58.

Neuman, Gerald. 1991–92. "'We Are the People': Alien Suffrage in German and American Perspective." *Michigan Journal of International Law* 13:259–335.

Ozdeger, Tulin, and Jewel Baltimore. 2006. "Homeless but Not Voiceless: Protecting the Voting Rights of Homeless Persons." *Clearinghouse Review* 40:313.

Raskin, Jamin. 1993. "Legal Aliens, Local Citizens: The Historical, Constitutional, and Theoretical Meanings of Alien Suffrage." *University of Pennsylvania Law Review* 141:1391–1470.

Robbers, Monica. 2008. "Ramifications of Felony Disenfranchisement on the Voting Population in the Commonwealth of Virginia." *Richmond Journal of Law and Public Interest* 11:1–29.

Street, Paul. 2003. "'Those People in That Prison Can't Vote Me Out': The Political Consequences of Racist Felony Disenfranchisement." *The Black Commentator.* http://www.blackcommentator.com.

Tocqueville, Alexis de. 1969. *Democracy in America.* Translated by George Lawrence. New York: Harper and Row.

Treaty of the European Union. 1997. Article 19. Amsterdam.

Walzer, Michael. 1983. *Spheres of Justice: A Defense of Pluralism and Equality 63.* New York: Basic Books.

9 THE COLOR OF TERRITORY

How Law and Borders Keep America Segregated

RICHARD THOMPSON FORD

HERE'S A DESCRIPTION OF ONE American city—worse than many, but still representative:

> Locals call the street the "Berlin Wall," or the "barrier," or the "Mason-Dixon Line." It divides the suburban Grosse Pointe communities, which are among the most genteel towns anywhere, from the East Side of Detroit, which is poor and mostly black. The Detroit side is studded with abandoned cars, graffiti-covered schools, and burned out buildings. Two blocks away, within view, are neatly-clipped hedges and immaculate houses—a world of servants and charity balls, two car garages and expensive clothes. On the one side, says John Kelly, a Democratic state senator whose district awkwardly straddles both neighborhoods, is "West Beirut," on the other side, "Disneyland." (Jackson 1985, 278)

If I had to identify only one social injustice that most cry out for redress, it would be the plight of the disproportionately black, urban underclass. Residential segregation is the most intractable legacy of America's struggle with racism. And unfortunately it makes many other problems—poverty, unemployment, crime, and educational disadvantage—harder to address. Isolated from mainstream society, ghettoized minorities suffer under several burdens. They are unable to establish the social networks that might alert them to better job opportunities. They remain unfamiliar with the social norms of the mainstream—hence they have difficulty favorably impressing employers—exacerbating employment discrimination. They eventually become socialized to a ghetto subculture in which employment in the mainstream doesn't seem to be a viable option. They lack role models who work in mainstream jobs, and they become acculturated to norms that are functional only inside the ghetto environment.

Anyone with an ounce of compassion deplores this situation. But most people have pretty much given up on trying to fix it. Segregation seems intractable—the consequences of human nature, centuries of custom and acculturation, and the inevitable inequities of modern capitalism. We've long since stopped enforcing racial segregation by law, but the problem hasn't improved much. In fact, in some ways it's getting worse. What can anyone do?

This attitude is understandable, but it's wrong. We haven't really stopped enforcing segregation by law. Yes, of course, we've eliminated blatantly race-conscious laws, but even today, legal rules keep segregation locked firmly in place. If we changed these laws, then we could change our impoverished and segregated inner cities. But the laws that keep neighborhoods segregated today are not as easy to identify as the Jim Crow–era laws were—they are laws we take for granted and that almost don't even seem like laws at all. This chapter will reveal those laws, point out how they keep our cities and neighborhoods segregated, and suggest how we can change them and reverse segregation without having to change human nature, history, or start a revolution.

Space Oddity: A Tale of Two Territories

I would like to begin with a relatively mundane legal dispute:

> Holt is a small, largely rural, unincorporated community located on the northeastern outskirts of Tuscaloosa . . . Alabama. Because the community is within the three mile police jurisdiction circumscribing Tuscaloosa's corporate limits, its residents are subject to the city's "police and sanitary regulations." Holt residents are also subject to the criminal jurisdiction of the city's court, and to the city's power to license businesses, trades, and professions. [The Holt residents] claimed that the city's extraterritorial exercise of the police powers over Holt residents, without a concomitant extension of the franchise on an equal footing with those residing within the corporate limits, denies [them] rights secured by the Due Process and Equal Protection Clauses of the Fourteenth Amendment." (*Holt Civic Club et al. v. City of Tuscaloosa et al.*, 439 U.S. 60 [1978])

With a very few exceptions, only residents of a city are entitled to vote in its elections. The territorial limits of the jurisdiction in which the elected body is authoritative also define the extent of the franchise, creating a reciprocal relationship between government and governed. But in *Holt* this typical solution to the question "who votes?" simply displaces the problem. Rather than expressing the conflict in terms of the right to vote, one could just as easily describe it in terms of the jurisdictional boundaries. Why should the boundary of the city of Tuscaloosa not include the residents of the community of Holt? *Holt* raises a vexing question: taking the principle of majority rule as a given, how are we to define the limits of the community within which a majority will rule? The answer to this question is typically taken for granted, but *Holt* reveals it as a highly contestable decision—a choice of a particular legal regime that works in the background of our social, political, and economic relationships. The background rules that determine the position and significance of territorial boundaries do some of the most important work in keeping America's cities racially separate and unequal.

At first glance there would seem to be only two possible answers to the question in *Holt*: either the relevant political community includes the residents of Holt, as well as those of Tuscaloosa, or it includes only the residents of Tuscaloosa.

There are in fact three possible answers, and the unlikeliest of the three is, according to the Supreme Court of the United States, the correct one.

It's tempting to insist that the relevant political community is the *police* jurisdiction of Tuscaloosa (including Holt). After all, what legitimate reason could Tuscaloosa have for excluding the residents of Holt from the political process? But this is misleading: in fact we *always* restrict the franchise to a select group; the question is how such a group is defined. Territorial boundaries typically define the boundaries of the political community and hence the limits of the franchise. Those boundaries are set by laws. In this case, the law puts the residents of Holt on the wrong side of the line.

So maybe the political community is the corporate jurisdiction of the city of Tuscaloosa (excluding Holt). Tuscaloosa's exercise of control over residents of unincorporated Holt does not mean the residents of Holt have a right to vote in Tuscaloosa's elections. As the majority opinion points out, any "city's decisions inescapably affect individuals living outside its . . . Yet no one would suggest that nonresidents . . . have a constitutional right to participate in the political process bringing [them] about" (*Holt*, 439 U.S. 60 [1978]). One might object that Holt residents are *directly* affected by Tuscaloosa's regulations, but this does not distinguish those living in Holt from a non-Tuscaloosans who own property in Tuscaloosa or enter Tuscaloosa to work, shop, visit friends, and so on. They, too, are subject to Tuscaloosa's police power. Some pay Tuscaloosa's property taxes and are subject to its land-use planning, drive through Tuscaloosa streets (and be subject to arrest by its police officers), patronize Tuscaloosa's businesses (and indirectly pay its business taxes and benefit from and bear the costs of its regulations), yet they are denied the right to influence its government through the ballot box. Local decisions affect outsiders because people trade and socialize across jurisdictional lines, "but . . . the fact that people trade with one another rather extensively does not mean that they care to be brought together in a more solemn association, as citizens in a common polity. Nor does it suggest that it would be good for them to joined in this way" (Arkes 1981, 325–26).

But the Court does not settle on this answer either. It resolves the dispute in a different way. The Court holds that the political community is neither the corporate nor the police jurisdiction of Tuscaloosa—neither Tuscaloosa alone nor Tuscaloosa plus Holt—but rather the state of Alabama: "This Court does not sit to determine whether *Alabama* has chosen the soundest or most practical form of internal government possible. Authority to make those judgments resides in the state legislature *and Alabama citizens are free to urge their proposals to that body*" (*Holt*, 429 U.S. 60 [1978], 73–74; emphasis mine).

Several things about this resolution are telling. Notice that the *Holt* Court describes the local government as a "form of internal government," "[a] convenient agenc[y] for exercising such of the governmental powers of the State as may be entrusted to it" (*Holt*, 429 U.S. 60 [1978], 71). Local government boundaries are simply another set of state laws subject to the state political process. It then follows that the only relevant political process occurs at the statewide level. All Alabama citizens, Holt residents and Tuscaloosans alike, are equally entitled to vote in Alabama elections and can "urge their proposals" to change the local jurisdictional arrangement at that level of government.

In a sense the boundaries that define territorial jurisdictions are both absolutely compelling and hopelessly arbitrary. In one sense all jurisdictional boundaries are arbitrary—including those separating France, Poland, or Switzerland from Germany or the United States from Mexico as much so as that separating Holt from Tuscaloosa. Yet at the same time faith in the necessity and legitimacy of those boundaries is almost a precondition of government. Our reaction to these territorial arrangements is rarely the skepticism or outrage that we direct at malleable human institutions (e.g., the Internal Revenue Service or the United Nations) but rather acceptance and resignation we reserve for natural phenomena beyond our control. When the von Trapps reach Switzerland, only the simplest child dares to ask, "Why don't the Nazis just cross the border to get them?" It is simply understood by those with a jurisdictional frame of mind (and how quickly we develop it, tutored by such compelling stories) that they *cannot* cross the line, that if they do, then their authority will vanish. The logic of government *is* the logic of jurisdiction—question it, and all that is solid melts into air.

This common understanding of legal boundaries forecloses any consideration of territorial jurisdiction as a contestable and revisable public policy. And that prevents us from seeing how law keeps our cities segregated.

Territory as a Bundle of Practices

It is tempting to examine legal territories solely in terms of their material/spatial attributes, as if they were simply an object or a built structure. But jurisdiction is also a discourse, a way of speaking and understanding the social world. As Thongchai Winichakul explains in the fascinating book *Siam Mapped*, "In terms of most communication theories and common sense, a map is a scientific abstraction of reality. A map merely represents something which already exists objectively 'there.' [But at times] this relationship was reversed. A map anticipated spatial reality, not vice versa. In other words, a map was a model for, rather than a model of, what it purported to represent . . . It had become a real instrument to concretize projections on the earth's surface" (Winichakul 1994, 310). Perhaps it is best to think of territorial jurisdiction as *a set of social practices*—a code of etiquette. Social practices must be learned and communicated to others. In one sense they exist in the realm of discourse; they are *representations* of approved behavior, as well as the behavior itself. For example, the social practice called "the tango" is a combination of the dance notation that "maps" the steps and the actual movement of individuals in rhythm (hopefully) to music ("when dancing the tango, the man leads and the lady follows; each partner should move according to the notation"). These representations have material consequences: they determine who leads and who follows as well as where one places her feet. It is both an actual spatial practice and the graphical representation of that practice. One could learn to dance the tango just by watching people actually dance, but the diagrams standardize the learning process and thereby in a real sense define the dance itself. It would be absurd to describe dance notation as "ideology" or "legitimation" as if it misled us as to the nature of the practice, yet it would also be incomplete to think of it as a innocent description, as if the graphical representation only describes and has nothing to do with *perpetuating and regulating* the "actual practice."

Similarly, territorial jurisdictions are a function of graphical and verbal descriptions; they are a set of practices that are performed by individuals and groups who learn to "dance the jurisdiction" by reading descriptions of jurisdictions and by looking at maps. This does not mean that jurisdiction is "mere ideology" and that the lines between various nations, cities, and districts "aren't real." Of course the lines are real, but they are real because they are constantly being *made* real (e.g., by county assessors levying property taxes, by police pounding the beat [and stopping at the city limits], and by registrars of voters checking identification for proof of residence). Without these practices the lines would not "be real"—the lines don't preexist the practices.

Of course, each of these practices can be described as "responding" to the lines or working within the lines rather than making them. When we think of the practices as happening "within the lines" and imagine that the boundary lines exist independently of the practices that give them significance, we begin to take them for granted. Thinking in this way, we imagine that jurisdiction *is* the space drawn on a map rather than a collection of rules that can be represented graphically as a map.

For many purposes, this way of thinking about a territory is perfectly reasonable: sometimes everyone understands the jurisdictional dance and knows where to step. At these times the map does seem to precede the practices. And of course, the representation of territory may at times precede the actual practices that give it life and meaning, just as when a city grid is mapped out before it is developed. But while lines on a map may anticipate a jurisdiction, a jurisdiction itself consists of the practices that make the abstract space depicted on a map significant. Moreover, when the stakes of a jurisdiction are in dispute, as they were in *Holt*, one cannot simply refer to lines on a map. In order to avoid taking legal territories for granted, we must constantly remind ourselves that territorial jurisdiction is itself a set of practices and not a preexisting thing in which practices occur or to which practices relate.

Segregation as an Effect of Territorial Practices

Now let's return the segregated neighborhoods. Many argue that although integration may be desirable, we can't mandate it; although segregation may be unfortunate, as long as it is not enforced by law, the Constitution does not speak to it. If people want segregation and accomplish it without overt state assistance, the argument goes, so be it: the Constitution demands only that government not become an agent of Jim Crow. This answer has a long juridical pedigree: it echoes the Court in *Plessy v. Ferguson,* the case that established the doctrine of separate but equal, considered good law in the United States for over half a century until it was overturned in the case of *Brown v. Board of Education*: "If the two races are to meet upon terms of social equality, it must be the result of natural affinities, a mutual appreciation of each other's merits, and a voluntary consent of individuals . . . Legislation is powerless to eradicate racial instincts, or to abolish distinctions based upon physical differences . . . If one race be inferior to the other socially, the constitution of the United States cannot put them upon the same plane" (*Plessy v. Ferguson,* 163 U.S. 537 [1896]). It also echoes Justice Potter Stewart's concurring opinion in *Milliken v. Bradley*—a case that effectively repudiated *Brown's* integrationist mandate by limiting the ability of the federal courts to join two or more districts in desegregation remedies when an entire district was almost racially homogenous: "The mere fact of different racial composition in contiguous districts does not itself imply or constitute a violation [of the Equal Protection Clause] . . . in the absence of a showing that such disparity was imposed, fostered or encouraged by the state or its political subdivisions. . . . [Segregation is now caused by] unknown and perhaps unknowable factors such as in-migration, birth rates, economic changes or cumulative acts of private racial fears" (*Milliken v. Bradley,* 418 U.S. 717, 756 [1974]). But to the contrary of Justice Stewart's suggestion in *Milliken* that racial segregation is the result of "unknown and unknowable" forces, segregation persists for reasons we can identify with some confidence.

Background Rules

It has been a staple of critical legal thought since the American legal realists of the early twentieth century that some of the most important legal controls operate in the background of social, economic, and political conflict. Legal rules that everyone takes for granted have a profound influence on social life and are arguably more potent precisely because they need not be explicitly discussed, defended, or even formally enforced. The private-law rules of property and contract were the main targets of this vein of legal realist thought. But public law is structured by background rules as well. We often speak of "democracy" as if the limits on the franchise and rules regulating the vote were self-evident, but anyone familiar with the electoral process knows it is nothing if not contestable.

Now to the point at hand: we take the territory, politics, and political prerogatives of cities and suburbs as fixed and given, but these are all determined by laws, which can be changed. The bundle of practices that make up American cities consists of three major moves: taxation and funding, land-use planning, and the residency rule for voting and access to most local services.

Taxes

We rarely question that property taxes collected locally should be spent locally (with the result that cities with desirable and expensive real estate have a lot more to spend than those with cheap real estate), but this is a legal rule that could be—and occasionally is—different. Most American cities collect and retain the revenues collected through taxes levied against property in their territorial boundaries and fund public services primarily through property taxes.

This provides a fiscal incentive for residents of wealthier jurisdictions to resist integration: because taxes levied against local property are retained for the benefit of schools exclusive to local residents, any merger with poorer districts makes the residents of the wealthier districts financially worse off.

Residency

They also are entitled to, and with very rare exceptions do, limit access to local services to residents of the jurisdiction. This means that cities have an overwhelming incentive to encourage people to move in who have resources to invest in real estate and thereby increase the value of property (and tax revenues) while requiring relatively little in terms of public services and to discourage people from moving in who have little resources and who will need a lot of public services. It scarcely needs to be said that the heavily minority-race urban poor fit the latter description.

Finally, as the controversy in *Holt* reminds us, only local residents may vote in local elections. As a result, policies that benefit local residents at the expense of outsiders are popular and widespread.

Land Use

Although American local governments do not have explicit immigration policies, they do have quite broad powers to restrict land uses. By excluding all or most high-density or multifamily housing, middle-class and wealthy suburbs can and do effectively screen out low-income (again, disproportionately minority race) potential residents by prohibiting the housing that they can afford. In some cases the desire to eliminate low-income housing may be motivated by classic land-use considerations such as a desire for open space and low-density development generally or a desire to avoid traffic burdens and environmental impacts. In many cases, the policies are driven by fiscal concerns: the background rules that allow localities to restrict the use of public services to residents and that allow localities to retain locally collected property- and sales-tax revenue give localities a powerful incentive to exclude low-income residents (who will require expensive public services but contribute little to the tax base) in favor of upper-income residential, commercial, and industrial uses (which will improve property values or generate taxable sales). And suburban local governments can and do resist regional public transportation, halfway houses, group-living arrangements, and rehabilitation centers—all services that many low-income people require.

Local land-use decisions are, needless to say, laws; moreover, the ability of localities acting autonomously (instead of through regional or state government or through shared or negotiated land-use authority) to make such decisions is itself a revisable legal rule.

These background legal rules are a fail-safe recipe for racially segregated neighborhoods. They are not the only reason segregation remains, but they alone are enough to keep America's neighborhoods segregated indefinitely.

It doesn't have to be this way. Local officials, state politicians, the federal government, and the courts have repeatedly confronted the web of legal rules that perpetuate segregation. With a few exceptions they have chosen to reinforce rather than reform these rules. In the following section, I will cite a few important Supreme Court opinions that reinforced segregationist background rules and thereby undermined the practical integrationist promise of *Brown*. In so doing I do not mean to suggest that the Supreme Court is the main culprit in the demise of *Brown*'s integrationism; instead I mean for the cases to illustrate the importance of legal background rules and to serve as an examples of lost opportunities to reform them.

As I noted previously, roughly twenty years after *Brown*, the most important implications of the landmark decision were repudiated by the Supreme Court in the case *Milliken v. Bradley*. In 1971 a federal district court held that Detroit's public schools were racially segregated and thus in violation of the Fourteenth Amendment. The district court found that because Detroit's entire school district was predominantly black, "relief of segregation in the public schools of the City of Detroit cannot to be accomplished within the corporate geographical limits of the city" (*Bradley v. Milliken*, 345 F. Supp. 914, 916 [1972]). Accordingly, the district court devised a desegregation plan that included the surrounding suburbs of Detroit. Affirming, the Sixth Circuit Court of Appeals noted that "if we [were to] hold that school district boundaries are absolute barriers to a Detroit school desegregation plan, we would be opening the way to nullify *Brown v. Board of Education*" (*Bradley v. Milliken*, 484 F. 2d 215, 298 [6th Cir., 1973]).

Apparently unafraid of blazing this trail, the Supreme Court reversed. In *Milliken*, the majority held that only Detroit could be required to remedy the segregation because "the record contained evidence of *de jure* segregated conditions only in Detroit schools" (*Milliken v. Bradley*, 418 U.S. 717, 745 [1974])—even though it was conceded that Detroit alone could provide an effective remedy. The questionable premise of this analysis is that local government boundaries define legally responsible entities with ontological continuity over time, such that a *city* can be thought of as responsible for "its" discriminatory practices in the distant past. This legal fiction is particularly implausible in the context of *Milliken*, in which the Court itself recognized that white flight had resulted in a dramatic change in the demography of Detroit in the years intervening between *Brown*'s invalidation of de jure segregation and the litigation at bar. It would not require too great a license to say that, morally speaking, the old city of Detroit, which had engaged in de jure segregation, had moved to the suburbs.

Moreover, local government and school-district boundaries are nothing more than laws—in this case, the laws of the State of Michigan. Supreme Court precedent stretching back to the landmark decision in *Hunter v. Pittsburgh* (207 U.S. 161 [1907]) establishes that, as far the Constitution of the United States is concerned, local governments are simply *policies* of state government. And more recently the court insisted that a locality is, as Chief Justice Rehnquist put it in *Holt Civic Club et al. v. City of Tuscaloosa et al.*, simply a "governmental technique" (*Holt*, 439 U.S. 60, 72 [1978]). It follows that the state is responsible for creating local governments—inner cities and autonomous suburbs (which are, thanks to the Court's decision in *Milliken*, isolated from economic or social responsibility for the inner cities).[1] Rather than indulging the flimsy fiction that the Detroit of the 1970s was responsible for its racial segregation, the Court could have acknowledged that the state of Michigan was the responsible entity and ordered the state to remedy the segregation. Following its own precedent, the Court could have held that the local government boundaries that divided Detroit from its suburbs, rather than barriers to an effective desegregation remedy, were themselves state action that predictably entrenched segregation.

The ability of localities to collect and retain revenues from taxes levied against property located within their territorial boundaries also contributes to segregation. In *San Antonio Independent School District v. Rodriquez* (411 U.S. 1 [1973]), the Court held that a school-financing system that was based in large part on local property taxes and produced large disparities in tax burden–expenditure ratios between districts did not violate the "Equal Protection Clause." Unequal school-district funding in a context (like that at issue in *Rodriquez*) in which districts are already racially segregated provides wealthier whites with a financial incentive for segregation. Far from "unknown and unknowable," the causes for segregation in this climate are as obvious as the observation that people prefer more money to less.

Finally, localities can use land-use planning as an effective immigration policy, predictably perpetuating segregation. In some cases, exclusionary zoning is driven, at least in part, by the desire to exclude low-income people in general and racial minorities in particular. At the very least, decisions with a significant racially segregative effects could be subject to intensified legal scrutiny. Such scrutiny is not, however, the state of the law. In *Village of Arlington Heights v. Metropolitan Housing Development Corp.* (429 U.S. 252 [1977]) the Supreme Court upheld a village's decision to bar the construction of multifamily housing despite that decision's demonstrable racially restrictive effects and despite evidence that popular support for the decision was motivated, in part, by racial animus. The village's formally race neutral but effectively racially exclusionary zoning was subject only to rational-basis scrutiny, which it easily survived.

Local land-use decisions are, needless to say, laws, and the ability of localities acting autonomously (as opposed to through regional or state government or through shared or negotiated land-use authority) to make such decisions is itself a revisable legal rule. Needless to say, a racially segregated municipality will, in most cases, have racially segregated public schools: although school district boundaries do not always match the municipal boundaries of local governments with zoning power, they rarely diverge so much as to take in communities of significantly different race or class demography.

Let us review: Most American cities fund public services primarily through property taxes. They also are entitled to and, with very rare exceptions, do limit access to local services to residents of the jurisdiction. This means that cities have an overwhelming incentive to encourage in-movers with resources who will invest in real estate and thereby increase the value of property (and tax revenues) and who require relatively little in terms of public services and to discourage in-movers without resources whose presence will tend to depress property values and who will need a lot of public services. It scarcely needs to be said that the heavily minority-race urban poor fit the latter description. And although American local governments do not have explicit immigration policies, they do have quite broad powers to restrict land uses. By excluding all or most high-density or multifamily housing, middle-class and wealthy suburbs can and do effectively screen out low-income (again, disproportionately minority-race) potential residents by prohibiting the housing that they can afford. And suburban local governments can and do resist regional public transportation, halfway houses, group-living arrangements, and rehabilitation centers—all services that many low-income people require. These background legal rules are a fail-safe recipe for racial segregation.

You'll notice that this recipe need not include something called "racism." It will taste just as bitter even in there's not a single racist person involved in the process. Therefore, we can expect the segregation of America's cities and all the consequences thereof to persist, despite the apparent waning of atavistic racial prejudice and even in the face of widespread goodwill. This is an example of what I have elsewhere called "racism without racists."

In fact it is, I think, *the primary* example of racism without racists because almost every other serious racial inequity in our society flows from it. The disproportionate representation of blacks in our nation's prisons and jails—what some have called a "new Jim Crow"—is actually less the result of Jim Crow–era racial prejudice than it is the result of the isolation of the disproportionately black, urban poor in neighborhoods with few job opportunities, where for many, a life of crime seems to be the only viable path out of poverty and hopelessness. High unemployment among blacks is again the result of isolation in neighborhoods where few people have connections with the mainstream economy and hence few can provide an entrée into the job market for their neighbors and relatives. Lower life expectancy is another issue, as this, too, can be attributed to high crime rates in poor neighborhoods, which lead to higher fatality rates and, of course, higher levels of unhealthy stress, combined with the already high stress of living catch-as-catch-can in the grey-market economy, without job security or health care. In the America that many celebrate as post-racist, the last major racial-justice struggle to be fought and won involves the isolation of the black poor. If we confront and fix this problem, then our children—or perhaps their children—may well be able to celebrate a postracist society without the aid of hallucinogenic drugs. If we don't fix it, they'll confront the same racial problems we confront today.

Note

1 My argument here is far from novel: the Supreme Court made precisely this argument when considering the decision on a school district to divide a county-wide jurisdiction into two separate systems: one for the city and one for the county. See *Wright v. Council for the City of Emporia*, 407 U.S. 451 (1972).

References

Arkes, Hadley. 1981. *The Philosopher in the City: The Moral Dimensions of Urban Politics*. Princeton, N.J.: Princeton University Press.
Arlington Heights v. Metropolitan Housing Development Corp., 429 U.S. 252 (1977).

Bradley v. Milliken, 345 F. Supp. 914, 916 (E.D. Mich. 1972).

Bradley v. Milliken, 484 F. 2d 215, 298 (6th Cir. 1973).

Holt Civic Club et al. v. City of Tuscaloosa et al., 439 U.S. 60 (1978).

Hunter v. Pittsburgh, 207 U.S. 161 (1907).

Jackson, Kenneth. 1985. *Crabgrass Frontier: The Suburbanization of the United States.* New York: Oxford University Press.

Milliken v. Bradley, 418 U.S. 717, 748 (1974).

Plessy v. Ferguson, 163 U.S. 537 (1896).

Winichakul, Thongchai. 1994. *Siam Mapped: A History of the Geo-Body of a Nation.* Honolulu: University of Hawai'i Press.

Wright v. Council for the City of Emporia, 407 U.S. 451 (1972).

10 CREATING JUSTICE FOR THE POOR IN THE NEW METROPOLIS

MARGARET WEIR

POVERTY, IN THE PUBLIC IMAGINATION and the academic literature alike, has long fixated on the system of "urban containment" that trapped the minority poor in low-income urban neighborhoods.[1] The face of poverty that became anchored in the American public mind was African-American, urban, and nonworking. The most voluble public debates singled out individual behavior as the cause of poverty. Transforming welfare into a temporary, work-oriented program became the cure. A less visible set of arguments did not blame the poor but rather the environment of the poor as the cause of poverty. Animated by concerns of fairness and equal opportunity, this perspective pointed to the concentration of poverty and the racially driven sociopolitical segregation of metropolitan areas as the prime causes for entrenched poverty. This alternative approach embraced policy solutions that ranged from reorganizing metropolitan area governments to deconcentrating poor people throughout the region.

It is now apparent that the economic, political, and demographic forces that made containment an apt metaphor during the last century have since shifted in complex ways. Assistance to the poor has been transformed by new time limits and work requirements and the social and political geography of poverty has shifted. Urban gentrification, the demolition of public housing under HOPE VI, and large-scale immigration have all combined to increase the racial and economic diversity of the suburbs. Poverty, never the sole province of the inner city, has spread beyond urban boundaries so that by 2005, 53 percent of the poor in large metropolitan areas lived in the suburbs, not the central city (Berube and Kneebone 2006, 4; Frey et al. 2009). Among this diverse group are African-Americans pushed out of the city by gentrification and public-housing reforms; immigrants seeking to settle near employment centers and searching for affordable housing; and white suburban residents buffeted by economic change. To be sure, concentrations of racially and ethnically identified urban poverty persist in cities across the country, but the challenges confronting the urban poor have also shifted as cash assistance becomes ever more rare and ongoing economic change moves jobs further from centers of urban poverty.

The new geography of need, together with policies that make the well-being of the poor contingent on market income, poses fundamental questions about justice. Is the more complex political geography of poverty creating new kinds of place-based inequalities? And if so, then how should they be understood? As poverty has taken on a more complex spatial configuration, what have we learned about the efficacy of the last decade's progressive solutions—regionalism and deconcentrating the poor—as antipoverty strategies? What are the implications for devising new approaches that build toward a more just metropolis? This chapter addresses these questions. It begins by examining the disappointing outcomes of efforts to promote regionalism and deconcentration of the poor. It then presents a typology for characterizing the economic and sociopolitical context that confronts the poor in different parts of metropolitan areas. I highlight in particular the dangers of "extrusion," a demographic–political pattern that leaves low-income communities with an even weaker social safety net and less access to opportunity than in the past. In so doing, I show how this array of public and private institutions violates basic principles of distributive justice. The final section of the chapter considers the political strategies and policy orientations that can help chart a path toward a more just metropolis.

The Disappointments of Metropolitan Reform

Since the rediscovery of regionalism in the early 1990s, advocates have touted its virtues as a solution to a diverse menu of urban, suburban, and national ills, ranging from economic competitiveness to global warming to growing economic inequality. One reason for regionalism's popularity was that it meant so many different things to different people. For some of its supporters, regionalism entailed new forms of collaboration among business elites; for others, it meant state regulations, such as tax-base sharing that links the economic fate of the region's localities together; for still others, regionalism evoked the image of authoritative institutions that can devise and implement plans for rational patterns of metropolitan growth and development.

For those concerned with urban poverty, metropolitan reform promised a way to challenge the twin pillars of urban containment: political boundaries and racial–economic segregation. Since the incorporation of the first suburbs, affluent communities have used political boundaries to protect themselves from the costs and inconvenience of lower-income residents. During the postwar era, the defensive localism of the suburbs not only constituted the flip side of urban containment but also began to establish an economically distinctive patchwork among suburban areas. Political boundaries meant that critical public goods, such as schooling and basic services, varied widely by jurisdiction. Boundaries also served as institutional bulwarks designed to produce homogenous populations (Lowrey 2000; Bickford 2000; Weiher 1991; Weir 1994). Earlier waves of regionalism had sought to erase those boundaries through governmental consolidation, but by the 1990s, most regional reformers dismissed this approach as politically unrealistic. Instead, they sought to promote policies and build regional connections designed to make existing boundaries less significant. One of the most important policies they embraced to reduce the economic significance of political boundaries was tax-base sharing that aimed to distribute the benefits of prosperity across the region (Orfield 2002).

To challenge the second pillar of containment, racial and economic segregation, a second set of policies, including inclusionary zoning and public-housing reform would help mix up populations that had been sorted by income and by spatial location (Rusk 1993; Turner, Popkin, and Rawlings 2008; Goetz 2003). Local control of zoning had long served as a powerful tool for carving metropolitan areas up into jurisdictions with distinct income profiles. The combination of urban renewal and segregated public housing had played a major role in creating "the second ghetto" of concentrated poverty in the postwar era (Hirsch 1983). Together, reforms requiring that affordable housing be built throughout the metropolitan area and that distressed public housing be replaced with mixed-income developments would break the pattern of poor black cities–wealthy white suburbs that characterized many metropolitan areas. By tackling the twin pillars of containment, this new cluster of reforms would begin to correct the policy biases that had long forced low-income communities to swim against the tide of policies that sent people and investment out of cities; instead, metropolitan reforms would help create new connections and fresh opportunities (O'Connor 1999).

Yet more than fifteen years after ideas about regionalism reappeared in policy debates, the achievements are disappointing. They are especially unsatisfactory when it comes to the protecting the interests of low-income residents and low-income communities. Indeed, many of the regional reform ideas that have been put into place in recent years either have been indifferent to low-income communities or have actually harmed them.

Efforts to reduce the economic significance of political boundaries have run into major political roadblocks. Only four metropolitan regions have adopted some form of tax-base sharing and only in Minnesota's Twin Cities does the policy redistribute significant revenue.[2] Despite the considerable interest these ideas provoked around the country during the 1990s, no metropolitan area adopted the broad tax-base sharing scheme put into place forty years ago in the Twin Cities..

Instead, business groups seeking to promote economic competitiveness became the most ardent backers of regionalism (Peirce, Johnson, and Hall 1993; Dodge 1996). Their central goal in reducing the significance of metropolitan boundaries, however, was not to promote redistribution but rather to decrease competition among jurisdictions in order to market the region as a single entity. On the whole, this type of regionalism has been indifferent to the issues facing low-income communities.[3] At worst, it has directed resources away from projects that would benefit low-income groups toward those that advantage businesses and upper-income residents. Recent developments in Pittsburgh provide an example of how regionalism can harm low-income communities. As the city moved toward bankruptcy in 2004, efforts at regional revitalization, overseen by the state-initiated Intergovernmental Cooperation Authority, focused on the development of regional assets, not the city and its neighborhoods. In the words of one critic, "Resident tax money goes to large regional projects like baseball and football stadiums, convention centers . . . [while] neighborhood assets like parks and recreation and senior centers are squeezed to the point where now they are threatened with total elimination" (McCollester 2005). A secondary impact of such regional revitalization is gentrification. New regional assets located in the central city may indeed help ailing central cities. But this approach may revitalize cities at the expense of low-income residents who find themselves displaced to new urban—or, increasingly, suburban—settings.

Efforts to dismantle the second pillar of urban containment—racial and income segregation—have confronted similar obstacles. Inclusionary zoning, the most far-reaching policy lever for mixing up populations by income and, by extension, race has been adopted in only a handful of settings, accounting for just 5 percent of the population by one count (Rusk 2005). A second set of policies that sought to "deconcentrate the poor" has achieved mixed results (Goetz 2003; Turner, Popkin, Rawlings 2009). Influenced by arguments about the dangers of concentrated poverty, the HOPE VI program promised to demolish the most "severely distressed" public housing and replace it with mixed income units (Hirsch 1983; National Housing Law Project 2002; Turner, Popkin, and Rawlings 2009). In practice, however, the program's successes have often occurred at the expense of the poorest residents (Popkin et al. 2004). Cities, with the blessing of the U.S. Department of Housing and Urban Development, have also used the program to demolish nondistressed housing in areas attractive to private investors (National Housing Law Project 2002). The failure to construct enough replacement housing for low-income residents and the restrictions attached to the new mixed-income developments have made HOPE VI a significant factor in reducing the supply of deeply subsidized housing and displacing the poor in some metropolitan areas (Popkin et al. 2004).[4]

In many metropolitan areas, ideas about regionalism have seeped into the domain of civic debate and sparked conversation about the region. But because these ideas are so diffuse and rarely attract a powerful constituency, they have had little impact on the public regulations and policies that have turned metropolitan areas into a patchwork of separate and unequal jurisdictions. Indeed, in some cases, policy shifts related to the aspirations of regionalism have exacerbated regional inequalities.

Conceptualizing the New Metropolitan Patchwork

Although ideas about regionalism and the policies associated with it have had limited impact, during the past two decades, dramatic demographic and economic shifts have altered metropolitan areas in ways that make the old picture of white suburbs–poor black city far too simple. Three forces that are remaking metropolitan areas include immigration, "demographic inversion," and "job sprawl." As the classic postwar city–suburb antimony becomes less meaningful in many metropolitan areas, new ways of conceptualizing regional inequality and access to opportunity become imperative.

The growing immigrant presence in the suburbs has begun to attract wide attention (DeParle 2009; Dawkins 2009). By the beginning of the twenty-first century, the majority of immigrants lived in suburbs, not cities (Singer, Hardwick, and Brettell 2008). Many of these immigrants were new arrivals who had broken the pattern of a century earlier by bypassing the city. Instead, they migrated directly to the suburbs, following job growth. Yet greater proximity to jobs does not by itself guarantee an escape from poverty. Given their lower education levels and greater presence among the working poor, the influx of immigrants has been a significant factor in the growth of suburban poverty. In 2009, 41 percent of poor immigrants lived in suburbs, not cities; 16 percent of the suburban poor were foreign born (U.S. Census Bureau 2009).[5]

The second force remaking metropolitan areas is what Alan Ehrenhalt has called "demographic inversion" (Ehrenhalt 2008). In his view, the influx of high-income whites back into cities and the movement of low-income African-American residents to suburbs is reconfiguring the basic demographic pattern that has characterized metropolitan areas during the postwar era. The movement of upper-income residents into the city reverses a more basic pattern established in American and British cities during the dawn of the industrial age (Fishman 1989). Among the drivers of this change are rising traffic congestion, which reduces the quality of life in suburbs; high energy costs, which made suburban life more expensive; and a heavily marketed cultural shift that has given "downtown living" an attractive, sophisticated patina (Leinberger 2007). For low-income African-Americans and some Latinos, these trends have caused displacement, one of the central causes for moving to the suburbs. The shift is a real, but as Ehrenhalt notes, it is an emerging trend that has only begun to alter the older demographic pattern.

The third factor reshaping metropolitan areas is ongoing "job sprawl" (Kneebone 2009). The exodus of jobs to suburban areas began in earnest during the 1970s. Since that time, analysts have studied the impact of "spatial mismatch" on the job prospects of African-Americans stuck in cities as jobs moved outward (Kain 1968; Stoll 2005). In subsequent decades, that pattern has become even more pronounced and more complex as more jobs have relocated to higher-income suburbs and more lower-income people have moved to suburbs in response (Holzer and Stoll 2007). In a study of metropolitan labor markets, Harry Holzer and Michael Stoll found that a majority of residents in lower-income suburbs commuted to higher-income suburbs or to the central city for work. Those residing in higher-income suburbs were more likely to work in the higher-income suburbs or in the central city, while central-city residents were overwhelmingly likely to work in the central city (Holzer and Stoll 2007, 5–6). The significance of these patterns greatly varies by metropolitan area. In some regions, such as Chicago, Atlanta, and Denver, the higher-income suburbs with job growth are located at the opposite end of the metropolitan area from the suburbs that are home to lower-income residents (Holzer and Stoll 2007). This pattern greatly exacerbates the problem of spatial mismatch by making employment opportunities even less accessible. In other metropolitan areas, such as Baltimore and Boston, the upper-income suburbs experiencing job growth are nearly contiguous to the lower-income suburbs. In such settings, the movement of jobs to upper-income suburbs is less likely to exacerbate spatial mismatch and may even help mitigate it.

As these three forces reshape economic and demographic patterns, they are rendering obsolete the older lens through which the challenges associated with poverty in metropolitan America have been interpreted. Established assumptions about the characteristics of particular places, such as cities and suburbs, no longer hold. Yet the older models are not easily replaced by new labels, since *the relationship* among places is central in shaping access to opportunity. Moreover, because the characteristics of place interact with the resources and connections of the people in them and because they vary in light of their history, places that are similar in some respects may, in fact, operate very differently when it comes to connecting residents to opportunity or providing safety nets to them.

These considerations suggest a two-dimensional model by which to characterize subsections of metropolitan areas. As Table 10.1 indicates, the first dimension measures the locational advantage of particular places. The vast literature on spatial mismatch has highlighted the

		Locational Advantage	
		High	Low
Organizational-political endowment	High	Inclusion	Urban containment
	Low	Segmented inclusion	Extrusion

Table 10.1. Two-dimensional characterization model for metropolitan areas

economic importance of proximity to jobs for low-income workers. Recent work demonstrates that greater job decentralization particularly disadvantages black residents (Stoll 2005).

The second dimension, which has received much less attention, characterizes the organizational–political endowment of particular places. The organizational endowment encompasses such factors as the fiscal capacity of political jurisdictions, the presence of public services such as clinics and hospitals, and the array and capacity of nonprofit organizations, which deliver many key social-welfare services (Allard 2009). After decades of devolution and contracting out of government services, it is this often jumbled and arbitrary set of institutions that serves as a social safety net and springboard to opportunity for people in low-income communities. The political endowment refers to the capacity and will within the area to articulate the interests of low-income residents and the ability to effectively represent those interests in the arenas where their concerns can be addressed.

The distribution of such organizational and political endowments across political jurisdictions is a crucial component of a just metropolis. Analyses of justice in the metropolis have touched on this issue in highlighting the uneven distribution of educational opportunities across political jurisdictions. For example, Stephen Macedo's chapter in this volume shows how reliance on the property tax to fund education creates sharp differences in educational quality across the metropolis, etching deep-seated inequalities into a foundational public program. Unequal access to education leads to fundamental injustices in life chances, especially in a nation where free public education has long served to justify a limited social-welfare state (Flora and Heidenheimer 1981; Steffes 2007).

But the significance of local organizational and political endowments for justice extends well beyond the institutions of public education. For low-income individuals and families, access to social services, provided by both public and nonprofit organizations, constitutes an essential aspect of the safety net that promotes more equal life chances. This role has become especially significant since 1996, when new provisions in welfare legislation sharply reduced access to cash assistance for families with children, put time limits on the number of years a recipient would be eligible to receive welfare, and made work the central goal of the welfare system. These reforms made the basic well-being of the poor more dependent on markets in a context where the jobs open to unskilled workers provide limited income and few of the "fringe benefits" associated with higher-wage jobs (Hacker 2006). But even to participate in those markets, many low-income people must rely (to varying degrees) on support from a range of publicly provided services, including transportation, health care, child care, food assistance, job training, and housing assistance. The location of these services matters. If food banks or child-care centers are located far from the residences of low-income people, then they will be of limited use to those in need. Those without access to such services are severely handicapped in their efforts to enter the workforce and remain in it, which is now a requirement for receiving benefits.

The density of organizations in a particular location matters as well. Mario Small's research on organizational networks shows how ties among organizations can play a critical role in providing needed services to low-income people (Small 2009). In places with a cluster of service organizations, clients are more likely find help in connecting to other needed services. Information sharing across service organizations lowers the barrier to securing services when clients need to access multiple bureaucracies. Places with more service organizations and a longer history of such organizations are more likely to have developed the ties that facilitate such information sharing. For this reason, low-income people living in a suburban location—even a prosperous suburban area—with few social services may be at a disadvantage when compared to their inner-city counterparts.

The political endowments of place are also a critical component of a just metropolis. The availability of public services that create the foundation of fairness for low-income people depends on the supply of resources to fund them. These services are funded by a complex set of public dollars from federal, state, local, county, and township governments. In some places, simple lack of fiscal capacity limits the availability of services for the poor. In other places, however, it is the willingness and ability of political leaders to address the needs of low-income residents that determines the supply of services. The calculations of politicians about whether to address the needs of poor residents depends on the structure of the local political system, the incentives of different types of political leaders, and on the mobilization of the poor.

Political analysts have long noted the ways that the characteristic elements of Progressive urban reform—at-large systems of political representation, appointed officials, and council–manager forms of urban government—disadvantage low-income residents. Voter turnout in such systems is notoriously low, and the basic institutional mechanisms of the ward system for boosting voter turnout are missing (Self 2003). To be sure, machine-style politics is no guarantee that a city will engage in broad voter mobilization, since both machine- and reform-style politics can work to suppress votes, as Jessica Trounstine has shown (2008). Even so, the structural features of politics in reform-style political systems make it more difficult to mount political campaigns that mobilize low-income voters.

Differently situated political leaders may also react differently to the needs of low-income constituents. As the political scientist Paul E. Peterson suggested over thirty years ago, city political leaders, responsible for managing the fiscal well-being of their city, may have more incentive to ignore the poor who are costly and contribute little to the city's coffers (Peterson 1981). This may be especially true in places that house residents with diverse incomes. Higher-income residents are more likely to have the political skills and connections to make their issues most politically relevant. But even in places with sizeable numbers of low-income residents, city leaders are often more interested in using scarce resources to lure higher-income residents to their localities. The incentives for ward-based city-council members, state legislative representatives, and members of Congress are different. In each case, these politicians may be more receptive to securing resources for low-income residents where they form a sizeable part of their electoral base.

The political mobilization of the poor is the third element of political endowment relevant to securing benefits for low-income residents. The poor are rarely poised to exercise power directly in urban politics: they can, however, benefit from the advocacy of experienced organizations dedicated to serving low-income residents. In many places, these service organizations function as the main voice for the poor. In some cases, nonprofits or public agencies directly advocate for the poor in city and state governments. In other cases, they forge ties with politicians in a machine-like system of political patronage. These "machine-community-based organizations can deliver substantial resources to poor neighborhoods (Marwell 2007). For example, Nicole Marwell's study of community politics in Brooklyn shows how one community-based organization was able to secure millions of dollars through its connection with powerful state and congressional representatives (2007). Another study of a CBO in Newark shows how the network of relations between a nonprofit and a politician built since the 1960s created a multifaceted, multimillion-dollar service organization

(Casciano 2009). These relationships have drawbacks: they may take a long time to develop, and they restrict the scope of political voice as the machine politicians set the political agenda.

The distinctive cross-cutting of locational advantages and organizational–political endowments creates different kinds of places within metropolitan areas for low-income residents. For much of the period after the 1960s, low-income people in metropolitan areas were concentrated in inner cities, where the war on poverty and the political mobilization of the minority poor created a hodgepodge of organizations designed to serve the poor. The capabilities of these organizations varied greatly across cities, and in many places, they deteriorated over time as resources dried up and political pressure to address the needs of the poor waned. As the pattern of metropolitan settlement has grown more complex with the settlement of low-income people across the metropolitan area, it has become essential to understand how the new combinations of location and organizational–political advantage affect the life chances of the poor. It is especially urgent given the transformation of social-welfare policy into a system that makes assistance conditional on work and leaves much of the provision of supportive services to state and local governments, who in turn contract much of them out to community-based organizations.

The Historical Legacy of Place and the Unjust Metropolis

A closer look at the development of distinct metropolitan places, illustrated with examples from the Chicago metropolitan area, suggests how and why these locational advantages and organizational–political endowments vary across subregions within metropolitan areas. The Chicago case also illuminates how difficult the task of creating new institutions in new places can be.

Whether suburban residence translates into opportunity for low-income people depends heavily on the locational advantage of the suburban area. This may vary sharply by race and ethnicity. For example, in Chicago, Latinos—who are disproportionately likely to be poor—have moved in the general direction of job growth over the past four decades, while African-Americans—also more likely to be poor—have moved in the opposite direction.[6] Growing numbers of poor African-Americans are moving to very poor suburban towns on the far south side of the city, far from the centers of job growth. Latinos, by contrast, have migrated closer to the centers of job growth in the north and west of the city. For low-income African-Americans and Latinos who remain in the city, the locational disadvantages are less extreme than for those in the poor southern suburbs, but the ongoing movement of jobs further north and west has increased the challenge they face in connecting to opportunity.

African-Americans in the poor south suburbs of Chicago are very likely to settle in areas with high levels of poverty and in political jurisdictions with extremely low fiscal capacity. For those who do, the disadvantages of location are extreme. They not only are far from jobs but also suffer from the attendant ills of concentrated poverty with meager local public resources available for remedying their situation. For immigrants, the story is more complex. Although they are more likely to live closer to job centers, many low-income immigrants are clustered in declining industrial cities (e.g., Waukegan, Elgin, Aurora, and Joliet) that have been engulfed by the expansion of the Chicago metropolitan area. Their locational advantage is thus tempered by the dangers of creating new concentrations of poverty and by the limited fiscal capacity of these suburban jurisdictions. When low-income residents are concentrated in separate suburban jurisdictions, meager local fiscal resources make it impossible to reproduce one of the key economic ladders available in affluent suburbs: good schools.

The organizational–political endowments of places may help compensate for or they may exacerbate locational advantages and disadvantages. Organizational and political endowments are historically developed characteristics of place that do not shift easily. In Chicago, as in many cities, earlier waves of European immigration and the more recent innovations of the war on poverty in the 1960s left an extremely varied legacy of organizations dedicated to serving the poor. Indeed many vital institutions that serve low-income communities, such as social-service agencies, hospitals, clinics, parks, and recreation centers, were the hard-won fruit of community struggles of the 1960s. These institutions—both public and nonprofit—have long played a vital role in providing services and opportunities for the poor. Recent research on New York City shows how second-generation immigrants can use these institutions to obtain a foothold on the economic ladder (Kasinitz et al. 2008). The organizational endowment of these places is strengthened by the presence of local philanthropy. Cities also were (and in many cases remain) the sites of enormous wealth creation, reflected today in the presence of community and national foundations that have invested in the social infrastructure for the poor.

In most suburbs, created as places of private middle-class and working-class life, access to services and community institutions is more difficult for low-income residents. Suburbs have no comparable history of immigrant settlement and the upheaval of the war on poverty that bequeathed to cities a set of institutions designed to serve low-income residents. As a result, the network of nonprofit organizations that has developed in cities since the 1960s has no counterpart in most suburbs. This means that these organizations have to be created from scratch. In many suburban areas, this is a daunting task. Even when region-wide institutions, such as the United Way, try to expand their reach into the suburbs, they often can find no counterparts with which to connect (Reckhow and Weir forthcoming). Compounding the difficulties of creating new services is the fact that suburbs do not have the philanthropic infrastructure to help support organizations that provide services to the poor. Moreover, the suburban public sector—apart from schools—is generally weak. In the Chicago metropolitan area, for example, this is evident in the absence of a public hospital in the suburban counties and a generally weak system of suburban transportation.

A similar contrast is evident when it comes to political voice for the poor. Public bureaucracies, for which service to the poor is a central mission, may also serve as influential advocates for the poor. For example, in Chicago, Stroger Hospital, the main public hospital, and its employees have offered significant muscle to support institutions that provide health care to the poor. The challenge of building new clinics to serve uninsured residents of the suburbs has proven much more difficult. The weak organizational infrastructure of the suburbs makes it much more difficult to advocate on behalf of low-income residents. Lacking the residue of machine politics, the Chicago suburbs typically offer few handholds for mobilizing new voters. Mayors and other politicians in very poor towns may be attentive to the needs of their residents but have little power to address them. In some northern suburbs, politicians have devoted more effort to discouraging the poor from settling there than to addressing their needs (Kotlowitz 2007). Local officials are particularly prone to react this way when the low-income residents are immigrants, many of them undocumented. The tactics that local officials have used to discourage low-income residents are many, ranging from restrictions on the number of residents who can live in a single-family home, to English-only rules, to requirements that landlords check legal status before renting (Dawkins 2009). The private and nonprofit institutions that do provide services in the suburbs, such as health care, are geared to more-affluent clients and may be poorly equipped to serve those with less income.[7]

I have presented these differences in organizational and political endowments as features that distinguish cities and suburbs, but it is important to note that not all cities share these characteristics. Many cities, particularly the sunbelt cities that grew dramatically in the second half of the twentieth century, such as Houston and Phoenix, have no organizational legacy comparable to that of cities in the Northeast and Midwest. With distinct histories and political systems, these cities were late to develop a nonprofit sector and often lack a strong philanthropic community. And as Amy Bridges (1997) has pointed out, the political systems of these cities are more akin to those of reform suburbs, where rule by a narrow set of elites was the norm and political institutions were designed to discourage political participation.

In the development of postwar Chicago, as in many other metropolitan areas, the majority of suburban areas functioned as the bedroom community for the growing middle class. Some suburbs, particularly south of the city, were also home to workers and the industrial manufacturing sector, notably steel and autos, that employed them. But as immigrants and low-income residents have moved to these places and as economic transformation has left some suburbs without jobs or public resources, the quest to create a more just metropolis must put the challenges of these new places front and center.

The Dangers of Extrusion

The two-dimensional model creates four distinct patterns of locational advantages and organizational–political endowment. The first is the model of inclusion that has inspired reformers since the earliest efforts to open the suburbs to minority and lower-income residents. The next two are variants of containment. One is the familiar model of "urban containment," where low-income communities are stuck in cities, where access to employment is difficult, and where concentrated poverty exacerbates the problems of the poor. In this model, a relatively developed system of social services helps to mitigate poverty, but in many cities, that system has deteriorated under the strain of increased demand and restricted resources. The second pattern is "segmented inclusion." In this model, which describes the situation of many immigrants and some African-Americans in the suburbs, the crucial locational advantage is proximity to employment and a lower likelihood of residing in a community of concentrated poverty. But with a weak system of social services, few institutions to promote economic mobility, and low political influence, low-income residents in such settings find economic security and mobility difficult to obtain. For them, suburban residence does not convey the opportunities commonly associated with it.

The model also introduces a new pattern: "extrusion." This pattern occurs when immigration, job sprawl, and demographic inversion (or some combination of the three) interact to produce extreme disconnection from the rest of society. In this pattern, characteristic of some African-American and immigrant suburban settlements, as well as some sunbelt cities, low-income residents live far from employment centers; they are likely to reside in communities of concentrated poverty and in jurisdictions with low fiscal capacity. In contrast to the older model of urban containment, places of extrusion have weak organizational and political endowments to assist residents in coping with or remedying the social and economic problems they confront.

The potential for extrusion has been amplified by two additional factors affecting African-Americans and immigrants. For African-Americans in particular, the dramatic growth in the prison population, the sharply restricted employment opportunities for those released from prison, and the legal limits on their political engagement greatly exacerbate locational disadvantages. Given their handicap in the job market, those with felony records are especially likely to need social and employment services to reintegrate into the community. Immigrants face a different issue that exacerbates extrusion: the fact that an estimated one-third of all immigrants are unauthorized. This legal status undermines locational advantages for those that have them and intensifies the challenge for those in disadvantaged locations.

As these considerations suggest, the elements of this new metropolitan typology do not represent pure models but rather a continuum of possibilities, with extrusion at the extreme pole. Many features of extrusion may also exist in the two containment models. The movement of jobs further from cities exacerbates spatial mismatch; gentrification can begin to erode the nonprofit infrastructure of cities (or, in the case of hospitals, reduce their willingness to serve low-income clientele); and inadequate resources can overburden public institutions, such as hospitals and clinics. Immigrants in suburban areas may locate closer to jobs but live in communities of concentrated poverty and low fiscal capacity, magnifying obstacles to economic security or upward mobility.

As the typology suggests, the demographic and economic changes of the past two decades have not tempered the inequalities of the older political–spatial system: in important respects, they have exacerbated those problems. And in numerous ways, they have altered the nature of the problems associated with inequalities and, as such, call for new kinds of solutions.

Conclusion: Institution Building for a Just Metropolis

The new geography of poverty and opportunity suggests the need to rethink key aspects of the way we approach metropolitan inequalities. Three elements of a new approach include a focus on institutions as well as individuals, renewed attention to the way the federal policy sets the rules of the game for how metropolitan areas operate, and recognizing how federal policy can strengthen the voice of low-income Americans.

During the 1990s, the debate about the problems associated with concentrated poverty led to support for its opposite: the solution to concentrated poverty was to deconcentrate it. Yet as suburban poverty has grown (as a result of both policy and individual migration choices), it has become clear that deconcentration focused too much on individuals and not enough on institutional infrastructures. The language of self-sufficiency that has permeated policy debates since the 1990s helped to obscure the ongoing need for a range of services even for the working poor. It also concealed the antipoor bias already built into the infrastructure of American metropolitan areas from the organization of transportation to the location of work. Strategies to promote inclusion require attention to the location, capacity, and purposes of institutions and the fit of each with the needs of low-income residents.

Second, it is striking how much of the debate about regional inequality in the past two decades focused on local policies, such as zoning. Local decisions are, without a doubt, critical in shaping the structure of opportunity throughout metropolitan areas. But it is important to remember that the federal government was central in creating the policies that underpinned urban containment in the postwar era (Hirsch 2000). Because federal policy plays such a key role in setting the rules of the game for local decisions, it is essential to understand how federal rules magnify the disadvantages of the poor and how they could instead mitigate those disadvantages. For example, the geographer Mark Hughes has argued that the federal government has amplified the obstacles that local boundaries create with the "administrative geography" it sets up for key programs such as workforce training (Hughes 2000). Alternative organization of federal programs can facilitate access to resources throughout the metropolitan area rather than making it more difficult.

Finally, the obstacles and needs of low-income residents vary so much within and across metropolitan areas that amplifying the voice of low-income people themselves is crucial to designing appropriate policies (Pastor, Benner, and Matsuoka 2009). The federal government can play a role here as well. Provisions in federal laws may open doors for the participation of groups that would otherwise have little power in decisions. Recent efforts in the domain of transportation provide some evidence of the difficulties and possibilities for building "vertical power" that allows advocates for low-income interests to enter policy arenas that had been closed to them (Swanstrom and Banks 2009; Weir, Rongerude, and Ansell 2009).

The postwar metropolitan form of middle-class, white suburbs and poor, minority cities has been shifting for several decades. As it does so, it presents new dangers of an even more divided metropolis, where "extrusion" of the poor renders poverty more even intractable and less visible than in the past. Even for those who live closer to work opportunities, suburban residence is no guarantee of economic security or upward mobility. Recognition of these facts is a first step in designing policies and institutions that promote inclusion.

Notes

1 Arnold Hirsch uses the term "containment" to describe the impact of federal and local policies on African-Americans in postwar Chicago (see Hirsch 2000).

2 http://www.naiop.org/governmentaffairs/growth/rtbrs.cfm

3 The aspirations of the Chicago Metropolis 2020 effort, a business-linked group, have been especially attentive to issues related to low-income groups, but their achievements in this regard have been limited.

4 A major Urban Institute study of HOPE VI has found that some residents used housing vouchers to move to urban neighborhoods with less-concentrated poverty.

5 Thanks to Ryan Hunter for for providing this data.

6 Chicago Metropolis 2020, "Change in the Centers of Employment and Population in the Six-County Chicago Region: 1980–2006," unpublished map, in author's possession.

7 Michael Jones-Correa's recent research (2008) on immigrants in the suburbs suggests that professionals in bureaucracies may be more proactive in serving new clients whose needs differ from those of existing residents.

References

Allard, Scott. 2009. *Out of Reach: Place, Poverty, and the New American Welfare State.* New Haven, Conn.: Yale University Press.

Berube, Alan, and Elizabeth Kneebone. 2006. *Two Steps Back: City and Suburban Poverty Trends, 1999–2005.* Washington, D.C.: The Brookings Institution.

Bickford, Susan. 2000. "Constructing Inequality: City Spaces and the Architecture of Citizenship." *Political Theory* 28, no. 3: 355–76.

Bridges, Amy. 1997. *Morning Glories.* Princeton, N.J.: Princeton University Press.

Casciano, Rebecca. 2009. "'By Any Means Necessary': The American Welfare State and Machine Politics in Newark's North Ward." Ph.D. dissertation, Princeton University.

Dawkins, Casey J. 2009. "Exploring Recent Trends in Immigrant Suburbanization." *Cityscape* 11, no. 3: 81–126.

DeParle, Jason. 2009. "Struggling to Rise in the Suburbs Where Failing Means Fitting In." *New York Times,* April 19, A1.

Ehrenhalt, Alan. 2008. "Trading Places: The Demographic Inversion of the American City." *The New Republic,* August 13.

Fishman, Robert. 1989. *Bourgeois Utopias: The Rise and Fall of Suburbia.* New York: Basic Books.

Flora, Peter, and Arnold J. Heidenheimer. 1981. "The Historical Core and Changing Boundaries of the Welfare State." In *The Development of Welfare States in Europe and America,* ed. Peter Flora and Arnold J. Heidenheimer, 17–34. New Brunswick, N.J.: Transaction Publishers.

Frey, William H., Alan Berube, Audrey Singer, and Jill H. Wilson. 2009. *Getting Current: Recent Demographic Trends in Metropolitan America.* Washington, D.C.: The Brookings Institution.

Goetz, Edward G. 2003. *Clearing the Way: Deconcentrating the Poor in Urban America.* Washington, D.C.: The Urban Institute Press.

Hacker, Jacob S. 2006. *The Great Risk Shift.* New York: Oxford University Press.

Hirsch, Arnold R. 1983. *Making the Second Ghetto: Race and Housing in Chicago, 1940–1960.* Chicago: University of Chicago Press.

———. 2000. "Containment on the Home Front: Race and Federal Housing Policy from the New Deal to the Cold War." *Journal of Urban History* 26:158–89.

Holzer, Harry J., and Michael A. Stoll. 2007. *Where Workers Go, Do Jobs Follow? Metropolitan Labor Markets in the U.S., 1990–2000.* Washington, D.C.: The Brookings Institution.

Hughes, Mark. 2000. "Federal Roadblocks to Regional Cooperation: The Administrative Geography of Federal Programs in Large Metropolitan Areas." In *Urban-Suburban Interdependencies,* ed. Rosalind Greenstein and Wim Wievel, 161–80. Cambridge, Mass.: Lincoln Institute for Land Policy.

Jones-Correa, Michael. 2008. "The Bureaucratic Incorporation of Immigrants in Suburbia: The Role of Bureaucratic Norms in Education." In *New Faces in New Places: The Changing Geography of American Immigration*, ed. Doug Massey, 308–10. New York: Russell Sage Foundation Press.

Kain, John F. 1968. "Housing Segregation, Negro Employment, and Metropolitan Decentralization." *Quarterly Journal of Economics* 82:175–97.

Kasinitz, Philip, John H. Mollenkopf, Mary C. Waters, and Jennifer Holdaway. 2008. *Inheriting the City: The Children of Immigrants Come of Age*. New York: Russell Sage Press; Cambridge: Harvard University Press.

Kneebone, Elizabeth. 2009. *Job Sprawl Revisited: The Changing Geography of Metropolitan Employment*. Washington, D.C.: The Brookings Institution Metropolitan Policy Program.

Kotlowitz, Alex. 2007. "Our Town." *New York Times*, Section 6; Magazine August 5, 30.

Leinberger, Christopher B. 2007. *The Option of Urbanism: Investing in a New American Dream*. New York: Island Press.

Lowery, David. 2000. "A Transactions Costs Model of Metropolitan Governance: Allocation Versus Redistribution in Urban America." *Journal of Public Administration Research and Theory* 10, no. 1: 49–78.

Marwell, Nicole P. 2007. *Bargaining for Brooklyn: Community Organizations in the Entrepreneurial City*. Chicago: University of Chicago Press.

McCollester, Charles. 2005. "The Glory and the Gutting: Steeler Nation and the Humiliation of Pittsburgh." *Monthly Review* 57, no. 7. http://www.monthlyreview.org/1205mccollester.htm.

National Housing Law Project. 2002. *False Hope: A Critical Assessment of the HOPE VI Public Housing Redevelopment Program*. Washington, D.C.: National Housing Law Project.

Orfield, Myron. 2002. *American Metropolitics: The New Suburban Reality*. Washington, D.C.: The Brookings Institution.

O'Connor, Alice. 1999. "Swimming against the Tide." In *Urban Problems and Community Development*, ed. Ronald F. Ferguson and William T. Dickens, 77–138. Brookings Institution Press.

Pastor, Manuel, Jr., Chris Benner, and Martha Matsuoka. 2009. *This Could Be the Start of Something Big: How Social Movements for Regional Equity Are Reshaping Metropolitan America*. Ithaca, N.Y.: Cornell University Press.

Peirce, Neil, J. Johnson, and H. Hall. 1993. *Citistates: How Urban America Can Prosper in a Competitive World*. Washington, D.C.: Seven Locks Press.

Peterson, Paul E. 1981. *City Limits*. Chicago: University of Chicago Press.

Popkin, Susan J., Bruce Katz, Mary K. Cunningham, Karen D. Brown, Jeremy Gustafson, and Margery A. Turner. 2004. *A Decade of Hope VI: Research Findings and Policy Challenges*. Washington, D.C.: Urban Institute.

Reckhow, Sarah, and Margaret Weir. Forthcoming. "Building a Resilient Social Safety Net." *Building Resilient Regions: Urban and Regional Policy and Its Effects*, vol. 5, ed. Margaret Weir, Nancy Pindus, Howard Wial, and Harold Wolman. Washington D.C.: Brookings Institution Press.

Rusk, David. 1993. *Cities without Suburbs.* Washington, D.C.: Woodrow Wilson Center Press.

———. 2005. "Nine Lessons for Inclusionary Zoning." Keynote remarks, National Inclusionary Housing Conference, Washington, D.C., October 5.

Singer, Audrey, Susan W. Hardwick, and Caroline B. Brettell, eds. 2008. *Twenty-First Century Gateways: Immigrant Incorporation in Suburban America.* Washington, D.C.: The Brookings Institution.

Small, Mario Luis. 2009. *Unanticipated Gains: Origins of Network Inequality in Everyday Life.* New York: Oxford University Press.

Steffes, Tracy L. 2007. "A New Education for a Modern Age: National Reform, State-Building, and the Transformation of American Schooling, 1890–1933." Unpublished Ph.D. dissertation, University Of Chicago.

Stoll, Michael. 2005. *Job Sprawl and the Spatial Mismatch between Blacks and Jobs.* Washington D.C.: Brookings Institution Metropolitan Policy Program.

Swanstrom, Todd, and Brian Banks. 2009. "Going Regional: Community-Based Regionalism, Transportation, and Local Hiring Agreements." *Journal of Planning, Education, and Research* 28:355–67.

Trounstine, Jessica. 2008. *Political Monopolies in American Cities: The Rise and Fall of Bosses and Reformers.* Chicago: University of Chicago Press.

Turner, Margery Austin, Susan J. Popkin, and Lynette Rawlings, eds. 2009. *Public Housing: The Legacy of Racial Segregation.* Washington, D.C.: Urban Institute Press.

U.S. Census Bureau. 2009. American Community Survey (3-year estimates). http://www.census.gov/acs.

Weiher, Gregory. 1991. *The Fractured Metropolis: Political Fragmentation and Metropolitan Segregation.* Albany: State University of New York Press.

Weir, Margaret. 1994. "Urban Poverty and Defensive Localism." *Dissent* 41, no. 3: 337–42.

Weir, Margaret, Jane Rongerude, and Christopher K. Ansell. 2009. "Collaboration Is Not Enough: Virtuous Cycles of Reform in Transportation Policy." *Urban Affairs Review* 44, no. 4: 455–89.

CONTRIBUTORS

SUSAN S. FAINSTEIN is professor of planning in the Graduate School of Design at Harvard University. She is completing a book, *The Just City*, which relates theories of justice to urban development. She is recipient of the Distinguished Educator Award of the ACSP.

RICHARD THOMPSON FORD is George E. Osborne Professor of Law at Stanford University. He writes on race and multiculturalism, combining social criticism with legal analysis. He is author of *The Race Card* (2008) and *Racial Culture: A Critique* (2005).

GERALD FRUG is Louis D. Brandeis Professor of Law at Harvard University, where he teaches local government law. He is coauthor (with David Barron) of *City Bound: How States Stifle Urban Innovation* (2008) and author of *City Making: Building Communities without Building Walls* (1999).

CLARISSA RILE HAYWARD is a political theorist at Washington University. She is author of *Defacing Power* (2000). She is currently completing a book focused on the ways democratic state actors shape identities by racializing and privatizing urban and suburban space.

LOREN KING is a political theorist at Wilfrid Laurier University. His research and teaching interests are in political philosophy, with a focus on the foundations of rational choice and theories of justice and legitimacy. His current work examines problems of justice in urban and global governance.

MARGARET KOHN teaches political theory at the University of Toronto. Her primary research interests are in the areas of colonialism, democratic theory, critical theory, and urbanism. Her books include *Radical Space: Building the House of the People* (2003) and *Brave New Neighborhoods: The Privatization of Public Space* (2004).

STEPHEN MACEDO is Laurance S. Rockefeller Professor of Politics and director of the University Center for Human Values at Princeton University. He writes and teaches on political theory, ethics, American constitutionalism, and public policy, with an emphasis on liberalism, justice, and public policy in promoting citizenship.

DOUGLAS W. RAE is Richard Ely Professor of Political Science and Management at Yale University. He is affiliated with Yale's Institute for Social and Policy Studies and Committee on Urban Studies and is author of *City: Urbanism and Its End* (2005).

CLARENCE N. STONE is research professor of public policy and political science at George Washington University. He is author of *Regime Politics: Governing Atlanta, 1946–1988* (2001) and coauthor (with Jeffrey Henig, Bryan Jones, and Carol Pierannunzi) of *Building Civic Capacity: The Politics of Reforming Urban Schools* (2001).

TODD SWANSTROM is Desmond Lee Professor in Community Collaboration and Public Policy Administration at the University of Missouri–St. Louis. He is coauthor (with Peter Dreier and John Mollenkopf) of *Place Matters: Metropolitics for the Twenty-First Century* (rev. ed. 2004).

MARGARET WEIR is professor of sociology and political science at the University of California at Berkeley. She specializes in the politics of social policy and inequality in the United States and Europe. She is currently completing a study of metropolitan inequalities in the United States.

THAD WILLIAMSON teaches leadership studies at the University of Richmond. He is coauthor (with David Imbroscio and Gar Alperovitz) of *Making a Place for Community: Local Democracy in a Global Era* (2002) and author of *Sprawl, Justice, and Citizenship: The Civic Costs of the American Way of Life* (2009).

INDEX

Addams, Jane, 82, 94; Hull House creation, 86–87, 89, 92, 97; on paternalism of elites, 91; on patriotism, 98; on prejudice, 97; on public spaces, 88–89, 94–95; on Pullman company town, 92

advocacy planning, 154

affected interests, principle of, 203

Allport, Gordon, 96

America, discovery of, 8

American Apartheid (Massy and Denton), 42

American dream, 22, 34, 47–48, 50, 54

American metropolis: Balkanized, 46–47; discriminatory effects in, 11; and economic restructuring, 22n3; and elasticity, 113; as fragmented, 13, 43, 53, 61, 71–72, 129; and immigration, 241–42, 251; inequality in/between, 20, 106–11; and justice debates, 3; left-biased, 111–14, 115–16; local institutions and inequality, 20, 33, 41–44, 45, 252–53; neighborhood diversity, 163; new metropolitan patchwork, 241–47; place in, 15–16; and political theory, 81–82; and procedural justice, 20; Progressives on, 82; reform, disappointing, 238–41; right-biased, 114–19; and segregation, 21, 237; status quo, 5, 6, 7, 9; suburbanization in, 13; and theories

of justice, 5–9; thick injustice in, 9, 13, 15–18, 111, 162. *See also* just city

Amin, Ash, 95, 97

Anarchy, State, and Utopia (Nozick), 8

antiurbanism, 87

Aristotle, 35

Barron, David, 202

Bénabou, Roland, 47, 48

Berman v. Parker, 68

Bettman, Alfred, 151

Bickel, Gil, III, 108–10

black population: architectural heritage, 11; civic involvement, 192–93; displacement of, 11, 12, 24; exclusion of, 2, 10; ghettos, 1–2, 16; incarceration, 207; and poverty, 15, 24, 186, 237; in suburbs, 242, 251; unemployment, 235; youth violence, 138

boundaries: jurisdictional, 226–27; local government, 226; and regionalism, 239; territorial, 225. *See also* territorial jurisdiction

Box, Richard, 186

Braga, Anthony, 139

Brandeis, Louis, 219

Bridges, Amy, 250

Brighouse, Harry, 49–50

Brodkin, Margaret, 130–32

Brown v. Board of Education, 229, 232–33

principles for, 169–70; and prisons, 207; and social welfare, 149, 164–65; and sports venues, 159–60; and tax revenues, 149; and workforce development, 134–35

Economic Opportunity Act (1964), 153

Edsall, Mary, 46

Edsall, Thomas Byrne, 46

education: of democratic citizens, 20; discrimination, 10; and economic success, 48–49; equal opportunity for, 40; equitable funding, 51. *See also* schools

efficiency: and economic growth, 62; and fundamental interests, 70; of market processes, 157; reliance on, 127; trade-off with equality, 20, 125, 140–41, 143

Ehrenhalt, Alan, 242

elasticity, 113

Elkin, Stephen L., 45

Emerson, Ralph Waldo, 93

eminent domain, 11, 14, 212

employment: discrimination, 10

empowerment zones, 157

Engels, Friedrich, 81

EOA. *See* Economic Opportunity Act (1964)

E Pluribus Unum (Putnam), 95–96

equality: arguing against, 9; of conditions, 35; and liberty, 44, 81; of opportunity, 38–39, 63, 70; and property ownership, 35; and redistribution, 81, 126, 177; trade-off with efficiency, 20, 125, 140–41, 143

Equal Protection Clause (Fourteenth Amendment), 1, 60, 219, 224, 229, 233

European Court of Human Rights, 207

Exit, Voice, and Loyalty (Hirschman), 112

exposure and change, 95

extrusion, 21–22, 238, 250–52, 253

Fair Housing Act (1949), 50, 150

Faulkner, William, 9

Federal Housing Act (1949), 68

Federal Housing Administration (FHA), 2, 10

felons and voting laws, 206–8, 217

FHA. *See* Federal Housing Administration (FHA)

Fifth Amendment, 68

Fight Crime: Invest in Kids, 136

Flint, Mich., redevelopment project, 69–70

Flynn, Rachel, 21, 186–93, 194

Flyvbjerg, Bent, 149, 154

Ford administration, 154

Fourteenth Amendment, 1, 60, 232

Gans, Herbert, 152

gentrification, 14–15, 156, 162, 214, 237–38, 240, 251

ghettos: blacks in, 1–2, 16; poverty in, 3; and white society, 3

Glass, Ruth, 156

Glazer, Nathan, 49

Gordon, Colin, 2, 60, 61

GreatSchools.org, 33–34, 43

Harvey, David, 5, 71

Head Start, 133

Hills v. Gautreaux, 60

Hirschman, Albert O., 112

historical amnesia, 9, 12

historic preservation, discrimination in, 11

Holt Civic Club et al. v. City of Tuscaloosa et al., 224–25

homeless: panhandling by, 181; and voting, 208–9, 217

home rule, 46, 70

homes: and advantage, 41; equity, 10; prices, 43; value and schools, 34. *See also* property ownership

HOPE VI program, 160–61, 237

housing: affordable, 155–56, 169; discrimination, 10–11, 16; fair housing laws, 51; New Deal policies, 10; prices, 43; public, 60, 69, 152, 160, 164, 169, 237, 239, 241; subsidized, 154, 156, 169, 241; and zoning laws, 43–44

Housing and Community Development
    Act (1974), 154
Housing and Urban Development
    (HUD), 241
Howe, Frederic, 87
HUD. *See* Housing and Urban Develop-
    ment (HUD)
Hughes, Mark, 253
Hull House, 86–87, 89, 90, 92, 97
Hunt, James, 133–35, 140

identity: and local institutions, 20, 37;
    and political boundaries, 50
immigration: and demographic makeup,
    85; and dynamic cities, 119, 248; and
    extrusion, 251; patterns of, 35; poli-
    cies, 231, 233, 234; and poverty, 252;
    and segregation, 42; and suburban
    diversity, 237
income inequality, 105–6; Gini coeffi-
    cient, 108–9; and governance, 119–23;
    in left-biased cities, 111–14; Paretian
    distribution, 107; in right-biased
    cities, 114–19
inequality: debates on, 3; educational,
    49; as good, 106; and inclusion, 168;
    local engines of, 41–44; and local
    institutions, 20, 33, 40, 41–44, 45, 54;
    maintenance of, 12; within munici-
    palities, 20; nature of, 41; of resources,
    5–6; structural, 6. *See also* equality;
    income inequality
Ingram, Helen, 127
inheritance laws, 35–36, 41, 50
injustice: historical roots, 9–12; invisible, 6;
    and moral responsibility, 3, 9–10, 15, 19,
    59; spatial, 4. *See also* thick injustice
institutions: and citizen identity, 20,
    37; shift in, 15; and thick injustice,
    12–15. *See also* legal institutions; local
    institutions
integration: contact hypothesis, 95–96;
    and racial prejudice, 96; school, 53
invisibility, 6, 17, 18, 81, 82, 217

Jacobs, Jane, 70, 152
James, William, 93–94, 98
Jim Crow era, 9, 224, 229, 235
job sprawl, 241, 242, 251
Johnson administration, 153
Jones v. Mayer, 60
Jones Wood, N.Y., 84
jurisdiction. *See* territorial jurisdiction
just city: and distributive fairness, 62–72;
    future of, 77; as hierarchical, 81; and
    institution building, 252–53; and local
    politics, 60–62; and public reason,
    67–68, 75–77; and reason in practice,
    69–70; and regional planning, 70–72
justice: and changing institutions,
    20; debates, 3; decline of political
    discourse, 4; distributive, 61; and eco-
    nomic development, 170; as fairness,
    63–66; and increasing inequality, 20;
    libertarian conception of, 63; and
    market freedom, 9; principles, 38–41,
    44; procedural, 20; and status quo, 7;
    theories of, 4, 5–9; and voting laws,
    215–19. *See also* social justice; specific
    theories

Kahlenberg, Richard, 48–49, 52
Kelly, John, 223
Kelo, Susette, 12
Kelo v. City of New London et al., 11–12
Kerner Commission, 3, 19
Kingdon, John, 129
Kraemer, Fern, 1, 18–19
Kraemer, Louis, 1, 19

LAANE. *See* Los Angeles Alliance for a
    New Economy (LAANE)
legal institutions, racial dimensions of, 21
legal-political structure as fragmented,
    13–14
lending discrimination, 10
libertarianism, 8, 63
liberties/liberty: basic, 38; and democ-
    racy, 37; and justice, 44, 81

life chances: equality of, 63, 73, 244;
inequality of, 7, 50, 60–61, 106, 122–
23, 244; and just city, 64; and location,
128; and place, 16; of poor, 247; and
segregation by income, 111
LIHTC. *See* low-income housing tax
credit (LIHTC)
local institutions: and citizen identity,
20, 37; and democracy, 177; and exit
options, 44–46; and inequality, 20, 33,
40, 41–44, 45, 54; and living location,
44–47; private/public ownership, 43;
and redistribution, 47–51; scholars
on, 53
Los Angeles Alliance for a New Economy
(LAANE), 166
low-income housing tax credit (LIHTC),
158–59, 165
Luke, Jeffrey, 185

maps and jurisdiction, 227–28
Marcus Avenue Improvement Associa-
tion, 1, 19
Marris, Peter, 152–53
Marx, Karl, 5–6
Massey, Douglas, 42
McConnell, Grant, 46
metropolitan areas. *See* American
metropolis
Milliken v. Bradley, 12–13, 53, 229, 232–33
Model Cities. *See* Demonstration Cities and
Metropolitan Development Act (1966)
Model State Homeless Voter Registration
Act, 208–9
"Modern Lear, A" (Addams), 91–92
moral responsibility: for helping youth,
137; for injustice, 3, 9–10, 15, 19, 59
mortgage programs, 2, 6, 10. *See also*
specific programs
Moving to Opportunity program, 163

NAACP. *See* National Association for
the Advancement of Colored People
(NAACP)

National Association for the Advancement of Colored People (NAACP), 12
National Coalition for the Homeless, 208
National Commission on Federal Election Reform, 206–7
National Voter Registration Act (1993),
208
neighborhood diversity, 163
Neuman, Gerald, 205
New Deal, 10, 154
New Public Service, 177–78, 184, 185
Newsom, Gavin, 114, 133
NGOs. *See* non-governmental organizations (NGOs)
Nixon administration, 154
noncitizens and voting laws, 204–6, 217,
218
nondisclosure agreements, 67
non-governmental organizations (NGOs),
155, 158
North Carolina Partnership for Children,
133
no taxation without representation, 206
Nozick, Robert, 8

Obama administration, 22–23n6, 166
O'Connor, Sandra Day, 11–12
Okun, Arthur, 125, 140
Olmsted, Frederick Law, 82–85, 97–98
Omi, Michael, 9–10
"On a Certain Blindness in Human
Beings" (James), 93–94
Operation Ceasefire, 138–39
Operation Night Light, 137
Orfield, Myron, 110

Park, Robert, 94
paternalism of elites, 91–92
People's Institute, 87
Peterson, Paul, 113, 122, 125
Pfizer, 12
place: and invisibility, 17; and poverty, 15–
17; and public choice, 17–18; and thick
injustice, 15–18. *See also* public space

planning, periodization of, 123
Plato, 81
Plessy v. Ferguson, 229
political morality, 38
politics of exclusion, 43, 50
population statistics, 1–2
positive environmentalism, 89, 93
poverty: and black population, 15, 24, 186, 237; causes of, 47–48; consequences of, 15–16; and crime, 235; displacement of poor, 11, 14, 164; and extrusion, 21–22, 238, 250–52, 253; ghetto, 3; and immigrants, 252; invisible, 17; nature of, 41; and slum clearance, 151; suburban, 21–22, 242, 252; and urban containment, 237
power relations: boundary-crossing, 14; and past injustices, 12; and rationalization, 149; unjust, 4, 8, 9, 16, 18, 19
prisons: and economic development, 207; growing populations, 251
private development: deference to, 189, 194; and master plan, 189; public-private partnerships, 156–57, 159, 165; redevelopment, 14–15, 157–62; and security, 127–28; and segregation, 5; shift from public development, 14–15, 184; subsidized housing, 169; tax credits, 159
private investment: attracting, 165; influence/control by, 202–3; in urban renewal, 155–57, 159
privatization: and inefficiency, 184; and NGOs, 156; and thick injustice, 14
productivity, 6–7, 127, 140
progressivism: on American metropolis, 82; and paternalism, 91–92; on public space, 20, 82, 85–90, 93, 95, 97; on urban life, 85–86; use of term, 98n1
property ownership: advantages for, 5, 41; and democracy, 40; inheritance laws, 35–36, 41, 50; and just society, 39–41; local government laws, 37–38, 46, 61; and social equality, 35; transfer

of, 11–12; values, 10, 15. *See also* homes
Proposition J. *See* Children's Amendment (San Francisco, Calif.)
Proposition 13 (Calif.), 125
public choice theory, 17–18, 185
public finance, 43, 111, 113
public housing. *See under* housing
public interest: and distributive justice, 187; elites on, 85; knowledge of, 154, 177, 190–91; promotion of, 21; and public use, 68; and social justice, 178–85; and use values, 180
public policy: and American dream, 33; control of, 212; ideas in, 129; on local institutions, 53; and public interest, 179; shift in, 125; and territorial jurisdiction, 227
public–private partnerships, 156–57, 159, 165
public reason: and agreement, 66; cost of, 62, 72; described, 20; and just city, 67–68, 75–77; and metropolitan governance, 75–77; in practice, 69–70; and reasonableness, 68, 75
public sector: activist, 178; case study, 186–93; and governance, 177; relegitimating, 184–86
public space: and democratic citizenship, 20, 82; Olmstedian, 82; Progressives on, 20, 82, 85–90, 93, 95, 97; rationale for, 89. *See also* urban spaces
Pullman, George, 91
Pullman Palace Car Company, 91; company town, 91–92
Putnam, Robert, 95–96, 163

race: categorization, 42; hierarchy in, 3, 12, 95; neutrality, 10, 11, 234. *See also* equality; inequality; segregation
racism: and deed restrictions, 1, 2, 8, 18, 60; localism as, 46; and mortgage programs, 1; and racial hierarchies, 95; segregation as, 21, 72–73, 235

Soja, Edward, 4

Southern Christian Leadership Conference (SCLC), 12

Spheres of Justice (Walzer), 7

sports venues, 159–60

Steward, Potter, 229

St. Louis, Mo.: exclusion of blacks, 10; as left-biased, 111–13; population loss, 1–2; racial zoning in, 59–60; segregation in, 19

St. Louis Real Estate Exchange, 59–60, 67

Stone, Clarence, 119

stratification, 42, 46, 49, 50

Street, Paul, 207

Stuart, Carol, 138

suburbs: black populations, 242, 251; as diverse, 42; and extrusion, 21–22; and immigration, 241–42; inequality in decision-making, 14; localism of, 239; poverty, 21–22, 242, 252; sprawl, 74; suburbanization, 13; white flight to, 46

Supreme Court decisions. *See* U.S. Supreme Court decisions

sustainability, 51, 53, 55, 74, 169, 181

Swift, Adam, 49–50

sympathy, 94, 95

Takings Clause, 68

taxes: and economic development, 149; incentives, 159; inheritance, 47; mortgage interest deductions, 11; by municipalities, 14; subsidies, 157; and voting laws, 206

Tax Reform Act (1986), 159

TenPoint Coalition, 139

territorial jurisdiction: background rules, 229–30; and boundaries, 226–27; and land use, 231; and maps, 227–28; and residency, 230–31; and segregation, 229–30; and taxation, 230

Theory of Justice, A (Rawls), 106

thick injustice: conditions for, 12, 59; defined, 4, 9; and fragmentation, 53; historical roots, 9–12; ignoring,

61; and institutions, 12–15; and invisibility, 17, 18; and legal-political structure, 13, 19; and place, 15–18; and privatization, 14; and urban development, 162; and voting, 201–2

Thirteenth Amendment, 60, 67

Thomas, Clarence, 12

Tiebout, Charles, 44

Tirole, Jean, 47

Title I. *See* slum clearance

Tocqueville, Alexis de, 35–37, 38, 41, 43, 50, 58

Toennies, Alfred, 85

Treaty of the European Union (1997), 205

trickle-down policies, 6, 125, 154, 161

unemployment: black population, 235; Detroit, 155; in St. Louis, 2

Uniform Relocation Assistance Act (1970), 153

urban containment, 237, 239, 241, 250–52

urbanist movement, 71

urban parks, 82–85, 87–88

urban policy: debates on, 3; and economic restructuring, 22n3; and equality vs. efficiency, 20–21; principles, 167, 169–70; and social programs, 164–67

urban renewal programs, 11; benefits, 150–52; criticism of, 152–53; and private investment, 155–57, 159; public housing as targeted, 160; and public reason, 68; and relocation, 161; Republicans on, 154–55; and second ghetto, 239; as shortsighted, 61; termination of, 154

urban spaces and resistance, 6. *See also* public space

U.S. Supreme Court decisions, 1, 11, 12, 59, 206, 225. *See also specific cases*

VA. *See* Veteran's Administration (VA)

veil of ignorance, 38

vertical power, 253

Veteran's Administration (VA), 2, 10

Vladeck, Bruce, 128

voting laws: defining residents, 208–12; exclusionary, 21, 204–15; and felons, 206–8, 217; homeless, 217, 208–9; and jurisdiction, 21; and justice, 215–19; and noncitizens, 204–6, 217, 218; and nonresidents, 212–15, 219; regional, 62; and taxation, 206; and thick injustice, 201–2

Voting Rights Act (1965), 206

Walzer, Michael, 7, 217

War on Poverty, 13, 153, 154

wealth, causes of, 47. *See also* distribution of wealth

white society: flight to suburbs, 46; and ghettos, 3

Winant, Howard, 9–10

Winichakul, Thongchai, 227

Winship, Christopher, 139

workforce development: and economic development, 134–35

Working Families Party, 166

World Bank, 106

Young, Iris Marion, 6, 183

Youth Violence Task Force, 138

zoning laws: and control over land, 44, 45; and diverse uses, 77; exclusionary, 2, 10, 14, 16, 33, 46, 60, 110, 123, 163, 233–34; inclusionary, 51, 239, 241; influence of, 201; and private investment, 157; racial, 59–60; and special-use permits, 189

Zublin, Charles, 87

Zukin, Sharon, 162

(*continued from page ii*)